A CANADI

INVESTMENT

TRAPS

and How to Avoid Them

HILLIARD MACBETH

PRENTICE HALL CANADA

Canadian Cataloguing in Publication Data

MacBeth, Hilliard
        Investment traps and how to avoid them: a Canadian guide

Includes index.
ISBN 0-13-022258-5

1. Investments – Canada. I. Title.

HG5152.M225 1999   332.6'0971   C99-931809-8

© 1999 Hilliard MacBeth

Prentice-Hall Canada Inc.
Scarborough, Ontario

ALL RIGHTS RESERVED

No part of this book may be reproduced in any form without permission in writing from the publisher.

Prentice-Hall, Inc., Upper Saddle River, New Jersey
Prentice-Hall International (UK) Limited, London
Prentice-Hall of Australia, Pty. Limited, Sydney
Prentice-Hall Hispanoamericana, S.A., Mexico City
Prentice-Hall of India Private Limited, New Delhi
Prentice-Hall of Japan, Inc., Tokyo
Simon & Schuster Southeast Asia Private Limited, Singapore
Editora Prentice-Hall do Brasil, Ltda., Rio de Janeiro

ISBN 0-13-022258-5

Editorial Director, Trade Group: Andrea Crozier
Acquisitions Editor: Paul Woods
Copy Editor: Catharine Haggert
Production Editor: Jodi Lewchuk
Art Direction: Mary Opper
Cover and Interior Design: Kevin Connolly
Author Photograph: Brenda Bastell Photography
Production Coordinator: Barbara Ollerenshaw
Page Layout: Monica Kompter

1 2 3 4 5   WC   03 02 01 00 99

Printed and bound in Canada.

This publication contains the opinions and ideas of its author and is designed to provide useful advice in regard to the subject matter covered. The author and publisher are not engaged in rendering legal, accounting, or other professional services in this publication. This publication is not intended to provide a basis for action in particular circumstances without consideration by a competent professional. The author and publisher expressly disclaim any responsibility for any liability, loss, or risk, personal or otherwise, which is incurred as a consequence, directly or indirectly, of the use and application of any of the contents of this book.

Visit the Prentice Hall Canada Web site! Send us your comments, browse our catalogues, and more. **www.phcanada.com**.

Table of Contents

Acknowledgments

I'd like to acknowledge the help I received from many people. In particular, Mary Walters spent many hours reading and commenting on several versions of this book. She gave good advice, support, and encouragement when I needed it most.

Don Loney, who took time to point me in the right direction.

Dean Hannaford, who saw something in this manuscript that caused him to pull it out of the pile, for which I am grateful.

Paul Woods and the publishers at Prentice Hall Canada, who brought their substantial expertise to the project.

My editor, Catharine Haggert, who asked the right questions and whose suggestions invariably resulted in improvements.

Doug Johnston, who filled in for me with competence while I was away writing.

My father, Hilliard C., who made insightful suggestions and corrections.

Nancy and Fraser, who always supported and encouraged.

Thank you.

Prologue

I joined the investment industry in 1978, at a time when the stock markets of North America were starting to recover from the worst bear market since the 1930s. For a couple of years, mutual funds never came to my attention since my initial group of clients expressed no interest in them. In the late 1970s mutual funds were completely out of favour with most investors.

After a couple of years I contacted fund companies to inquire about mutual funds, mostly from curiosity about all forms of investing. The fund companies, who were suffering from a decade-long cold shoulder from investors and investment advisors, were eager to give out information to any broker or investor who showed an interest.

In our small office my work area consisted of a desk and a chair near the front of the bullpen—a room of desks jammed together so that brokers could share expensive electronic quote machines. As a rookie I occupied the noisy space near the operators who entered buy and sell orders on teletype machines. The senior brokers remained near the back, where the light from the only windows in the room cheered their day.

The fund companies' quick response to my inquiries took the form of pounds of marketing information that piled up beside my desk. Soon this pile overflowed, partially blocking the aisle that senior brokers used when rushing to the front of the office to enter buy or sell orders.

Some of these more experienced brokers asked what I was doing with all this mutual fund information. Several of them told me to leave mutual funds alone and get rid of the pile of paper. While I do not remember exactly what was said, the general idea was that a lot of people were hurt by mutual funds in the past decade or so. The brokers unanimously asserted that offering a portfolio of stocks and bonds was the better route to take with clients. Since the wisdom of these older and wiser stockbrokers impressed me at the time and they were not in the habit of giving out free advice, I took the warning seriously and cooled my enthusiasm temporarily.

Their reaction opened up a mystery, though I did not give it much thought at the time. Why had so many brokers developed such a negative view of mutual funds? What had happened prior to that decade of decline for funds? As my career progressed I became interested in these questions. Finding more information about their chequered past became important for me as mutual funds began to gain in popularity. What lessons could be learned from past experience with mutual funds, especially for investors overwhelmed with advertisements promoting funds?

I eventually developed more experience with mutual funds through selling them and listening to clients who had owned them in the past and preferred not to get involved again. These clients led me to research the mutual fund cycles—periods of popularity followed by decades of disfavour. While I came to understand the reasons for past cycles of mutual fund popularity I realized it was important to understand other aspects of investing, such as the tendency for individuals to jump in and out of the stock markets, often at times that were detrimental to their investment success.

Individual investors showed evidence of other behaviours that limited their chance for investment success that I came to call investment traps. Some of these traps were related to the mutual fund phenomenon and others were connected to the challenges of selecting an investment advisor, managing an investment portfolio, and buying and selling stocks and bonds.

One of the best things about having investing experience is the opportunity to share that experience with other people to help them avoid some of the bigger mistakes that can do permanent damage to an investment program. The purpose of this book is to show investors a path that will avoid the pitfalls and to suggest alternative techniques that will allow them to achieve their goals.

The following fictional account describes some of the issues that are often raised by clients during discussions about mutual funds and what investors can do if they decide to take a more independent route with investing.

The two men walked through the large room, passing dozens of desks and chairs occupied by people wearing telephone headsets, some seated and others standing. Mostly male, these young-looking individuals all wore shirts and ties without jackets. A feeling of energy and activity flowed through the room as the conversation level produced a steady hum, highlighted by the quiet flickering of computer screens showing blue, red, and green letters.

The men entered a small room, private except for the glass wall that allowed everyone to see but not hear their conversation. The older man gestured to the other to sit at a small table next to a desk loaded with paper and more computer screens.

The younger man appeared to be in his late 20s or early 30s, and displayed lots of confidence as he settled into his chair. The older man started speaking as he also sat down.

"Your mother, Judy, told me that you have recently inherited a large sum of money."

"My grandfather was successful with his investments. When he died 12 years ago, the terms of his will allowed for the money to be held in trust for my mother to live on the income. On her death the money comes to me as an only child. She has decided that because there is much more than she needs she would like to see me get the chance to learn how to handle investments on my own while I am still young," the younger man replied.

"When I told her that I was thinking about putting the money into mutual funds she suggested I call you first. I should tell you that I am talking to several other financial advisors that were recommended to me."

His speech, which seemed prepared in advance, did little to relax the atmosphere in the room. His host, Tim Brighton, a young-looking 50-year-old, leaned forward in his chair and spoke.

"Why don't you tell me about what you've heard from those other financial advisors, especially the parts you don't like? I don't want to waste your time repeating things that you've already heard."

He hesitated as if debating whether it was right to give him this information. He might have been wondering if he was giving Tim an unfair advantage over the others by confiding his thoughts about the other interviews.

"You know that you don't have to tell me anything that you don't want to, Mike," Tim said, trying to put him at ease.

"Well, I don't really have a problem with their recommendations. They seem to like the idea of buying mutual funds and that makes sense to me. My problem is with my mother. She believes that since my grandfather made this pile of money by holding stocks and bonds I should continue with the same approach. She carried on with that method with her own money and more than doubled the value of her portfolio in the last five years. Her feeling is that the current popularity of mutual funds is a fad that will end and hurt a lot of investors when it does. She is encouraging me to invest on my own rather than turn the money over to a professional manager."

"Did you ever talk to your grandfather about this?"

"I did once or twice, but I wish I had paid more attention. I know that he enjoyed the challenge of deciding which companies to own and following their progress. He and his stockbroker would talk frequently on the telephone. I think he got to be quite knowledgeable about the stock market. I wish I knew enough to do the same."

After a short pause, Tim decided to pursue his earlier question. "I guess that most of the financial planners you met suggested you turn the investments over to a mutual fund or professional money manager." Mike nodded. "This happens today because the most popular form of investing is the mutual fund. The sales pitch usually focuses on professional management and worry-free investing for people who don't have the time or knowledge to manage their own money."

"Exactly," Mike said.

"You also heard that mutual funds give you instant diversification in your portfolio, even for small amounts of money. These are the standard sales benefits that are mentioned when discussing funds." He could see that Mike was interested now, perhaps impressed with his ability to know what others had told him. "It's not difficult to guess since these selling features are well-known in mutual fund circles. They've been used for many decades to sell funds."

"My mother's concern is that if I go with mutual funds I won't learn anything about investing. According to her the owner of a fund gets very little opportunity for involvement in the investing process so there is no chance to develop a feel for the stock market or learn anything about the companies, or when to buy or sell. My mother also mentioned that my grandfather was against funds because of what happened in the 1960s. She claims that most investors pulled their money out, causing mutual funds to lose a lot of money for people."

Tim nodded. "Judy is right about mutual funds, I think. One problem with funds is that once you buy a share you become partners with all the other people that own that fund. If they get too enthusiastic about stocks near a market peak and too pessimistic near a market bottom they can force the fund manager to do the wrong thing. This makes your success dependent on their actions to some degree, since you're in the same pool."

Tim continued, "But enough about funds. Have you thought much about what you would do if you decided to give portfolio investing a chance instead?"

Instead of replying, Mike produced a letter-sized folder and slid it across the table.

"This is a copy of my grandfather's portfolio that he kept at the stockbroker he dealt with. He also left a book where he recorded each purchase and sale. He was often talking about the companies he owned. The portfolio is now managed by a trust company and my mother. The money that is coming to me will come out of this portfolio. About half of the positions are the same as when my grandfather died. The trust company doesn't make a lot of changes."

Tim was examining the statement while the younger man was talking. He seemed very absorbed in the financial statements. "This is just the kind of portfolio I recommend to my clients. Not the same stocks but the type of holdings, balanced between stocks and bonds. There's even a nice distribution among the various sectors of the stock market. Thirteen different companies is enough for safe diversification. Your grandfather was obviously a wise and careful investor."

Mike jumped in, "The other financial planners all wanted me to get rid of this portfolio and buy mutual funds instead or hire an investment counsellor. They hinted that I'm not capable of managing a portfolio like this and I don't feel that I am. I don't want to stop following his method but I can't find anyone who can show me how to manage this." He paused, looking directly at Tim, "Perhaps you think that too; that I should turn it over to someone else to handle. I don't want to change the portfolio but maybe it is too complicated for me."

Tim glanced once more at the financial statements, then said, "I think that it's entirely possible for you to manage a portfolio like this, with some help from an advisor who believes in this method of investing. You've got a great starting point with this portfolio and your grandfather's records. I know your mother has become very capable of handling her own portfolio with my assistance. I'm sure she would be willing to help you get started."

"My grandfather used to say that you never really learn anything about investing until you have your own money invested."

"I agree completely. I would add one thing too; it's important to stay involved in the decision-making process, even if the stockbroker makes most of the suggestions, so that you still take the responsibility for what goes into your portfolio. After all, it's your money that's at risk."

Tim continued, "You need to know too that there are a number of traps or pitfalls that can trip up investors who go along with the crowd or try to gain their independence in investing. All of these traps are manageable, with some forewarning and more information. That's where a good stockbroker or coach becomes invaluable. Without any doubt though you can carry on with your investing program in the same manner as your grandfather. And you can have a lot of fun and satisfaction while your doing it."

Mike smiled, "I like the idea of staying involved with the investing. I know my grandfather thought that was very important. But isn't it very difficult to chose which companies to own? Isn't the investment world a lot more complicated now with all those professional money managers? I don't want to blow it with all this money."

"Yes, it can be a challenge to decide what to buy and when to buy it and when to sell. Some people get pulled in the wrong directions by their own emotions when buying and selling stocks. But believe it or not, individuals actually have some real advantages over the professional investors. All of these challenges are more easily met than most people think with a little help from an experienced and interested advisor."

There are a number of challenges facing investors who wish to retain some independence and stay in control of their investments:

- What to do about mutual funds?
- When to be in the stock market and when to get out?
- How to choose an investment advisor?
- How can an individual expect to do better than professional investors?
- What kind of stocks should be purchased and when should they be bought?
- How to know when to sell?
- What are the investment traps that must be avoided?
- What do successful investors do?

Starting with an explanation of the hidden traps in mutual funds, this book takes you through different traps with full explanations of how to avoid each one, followed by a straightforward technique that will ensure that you succeed.

Part 1

Keeping Your Independence

from the Mutual Fund Crowd

One
Mutual Fund Mania

The stock market places a drastically different valuation on companies at different stages in the company's growth and at different times in the economic cycle. Because of the huge swings in stock prices produced by these fluctuations, investors find that getting rich in the stock market is simpler in concept than in reality. Typically, during periods of rising values in the stock market, many people discover the benefits of stock market investing. When markets are falling, these same investors discover feelings of fear seldom encountered in everyday modern society. Most investors get involved with the stock market after a period of rising prices, when greed is more powerful than fear.

As an alternative to facing these challenges alone many investors turn to mutual funds. Mutual funds appear to provide help to the busy investor who wishes to avoid the time and trouble required to run his own investment portfolio. Unfortunately, mutual funds contain hidden pitfalls or traps that compromise the long-term success of an individual's investment program.

The term "mutual fund" refers to an investment holding company that pools the money of many investors, hires a staff, and administers and selects investments. Mutual funds invest in all types of investments. Common stocks, bonds, and money market instruments such as Treasury bills are typical mutual fund investments. A specific mutual fund usually invests in one asset class, such as common stocks. During bull markets most investors seek out mutual funds that invest in common shares. Since the stock market holds the best chance for reward and the most potential for trouble, this discussion of the benefits and pitfalls of mutual funds will focus on equity or common stock mutual funds.

MUTUAL FUND SELLING FEATURES

During the period from 1984 to the end of the 1990s, mutual funds became the most popular method of stock market investing for individual investors. In particular, the baby-boom generation embraced mutual fund investing wholeheartedly. In their book *The Wealthy Boomer—Life after Mutual Funds*, authors Jonathan Chevreau, Michael Ellis, and S. Kelly Rodgers (Key Porter, 1998) estimate that there are seven to eight million Canadian boomers, with 77 million more in the United States.

While there are many reasons for the boomers' interest in mutual funds, most observers agree on three characteristics of mutual fund investing that investors find most attractive: diversification, professional management, and "worry-free" investing.

THE MUTUAL FUND BENEFITS TRAP

According to conventional wisdom, mutual funds offer three advantages over other types of investing. Mutual fund investors are told to expect to receive diversification, professional management, and what is known as "worry-free" investing or peace of mind. Unfortunately, the only benefit that mutual funds deliver in all markets is diversification.

Diversification

The first of these, diversification, is a powerful benefit for investors with small amounts of money. Diversification refers to the strategy of spreading investment money over a number of different investments. At times in the history of investing, when the purchase of individual stocks presented hurdles not seen today, this feature was an important lure for investors. In the 1960s, for example, the cost of investing small amounts of money in the stock market prohibited some small investors from entering the game. Share prices for "blue chip" stocks were high, and a "board lot" of 100 shares required more funds than many investors had, if they wanted to buy into several companies. Purchasers of a block of less than 100 shares, known as an "odd lot," paid a premium in the form of higher sales commissions. Investors with limited means were forced to choose between putting "all their eggs in one basket" with a board lot or paying substantial costs on a number of small purchases.

Mutual funds appeared to offer the best opportunity to get involved with a small amount of money, while maintaining the added safety of diversification. This argument in favour of funds might have made sense then. But now, with discount brokers and electronic trading on the Internet, investors find it inexpensive to buy stocks. Today's increased ease of investing at reasonable cost makes it unlikely that a need for diversification draws large numbers of investors to invest in mutual funds. With mutual funds holding more money from investors than ever before, there must be other compelling reasons for this phenomenon. In the next chapter you will discover that the degree of diversification necessary for safety is much less than many investors think, and certainly the amount of diversification practised by most funds today is far beyond anything needed for safety.

Professional Management and Performance

Professional management means hiring full-time staff to select investments in the stock market. The investor delegates the responsibility for choosing stocks to the "professional," who is expected to do better than the investor could on his or her own.

Evidence shows that most professional managers in North America fail to achieve even an average performance. The indexes that represent the stock market, such as the Dow Jones Industrial Average (Dow), the Standard and Poor 500 (S&P), and the Toronto Stock Exchange 300 (TSE) outperform more than half of the mutual funds managed by professionals. In some periods, unmanaged funds that mirror a stock market index, known as index funds, provide a better return than 60% to 70% of the fund managers.

One study, conducted by Jeremy Siegel and reproduced in his book *Stocks for the Long Run* (McGraw Hill, 1998), reported that from 1971 to 1997 only 76 of the 198 funds that survived that period were able to outperform the Wilshire 5000 (an index that measures 5000 U.S. stocks). This study does not include the commissions associated with funds with front-end loads or rear-end loads, so the number of outperforming funds is overstated. Siegel does include the annual management fee that all funds charge. This fee, which averages over 2% for equity funds, is a major factor in the inability of most funds to meet or beat the market averages. In other words, professional mutual fund managers find it difficult to justify their own costs in incremental performance results.

Some investors avoid the cost of front-end or rear-end load commissions by purchasing no-load funds. In most cases these funds carry annual management fees similar to or higher than other funds, so the effect on performance is still important. No-load funds also are subject to a greater amount of sharp inflows and outflows of investment dollars during the market cycles. These money flows make the professional manager's job more difficult as you will see below.

Some fund companies offer index funds that try to match the performance of a specified index. These index funds cost less to acquire and own than performance-oriented funds. Index funds are able to charge a much lower annual management fee since they do not actively manage their portfolios. This lower annual fee makes it easier for them to match the performance of the market.

Many recent newspaper articles highlight the performance discrepancy. On December 11, 1998, the *Wall Street Journal* reported that a fund research firm found that over the previous five years, 273 out of 294 actively managed funds lagged the Standard and Poor 500 return of 22.27% per year.

Professionals try to deliver performance yet fail most of the time. They hold degrees in finance and business; they spend full time on their activities; they are usually above-average in intelligence. In spite of their best efforts, the pros fail to provide the gains that people expect.

Still, despite the frustration, most investors prefer to purchase professionally managed mutual funds. Since it is not difficult for an informed investor to find out that many professionals fail to provide even mediocre performance, there must be stronger reasons than the performance promise for the fund mania gripping the world today.

Worry-Free Investing (Peace of Mind)

The main reason for the explosive growth in mutual funds is found, I believe, in the third characteristic attributed to mutual funds. Funds owe most of their popularity to this feature: the promise of worry-free investing. Freedom from the burden of day-to-day management holds special attraction for those busy investors interested in the rewards of the stock market. People in their 40s and 50s prefer not to spend a lot of time on their investments. Baby-boomers wishing to participate in the positive returns advertised for the stock market make up a large portion of fund buyers. A lot of human psychology goes into this drive for "worry-free" investing. "Peace of mind" mixed with greed fuelled several previous booms in mutual fund investing too.

Convenience must be a major factor in the popularity of mutual funds also, because other investments besides stocks find their way into funds. In the United States alone, there are several trillions of dollars invested in bond funds, money market funds, and other types of non-stock market funds. Only about 55% of the $5.5 trillion (1999) dollars held in mutual funds in the United States are invested in equities. A similar proportion of the more than $350 billion in Canadian funds resides in bonds with the other half in the stock market.

During the last few years of the 1990s, the total investment in the stock market by households remained relatively stable. What changed dramatically was the vehicle used to hold those investments. Individuals sold direct stock market holdings during the 1990s while adding to their mutual fund holdings. With the exception of one year, 1988, mutual funds were net buyers of common stocks every year from 1982 to 1998 according to the Investment Company Institute (Factbook, 1998). To provide the money to make this buying spree possible, American investors added to their mutual fund holdings in every year since 1979. Quite clearly, the public fell in love with mutual fund investing. The stock market and mutual fund sales companies continue to benefit dramatically from the public's affection for funds.

Investors find comfort in being part of a large group of people when considering a leap into an unknown like the stock market. Any parent recognizes how powerful that peer group validation can be. Crowd psychology works in the stock market too.

This popularity of investing in pooled investments is not new. The periodic epochs of interest in common stocks go back several centuries. At certain stages of every economic cycle individuals notice that owners of companies earn significantly better returns than savers at the bank. When interest rates are low, and stock market indexes are soaring, people with some savings wonder: Should I get involved? Often this interest in the stock market leads to involvement in mutual funds.

MUTUAL FUNDS IN HISTORY

Markets in financial instruments have existed for centuries, and periodically groups of investors embrace the idea of hiring a professional to manage their investments. One early example of a pooled investment goes back to the days of Christopher Columbus and Captain Cook, when investors would buy shares in the plunder that ships might bring home from the new world. The phrase "when my ship comes in" that is still heard today originated at that time, according to some. Historical accounts of pooling resources to enter the stock market go back more than one hundred years. The present-day popularity of mutual funds is an extension of those types of investing activities. Promoters of mutual funds encourage investors in the belief that they are too busy and too unsophisticated to manage their own money. Investors come to agree that it is preferable to let the professionals do their investing for them. After all, to paraphrase a popular sales pitch: Would you remove your own appendix or would you go to a surgeon?

Mutual Funds Are Not New!

The seductive nature of this appeal to invest with "peace of mind" has been around as long as people have invested their money. Few investors today are aware that mutual funds (sometimes called by another name) were popular during the bull phases of previous market cycles. The "bull" phase of a cycle occurs when stock prices are generally rising. A "bear" market refers to the phase when prices of stocks are in decline.

Early references to mutual funds appeared in the 1800s, although investment entities with similarities to mutual funds probably started even earlier.

In the 1880s, mutual funds, known then as "investment trusts," were riding a wave of popular appeal in Great Britain. These investment vehicles started in Scotland around 1860. As reported in an excellent book about mutual funds, *Surviving the Coming Mutual Fund Crisis* by Donald Christensen (Little, Brown and Co., 1994), a man named Robert Fleming of Dundee, Scotland started to exploit the investment trust idea in 1873. Many Britons wanted to invest in the construction of railroads in North America. Investment trusts offered the ideal method for the small investor.

By 1888 others formed new investment trusts, drawing millions of pounds from savers. In just two years, thirty new trusts were formed as demand blossomed. New companies went public to take advantage of the demand for common stock that these trusts created. The fifteen-year track record of good results established by Fleming provided comfort to those who were nervous.

The trusts began to look into investments in other countries besides North America. These developments attracted additional investors to the investment trusts. After all, who could invest directly in those countries on their own? For several years this investment trust mania grew.

The end of this particular era struck suddenly in 1890. Baring Brothers & Co.—the same Baring Brothers whose rogue trader in Singapore almost sunk the company recently—started several investment trusts that purchased foreign bonds. These bonds promised to pay a higher rate than the dismal 2.5% available at the time in British government bonds. Unfortunately for the trust holders, the Argentinean government defaulted on their bonds, precipitating a crisis. The foreign bond trusts lost most of their assets due to these defaults and failed.

In North America, however, and especially the United States, this potentially enlightening episode went largely unnoticed. With the events of the First World War, the start of Communism in Russia with the Bolshevik Revolution, and concerns about inflation and depression during the 1920s, Americans were unlikely to be aware of obscure investment-related events 30 years old in another part of the world.

Having missed the chance to learn from the 1890 British fiasco, American and Canadian investors were given another opportunity to learn from that harshest of teachers, experience. In the period from 1924 to 1929 a type of mutual fund played a key role in the events leading up to the crash of October 1929 and the Great Depression that followed. The most popular funds in the 1920s were closed-end investment companies. At that time, the Americans continued to use the British name, investment trusts.

Closed-End Funds or Investment Trusts

A type of an investment trust known as a closed-end fund operates as a corporation trading on the stock market. These trusts issue shares to the public at the outset of their operation. With the money raised from the public the fund managers proceed to purchase common shares in many different publicly traded companies.

Many investment trusts in 1929 were so-called "blind pools" that invested money under the total discretion of the manager. In other words, the investor put up the money and the promoters said "trust me." As long as the performance remained favourable, investors preferred not to know what investments they had. Rules requiring specific disclosure did not exist in 1928. Investors were intrigued by the mystery of how these funds made their astonishing gains. Funds that revealed their investments were less popular at that time. The power of imagination beat reality when it came to greed in the stock market.

For closed-end funds, the purchase and sale of shares in the fund operate differently from the way today's style of mutual funds operate. The investment company calculates the "net asset value" of the company for information purposes, but makes no direct attempt to facilitate entry or exit for the shareholder. The net asset value is the total value of all the holdings of the investment company divided by the shares outstanding. To provide an avenue for investors to exit the fund, the promoters establish a listing on the stock exchange. There is no guarantee that the trading price of shares will equal net asset value. Demand and supply for the shares are the sole determinants of the price.

Closed-end investment companies were very popular in the 1920s. At times, their values on the stock market exceeded net asset values by a two to one margin.

In more normal times the fact that closed-end funds can only be sold through the stock market usually means the seller must accept a discount to net asset value if he is determined to sell his shares. You can see that a closed-end investment fund trading at more than its net asset value is an unusual situation because the shares are selling at a price that makes the company worth more than the value of the stocks that it holds. Any investor could just go into the stock market and buy those same stocks at net asset value directly. In the 1920s, for closed-end funds to trade at those inflated values the public must have been in the grip of a mania of greed that defied common sense.

This same situation developed in the 1990s with closed-end investment companies that specialized in equities sold on Asian stock markets, where the purchase of stocks directly was difficult and sometimes impossible. People were so eager to cash in on the Asian economic "miracle" they paid a premium for the privilege of participating. A couple of years later the "Asian Flu" developed, markets collapsed, and the investment companies' shares sold at a severe discount to net asset value. Investment company investors suffered two losses: first, the actual decline of the stock markets and then the slumping of the fund prices from a premium-to-asset value to a discount. Many Asian markets declined by more than 50% but fund shareholders saw a further 20% or more swing downwards in their holdings.

Remember, if you wish to avoid this type of unmitigated disaster never buy stocks in a sector or a country where investment funds are trading at a premium to net asset value.

The 1929 Crash and Investment Trusts

In an interesting book, *A Short History of Financial Euphoria,* by John Kenneth Galbraith (Penguin, 1993), the author reviews the events leading up to the famous 1929 event. In addition, Galbraith describes several other financial manias to demonstrate his thesis that all financial euphoria contain similar elements. He does a good job of showing the crowd psychology common to these crises and panics.

Interestingly, transportation developments and, more recently, communications advances are found in the middle of many financial booms and busts. A common theme of this type of stock market mania is the introduction of a new technology. The public embraces the new development, investing and speculating in shares of companies engaged in that field. Unfortunately for these early birds, the payoff from these new technologies arrives only many years later in the form of profits and dividends for companies working in that sector. In the interim, investors lose their shirts because they get in too early. Canals, railroads, the telegraph, and the telephone have created fortunes one year and destitution the next. Could the extreme popularity of Internet companies on the stock market, a most modern form of communication and a substitute for transportation, contain the seeds of the next crash?

The history of financial events includes numerous boom and bust cycles. But there is no bigger event in the history of cycles than the 1929 crash.

The build-up to the 1929 crash started with rising stock market prices in 1924. Prices rose steadily during those years with one sharp, short break in 1926 that may have been connected to a Florida land boom that ended with collapse. After the 1926 break, stock market investing grew steadily in popularity right up to the crash in late 1929.

The use of leverage by closed-end investment companies deserves special mention. Several of these funds used a capital base raised from the public as an equity underpinning for additional borrowing. All of these monies were then invested in common stocks in the rapidly rising market of 1928 and 1929.

At that time the margin requirement for buying stocks was 10%. Margin refers to the deposit required to secure a loan for the purposes of stock market investment. In other words, an investor with $10 000 could buy $100 000 worth of stock or investment trusts, with the loan of $90 000 by the brokerage firm. If the market dropped 10% the equity portion of the investment disappeared, leaving only the loan. The investor lost the equity stake, but still owed the debt from the loan. Many investors were wiped out in just this manner.

In the late 1920s, the potential for leveraging investments reached greater heights. Since the closed-end investment trust traded on the stock market, an investor who borrowed 90% of the cost achieved a 10 to 1 leverage. The closed-end investment company then applied leverage again, borrowing money within the trust to enhance the potential for gain (and loss). This leverage on leverage worked wonderfully well in the rising market but devastated the trusts and their shareholders when the collapse came. As the stock market collapsed, loans within the trust were called, forcing the sale of shares by the trust. As trust shares fell, individuals received demands for more money. Failure to meet those demands resulted in a sell out of the trust shares, at a loss.

Christensen describes the key role that investment trusts played in the days and months leading up to the history-making events of October, 1929. One of the dominant figures mentioned by most observers in connection with the 1929 crash is Dr. Irving Fisher, who was an economics professor at Yale University. His memory continues in financial circles for his famous statement, made in a speech just before the crash: "stock prices have reached what looks like a permanently high plateau." Articles in the *New York Times* just one week before the crash quote him as saying that "stock prices have not yet caught up to their real values."

Less well known is the fact that Fisher was heavily connected to the investment trusts of the day. He held paid positions as advisor to some investment trusts. Fisher lectured extensively on the state of finance, making supportive comments about investment trusts. Fisher declared authoritatively in the *North American Review* in July 1929: "The investment trust principle acts to reduce risks by utilizing the special knowledge of expert investment counsel. It also operates to shift risks from those who lack investment knowledge to those who possess it." Clearly, Fisher had the zeal of a true believer when he made those statements. Of course, the false assertion that risks shifted from the less knowledgeable to others is unforgivable for someone of his background. Obviously, in any type of fund the risks stay with the investor who puts up the money. Only the control over the selection of investments and the management fees transfer to the "expert" manager.

There is little reliable information about mutual fund performance during the era of the 1920s. Funds were new in North America and records, if they were kept, were not reported. Newspapers carried stock quotations in 1929 but no mutual fund performance figures. One can deduce that performance, for awhile, was spectacular, due to a rising market and exponential leverage.

One example of this roller coaster performance was a large investment fund launched by Goldman Sachs in late 1928. The fund was issued at $104, traded up to $220.50 in 1929 and fell to $1.75 by 1932. To use the Goldman Sachs fund as an example of leverage, consider the investment of $10 000 in the fund at issue, using the maximum leverage. A margin deposit of $10 000 allowed the purchase of $100 000 worth of units. Just prior to the crash the units traded over $200, which made the investment worth $200 000. If sold near the peak that $10 000 grew to $110 000 after repaying the $90 000 loan.

You can easily imagine that, as the stock market rose, and as prominent figures like Fisher promoted the use of funds, the eager and greedy public accepted the idea that funds allowed them to participate in a stock market boom. Anecdotal accounts indicate that most adults became enthralled with the possibility of making riches on the stock market.

The amount of money involved in these trusts grew exponentially. By 1928, the total amount involved exceeded $8.5 billion as reported in *Forbes* in May 1928.

And then the curtain fell on one of the most exciting periods of financial excess in the history of the world. In the ensuing three years the Dow, made up of 30 of the largest U.S. companies, lost 89% from the peak in September 1929 to the bottom in October 1932. Using the broader index, the S&P 500, and assuming that dividends were reinvested, the decline was 61.5% from December 1929 to December 1932.

Economic activity suffered a similar devastation. Industrial production in the darkest days of 1932 measured just one third of that prevailing in 1929. Debates among economists continued for many years over the chicken and egg question of whether the stock market crash triggered the depression or vice-versa. Some economists argue that a normal business cycle downturn that started in 1929 developed into something much worse because of the end of the stock market speculation.

As a result of the crash and the depression that followed the public lost interest completely in investing and investment trusts. Most trusts just disappeared, along with the money invested. From the peak of approximately $8.5 billion the total amount of money in all mutual funds declined to almost nothing during the 1930s. Eventually the total bounced back a little, to only $2.5 billion in 1950, over 20 years later.

A myriad of post-mortem analyses rehashed the events of 1929. Banks and brokerage firms bore the brunt of many negative attacks after the debacle. Many senior banking and brokerage officials either committed suicide or went to jail. An intense search for scapegoats lasted for several years.

After the personal experiences of millions of investment trust speculators and the bad press after the crash in 1929, the mutual fund industry fell into complete disfavour during the 1930s and 1940s. By 1940 the total dollars invested in mutual funds of all types—stock, bond, and money market—was around $400 million, a 95% decline from 1928. The memory of the crash and the Great Depression overwhelmed the consciousness of almost everyone in North America and Europe. The few people who had money opted for safer types of investing. The investment trust, or closed-end investment company, would carry a black mark in investors' minds for at least 30 years. After the 1929 crash the stock market carried a reputation for speculation and greed that made respectable people avoid it. As recently as the 1960s some investment dealers in Canada remained specialized in government bonds and refused to deal in common stocks, labelling them too risky and unsuitable for the wealthier clients they favoured. Stock market investing was considered an activity for desperate, greedy people, not for the coupon-clipping elite.

It was not until long after the Second World War that investing in stocks came back into favour. By 1950 North Americans felt more confident. They used most of their new income to acquire material things—houses, cars, refrigerators, appliances, televisions (a little later), and furniture. With the strong economic growth of the 1950s and 1960s and with the lessons taught by the Great Depression, middle-class people built up savings, even after their spending spree and the costs of rearing what was to become known as the baby boom generation.

After fifteen reasonably good years of rising markets, a period of financial euphoria developed again, in the 1960s. Investment trusts, now changed in name to mutual funds, made a new entrance onto the scene. The most popular fund emerged as the "open-end" fund, which remains dominant today.

Open-End Mutual Funds

The open-end fund, which is the type people usually mean when discussing a "mutual fund," is a pooling of resources similar to the closed-end fund. The fund managers assume responsibility for management of the assets, including stock selection and distribution of dividends. Record keeping and administration are provided also.

One of the main distinctions between the "closed" type popular in the 1920s and "open-end" mutual funds centres on the possibility of adding new money at any time to an "open" fund. In a "closed" fund new money was added only rarely, in the form of a new stock issue. Open-end fund companies, on the contrary, try to add new money every day. They spend a good deal of time and energy looking for new money.

Advertising for new money consumes a major portion of the revenues of mutual fund companies.

New money is desirable for growth and profits. New money helps also to replace money lost through "redemptions." Redemption rights mark the other main distinction between "open-end" and "closed-end" funds. The investor who wishes to exit the open-end fund redeems or sells his shares back to the fund. When the investor sells shares, the mutual fund company pays out money to the investor, cancels the shares sold, and the number of shares outstanding shrinks. The fund company pays "net asset value" to investors wishing to exit. Mutual fund companies calculate the net asset value of each fund at the end of each day, based on the closing price of each share.

The open-end type of fund is continuously in distribution. Salespeople are selling new shares each day adding to the total dollars under management. When an investor decides to put money into a mutual fund, a number of entirely new shares are created. This may add to the total of shares outstanding depending on the level of "redemptions" that day.

On any given day there are new shares being created with new money going into the fund and, simultaneously, money is being withdrawn by other investors. If the total money going in is larger than the money going out, as it has been for several years now, the fund is in a "net sales" position. Fund administrators give some of the new money coming in to the investor who is leaving, which allows the portfolio of stocks to remain undisturbed.

If there is more money going out than coming in it is known as a "net redemption" status. This is a tricky situation for a fund manager as there will be a need to sell shares in some of the stocks owned by the fund.

For a period of 16 years (1982 to 1998) mutual funds had been in a net sales position all of the time, except for 1988. There were no periods of prolonged, heavy redemptions, except briefly after the 1987 crash. The last long period of net redemptions was from the early 1970s to the early 1980s, when redemptions continued right through the bull and bear cycles. Immediately prior to this period of redemptions, mutual funds enjoyed an unprecedented surge of popularity. Looking at this era, and its aftermath, will help give us some clues to what might happen after the end of the current mania for funds.

The Go-Go Years

Mutual fund assets grew over 20 times from 1950 to the peak in 1971, from $2.5 billion to $55 billion. These times came to be known as the Go-Go years of mutual fund popularity.

Fund managers became known as celebrities, reaching heights of renown and income surpassed perhaps only by baseball and hockey stars today. Funds' performance attracted more money than ever before, helped by the 15-year record of steady gains in the market. History has shown that a multi-year period of steadily rising stock prices is key to a successful mutual fund industry.

Mutual fund popularity coincides with heavy public participation in stock market investing, and the 1960s were no exception. Equity assets as a percent of total household financial assets rose from 18% in 1953 to 34.35% in 1968. This public fascination with stocks increased the total size and influence of the mutual fund industry in the 1960s. Money flowed into mutual funds steadily for 25 years after the Second World War. Investors chose funds during both bull and bear market cycles throughout this period.

Many interesting books record the events of the Go-Go years of mutual fund excitement. One book tells the story of Bernie Cornfeld, head of Investors Overseas Service, a failed mutual fund that preyed on unsuspecting investors. The title of the book, echoing the recruiting pitch to aspiring mutual fund salespersons—*Do You Sincerely Want to Be Rich?*—captures the mania that gripped much of the public during this period.

The Aftermath

What happened next shocked everyone who believed in mutual funds. The U.S. mutual fund industry continued to grow until 1971, when it entered a decade-long decline. Redemptions exceeded sales in every year from 1972 to 1979, except for 1977. For mutual funds investing in the category known as "equity, bond, and income," assets in 1971 were $55 billion, declining to $49 billion by 1979. Separate figures for equity funds alone were not available but it is safe to assume that equity funds as a separate class would have fared much worse. Frightened investors like to switch their holdings to bond and income funds out of equity funds during uncertain times.

Canadian data from the *Financial Times* "Survey of Funds" (1977, 1982) confirms this shrinkage of the industry. Total equity fund assets in Canada declined from $2.95 billion in 1972 to $1.92 billion in 1976. The largest equity mutual fund in Canada shrank from $407 million in 1972 to $210 million in 1976. This fund continued to lose assets until 1982, when assets were a mere $157 million. This fund lost more than 60% of its assets in a ten-year period that included at least two major bull markets. While the performance of this fund was mediocre, the heavy redemptions were not due solely to performance.

The best-performing Canadian mutual fund in its category was the AGF Special Fund, managed at the time by Richard Whiting, a talented fund manager. AGF Special ranked number one in its category every year from 1974 to 1980. During those years, annual percentage increases in net asset value ranged between 22% and 61%, with just one losing year of –46.5% in 1974.

This leading fund manager watched assets drain away throughout the whole period of 1972 to 1981. The extent of these withdrawals is impossible to determine exactly, as it is difficult to separate market gains from asset redemptions. It is reported that the fund, which held $27.2 million of assets in 1972, dipped to $13.5 million in 1976, even after performance gains in 1975 of 50% and 1976 of 27.6%. By 1981 there were still only $21.6 million of assets in total in this top-performing fund. Investors obviously redeemed shares in good years and bad. Both mediocre funds and best-performers lost assets throughout the 1970s in Canada.

In the United States, the fund industry lost assets at an alarming rate during this period as well. The net flow to equity mutual funds was negative from 1971 to 1981 every year. This outflow continued through the bear markets of 1974 and 1977–78, as one would expect.

Surprisingly, redemptions exceeded sales also during the bull markets of 1972, 1975, and 1978–81. In fact, the heaviest redemptions occurred during the longer period, mostly bullish, from 1975 to 1981. This happened at a time when, from December 1975 to December 1980, the S&P 500 almost doubled.

Equity funds in the United States lost 27.2% of their assets during the bull market between 1978 and 1980, more than twice the 13.1% lost in the bear market of 1976–78. By contrast, the 1987 market crash triggered a net outflow of small proportions, only 3.5% of assets.

The stock market as a whole lost money due to these massive redemptions of equity mutual fund assets by the public during the 1970s. Mutual funds were net sellers of common stock in the United States every year from 1972 to 1981. More than $17 billion in common stock was sold by funds during this period, with the heaviest selling hitting the market during 1973, 1976, 1977, and 1979, when the market was rising most of the time. During the worst year of stock market performance, 1974, the funds sold the smallest amount of stock. This happened because the public redeemed the largest amount of funds in the years when the market was up, not down. This fact comes a surprise to even veteran market watchers.

The most plausible explanation is that mutual fund investors experience a bear market, triggering a desire to get out of mutual funds. Dismayed with the prospect of taking a loss, they make a decision to sell when the market gets back to even. Then they wait until they get this price level. This level probably reflects the value of their savings when they first entered the markets.

Obviously, the popularity of mutual funds is tied to the stock market cycle. In the 1888 mutual fund boom in Scotland, there had been a 15-year period of rising stock prices and good fund performance. In the 1920s, a shorter period of seven years of positive stock market returns preceded the mania. In the late 1960s, stock prices performed well throughout the 1950s and 1960s prior to the spectacular growth in fund assets. And, in the 1990s, the stock market recovery from the 1982 low gave an unprecedented 15-year record of double-digit annual market gains. As a consequence, mutual fund assets doubled from 1995 to 1999 in the United States to over $3 trillion in equity funds alone.

These cycles of widespread popularity and disillusionment are not healthy for the mutual fund industry or fund investors. The actions of the crowd invested in funds as they adjust to the cycles create the climate for an investment trap that catches many investors unaware.

WHAT MAKES MUTUAL FUNDS INTO TRAPS?

As a bull market picks up momentum, mutual funds start to advertise their attractive performance. Better track records attract more money for investment. The very success of the fund leads to rapid increases in the size of the fund.

If the fund is one of the few that outperforms the market averages, additional money flows into that particular fund. A long rising trend, without serious breaks or downturns, causes a feeling of confidence among investors. Along with this positive feeling toward the stock market comes a willingness to put more money into funds, particularly during the later stages of the rise. Funds advertise their track records more heavily after a long rise in the market when they have a positive story to tell. Advertising focuses on performance and "peace of mind" issues. Advertising success is much greater in the years when the stock market is doing well, leading to a trap I call involuntary market-timing.

Involuntary Market-Timing

This inflow of money during the bull market phase is an example of a "market-timing trap," discussed in more detail in chapter 7. Investors feel more comfortable adding money to the stock market when prices have been rising for some time and stocks have a reputation as safe and rewarding.

THE INVOLUNTARY TIMING TRAP

Just as the market is getting expensive, and reasonably-valued stocks are getting difficult to find, the public floods the manager with even more new money to invest. The public forces the fund manager into a "buy high" attitude.

Fund Managers Are Human

Fund managers control very little of the timing of the inflow of money. After a long, slow period of difficulty in attracting new money, a fund couldn't be expected to turn money away when it means more management fees from new clients. If the fund company takes the new money, they have an obligation to invest it.

Heavy advertising of the advantages of mutual fund investing in a booming market is normal. It happened in the 1880s, 1920s, and 1960s, expanding to new levels of powerful promotion in the 1990s. Fund management companies have the dollars available to advertise when their assets are soaring. Investors are more receptive after a long period of rising markets so advertising dollars go further.

Advertising portrays fund managers as superhuman idols, highlighting their stock picking ability. Advertising executives and the public remain blissfully unaware of the old adage, "never confuse genius with a bull market."

Performance Pressures

The fund manager chases more and more speculative securities as the bull market ripens. In the continuous quest for performance, the funds buy the stocks that rise the most quickly. Often the type of company that moves up in price rapidly tends to be smaller and less liquid than the big, slow-moving blue chips. Some fund managers reach for aggressive stocks, in an attempt to outperform the indexes and attract even more money, or not lose money to the competition. Some mutual fund managers try to resist this pressure to reach for performance but they often suffer substantial redemptions as the investing public is impatient with an under-performing fund.

Few fund managers stick to a resolve to do the "right thing" and stay with solid blue chip companies if the assets of the fund are rapidly depleting. Every fund manager lives with the reality of performance pressures. Investors look at the one year performance especially closely in a bull market. Managers develop what I call "short-term performance anxiety." While this may sound like a problem for a sex therapist it refers to the necessity of keeping up with the more aggressive funds. When a fund buys some speculative securities, which move up rapidly and enhance performance, can a competitive manager afford to be left out? What if that sector keeps moving up and the relative performance numbers move even further in the other manager's favour?

An article titled "Like it or not, Mutual Funds are Buying Internet Stocks," by Charles Gasparino in the *Wall Street Journal* on December 16, 1998 illustrates the problem. The article quotes Mary Meeker, a top-ranked research analyst specializing in Internet companies. She attributes "at least part of the huge recent run-up in the price of Internet shares to money managers who have chased performance in order to boost returns." Ms. Meeker went on the say that the "underperformance by 90% of all money managers has forced many to purchase Internet stocks, thus boosting shares above and beyond their already lofty levels."

While any investor can understand the performance and market-timing pressures facing the portfolio manager, investors want their money going into good quality stocks when they are reasonably priced. Investors have a right to expect this from fund companies that advertise conservative investing. Shocking stories inevitably appear after the end of a bull market about the excesses, legal and illegal, that crept in during the latter stages of a bull market.

After the Go-Go years of mutual fund popularity in the 1960s, superstar fund managers like Gerald Tsai developed feet of clay. Tsai was considered an investment genius by many when he managed the Fidelity Capital Fund. Tsai left Fidelity in 1966 to form his own fund, called the Manhattan Fund.

The Manhattan Fund attracted $250 million by opening day, a record for its day. Within a short time nearly one hundred new funds sprouted, copying Tsai's style of management. Tsai's performance record was built on risk-taking that was unusual for the mutual fund industry up to that time, at least since the 1920s. Of course, other funds took notice as they watched their assets drift away toward these new, aggressive funds. A performance cult developed in the fund industry.

Christensen reports that "one trick that was popularized by Tsai and copied by others was to concentrate the shareholders' money in a small number of stocks." The companies selected often were new or obscure with a small float (number of shares trading on the market) so the funds' buying pressure pushed prices up. This technique worked wonders for performance in a bull market as thinly-traded stocks were pursued by several fund managers simultaneously, guaranteeing a rapid and substantial price rise. The public was not aware of these practices, preferring to concentrate on the excellent performance numbers reported by Tsai and his copycat competitors.

Another development that became important for the stock market that can be traced to these fund practices is the emergence of the "Nifty Fifty" stocks in the early 1970s. Portfolio managers of all types of money concentrated their buying in a few stocks, known as the Nifty Fifty. These stocks delivered good performance for several years, again as a consequence of the concentrated buying of professional managers. When redemptions started in the early 1970s, however, the fund manager had only a few stocks they could sell to generate cash to pay off the departing investors. All the fund managers owned the same stocks, forcing their prices much lower than the market averages.

Many investors were left with severe losses. Tsai's Manhattan Fund lost 73% of its value from September 1969 to September 1974, compared to the Dow's decline of 25%.

The Party Winds Down

The incredible excitement of the 1960s, which drew so many into investing through mutual funds, waned eventually. The bear market of 1968–70 moved the Dow 36% lower, affecting investors' outlook and optimism. As the market slowed, less money came into funds, and the cycle rolled over. Initially, fund managers were probably unaware that a slide had started. While the stock market as a whole was in decline, many individual stocks continued to rise and some even reached new highs. Money continued to flow into funds up to 1972, even though the markets were in decline for several years by then.

Involuntary Market Timing in a Bear Market

As mentioned earlier, a bear market is a phase in the stock market cycle when prices are generally declining, although some individual stocks do move higher. Bear markets usually last a shorter time than bull markets, with average market declines from 20% to 50%.

In the early stages of a genuine bear market the public and the fund managers may think it is nothing more than a mild correction. After many years of bull markets the public is accustomed to "buying the dips." In 1999, for example, the public believes that the right thing to have done in 1987, 1990, 1994, and 1998 was to buy when the market dropped. Few investors have experienced a genuine bear market, such as the one of

1973–74. Bear markets of this severe type convince many investors that ownership of common stocks is too painful. This change of perception in the mind of the public takes more than a few months to develop. A minimum of one year of declining markets is usually required.

Fund managers too are nervous in the early stages of a bear as they suspect that prices in the stock market are high and the bear market may be underway. However, just when they feel like selling they continue to get money in the door, unsolicited. A manager convinced that stock markets are in trouble will stop buying stock and let a cash position accumulate. The manager's inability to know if it is a temporary correction or the start of a big, bad bear market creates a serious problem. If it is just a correction, performance will suffer dramatically because of the manager's caution, jeopardizing future asset growth and job security for that manager.

The longer the bull market lasts with only mild corrections the more likely a manager and the public are to buy more shares of favourite stocks during a falling market.

If the correction lasts long enough to cause the public to redeem shares, the manager must start thinking about selling some stocks, depending on the size of the cash cushion, if any, in the fund. Uncertain if the decline is only a pause or the start of a savage bear, the manager is loath to sell his favourite growth stocks. Those stocks usually are the ones that gave the manager special recognition and bonuses during the bull. The manager also knows all too well that other investors know of his sizeable position in those stocks. Other managers watching closely would rush to sell if word got out that one of the key supporters of that stock was selling.

The manager of a major mutual fund company related to me an experience with market liquidity, describing how it took three months to dispose of a large block of stock. He used third-party intermediaries so that no one knew that his fund was the seller. The fund did not want anyone else to know as this would cause others to start selling the stock, making it more difficult for this manager to unload his position. The most disturbing part of the story was that the sale happened in 1993 when the market had one of its best years in a decade. These shares were in a leading growth company with a very liquid float. It makes one shudder to think of the disaster this would be in a declining market with a less liquid company. When I examined the other holdings of this fund, I found there were many stocks with less liquidity than the one that took three months to sell.

A fund manager knows that blue chip stocks are easy to sell and replace later. The sale of a large block of these actively traded stocks affects the market price for that company's shares only a small amount. On the other hand, the market for a high-performing growth stock can be severely hurt by a large block trade in a weak market. So at the early stage of a correction the manager opts to sell liquid, blue chip stocks if cash is needed to meet redemption demands.

At some point in the cycle a correction is no longer a correction and a genuine bear market gets established. After a few quarters of market decline the public starts to be aware that something is wrong and the money flow stops. The effect on mutual fund companies can be profound.

Redemptions are a constant reality for mutual funds. For reasons unrelated to market conditions, such as taxes and estate liquidation, a certain amount of selling of fund shares is ongoing. To replace this money mutual fund companies rely on a massive sales effort that maintains a constant inflow of new money. In a bear market this sales effort is often not enough. The public becomes cautious, frightened, or just broke. Net redemptions are triggered when investors take money out and there is not enough offsetting new money to cover. Shares must be sold in the stock market to provide money to pay off departing investors. If this net redemption state lasts for more than a few days, the fund manager needs to make decisions about which securities to sell into the market.

Continuous net redemptions create a problem for the mutual fund manager. The manager must sell some holdings to pay out cash to the investors who want to get out. In the beginning of the down phase of the market it is relatively easy as there are many choices of stocks to sell without unduly affecting the market. The manager usually sells the most liquid stocks first, and blue chip stocks are ideal sale candidates. Examples of the type of shares sold during this phase are telephone companies, large manufacturers, consumer product companies, integrated oil companies, banks, and any large company with market liquidity. Some of these companies pay generous dividends. Buyers for these types of shares are usually available in any type of market.

After a fund manager sells most of the blue-chip portions he faces a dilemma. Managers go to great lengths to avoid selling stocks that are thinly-traded or favourites. If the cash cushion is gone, the manager utilizes bank loans to avoid selling. Some managers take the drastic step of suspending redemptions, depending on the legalities permitted in the prospectus. All funds reserve the right to suspend redemptions in certain circumstances, such as closure of the stock exchange. After a prolonged period of redemptions however, there is no alternative but to sell stocks.

A public insistent on getting out of mutual funds redeems shares in a day-after-day, grinding fashion. Redemption requests received late in the day may not be forwarded to the manager in time to trigger a sale that day. The fund must honour the prices of that day's close, even though the manager may not have sold enough shares before the close. As sometimes happens during a market slide, the opening prices on the market the next morning may be lower than the closing prices of the night before. This situation is known as "gap down." This creates a problem for the holders of fund shares. For example, if each share fell by 5% overnight, it could take 5% more shares sold to meet the cash requirement of that redemption demand. Mutual fund managers must sell more shares than would have been necessary at yesterday's prices. The loyal shareholders staying with the fund are subsidizing the investors who redeemed their shares the day before.

Investors in mutual funds are not generally aware of the fact that they must enter an order to sell during the trading day of the market, before they know the price they will get that night. On Monday, October 19 1987 the market fell 20% in one day, as measured by the Dow. From the investor's point of view he would be thinking of the price for his mutual fund reported in the paper on Monday morning. This price was based on the closing prices from Friday, October 16. By Monday night, when his sell order was valued, average prices were 20% or more lower. What a shock for those who sold that Monday thinking they would get Friday's price!

Managers suffering heavy redemptions will be forced to get liquid in a hurry. Any remaining decent-sized blue chip position that can be liquidated easily will be sold. The more speculative securities are not easily sold when there is an urgent need for the money.

Fund portfolios become less liquid and progressively more speculative as the bear market continues. In a typical bear market, the slide in stock prices picks up steam as many investors try to sell at the same time. The only kind of companies people are willing to buy in these fear-driven markets are the blue chips. So anyone forced to sell must sell blue chip stocks, crossing their fingers that the bear will end before they are forced to start selling some of the less liquid positions.

This forced selling by fund managers to accommodate the fear-driven fund shareholder redeeming at the bottom of the cycle completes the involuntary market-timing syndrome of "buy high, sell low." The public demands that fund managers buy stocks heavily near the top of the cycle and sell stocks heavily near the bottom of the cycle. This is a recipe for disaster. This buy high, sell low syndrome is one of the reasons that funds fall out of favour during long bear markets.

You may feel as if this scenario is far-fetched, a product of an over-heated imagination. In fact, versions of this scenario were played out in the 1880s, 1929, and 1969–74. For this reason, by 1982 there was rela-tively little money left in equity mutual funds.

They Held the Wrong Stocks

From 1971–73 most mutual funds missed the bull market as they held the wrong kind of stocks. The funds continued to hold the growth stocks of the last bull market (the Nifty Fifty), having sold all of their liquid, blue chip stocks to meet redemption demands.

When investors came back into the market in 1975 they wanted nothing to do with the Nifty Fifty. And new investors in the stock market avoided mutual funds because of the recent bad publicity. Since they were frightened by the recent memory of the bear market, they would only venture into the bluest of the blue chips, shares that mutual funds had dumped during the bear phase to meet redemption requests. Left with only the more aggressive and speculative securities the funds were positioned completely at odds with the market cycle. And they could not switch their investments to the right kind of stocks because they could not find buyers for the stocks they held. So they missed the big move in the blue chips and dramatically underperformed the market. This under-performance triggered more redemptions throughout the late 1970s as fund holders realized they were paying annual management fees to make less money than the market averages. As some investors related to me at the time, "I can lose money on my own, I don't need to pay somebody to do it for me!"

Mutual fund holders fall into a class of investors known as momentum players, according to one theory. The definition of a momentum investor is one that looks at recent past performance to determine what to buy in the markets. Momentum investing is discussed in more detail in chapter 9. Investors who follow this investment style tend to come into markets late, as the trend takes a long time to establish and also tend to leave the markets late. A long period of underperformance usually is required before a momentum player, who follows the markets from a distance, realizes that the trend has shifted. By the time the momentum player decides to get out, the down cycle is already well underway.

I believe that mutual fund investors place too much emphasis on past performance. The really successful investors look to the future, trying to find out which investments will do well over the next ten years. Since forecasting the future is a daunting challenge, and past performance figures are readily available, many fund investors fall into the trap of relying on past performance to pick investments.

Any long-term investor in mutual funds is along for the ride with these momentum investors. When the next bear market arrives, some fund holders sell their shares immediately, avoiding some of the negative consequences of underperformance and redemptions. These same investors were forcing the managers to buy when prices were unusually high, by buying shares in the mutual fund when it was performing well. Many investors will remain invested however, and as long-term holders they will suffer the performance consequences caused by others who are forcing the managers to sell. The crowd mentality determines the investment experience.

As part of the crowd, and partners with all those other fund holders, the fund shareholder must accept fate passively. The actions of others, whether redeeming or staying, will largely determine the outcome for all holders in that fund. Few investors would be happy about being in such a position of complete loss of control.

WHO WANTS TO BE IN PARTNERSHIP WITH A GROUP OF MOMENTUM PLAYERS?

The manic-depressive nature of momentum investors who dominate the mutual fund game is analogous to a large group of people deciding to go into business together. Imagine that you and a group of 100 others decide to go into the widget manufacturing business. As luck would have it the widget business gets better shortly after you buy your first factory. Prices for widgets go up, demand is up, and the factory is running full out, creating lots of profits.

The group holds a meeting of all the owners with the discussion focusing on adding another widget factory. The manager hired to run the factory points out that if only he had more capacity to produce widgets he could make more and sell more. Your partners decide to build another widget factory to meet the demand. You argue, in vain, that the widget business is cyclical and a downturn would cause real problems if a new factory were just coming on stream.

The factory is built, and all seems well. But after strengthening for a while longer, the widget business enters the down part of the cycle. The debt incurred to build the new factory cannot be serviced by the reduced cash flow of the business, so another meeting is held. The managers of the business explain that a cash injection is needed from the owners to survive the cycle. The other partners balk, saying that they would prefer not to put any new money in. Many of them actually start talking about getting out of the widget business.

As the partners argue back and forth a feeling of panic starts to develop in the room. Several vocal speakers portray the widget cycle as entering new territory, a period of lack of demand for widgets never before seen. Other speakers relate how competitive widget manufacturers have put their factories up for sale.

The group decides to put both factories up for sale too, against the advice of the managers. The price for widget factories is very poor and there are too many already for sale. You argue that the better course of action would be to add more money to the partnership to support the existing business and in addition, add an additional amount to finance the purchase of a third factory, which is available at a bargain price. The group shouts you down, with suggestions that you might have lost your ability to reason.

After some time the factories are sold, at a large loss. Your share of the money left in the pool after paying off the debt and the managers is a mere fraction of your original investment.

Throughout the experience you had the right idea of how to manage the widget business. However, because you were in a partnership with a large group that was caught up in greed at the top of the cycle and fear at the bottom, your investment suffered. The professional managers also knew what to do but were unable to change the outcome. At least they got paid while the events unfolded; you just lost money.

BECOME AN INDEPENDENT INVESTOR

Now that you are aware of the traps hidden in the mutual fund game you are in a better position to make a decision. If you are invested in mutual funds now you can hold on, hoping that history will not repeat itself. This time your mutual fund partners may do the right thing and not cause your investments to suffer. Do you really want your investment program, and perhaps your retirement, dependent upon the actions of these other investors? If you are willing to take that chance, you need not sell out of your mutual funds now. But there are alternatives that avoid these mutual fund problems.

One little-known alternative that is becoming more popular is outlined in the book *The Wealthy Boomer: Life after Mutual Funds*. For centuries wealthy individuals have hired money managers directly to select investments on their behalf. This practice carries the name of discretionary portfolio management or managed money. Investment counsellors manage your portfolio, charging an annual management fee. You get diversification, professional management, and peace of mind without the risks of pooling your money with thousands of inexperienced investors. Each portfolio is kept separately from the others.

This method was previously available only to those with $1 000 000 or more in assets. For those people the cost was reasonable at 1% to 2% per annum. Now the service is available through some investment firms for minimum amounts of $150 000 with annual fees of 2.75%. Although a little high, this cost is still in the same general range as the management fees of many mutual funds.

Investors find the discretionary aspect of the service attractive. They are not required to participate in decisions about which stocks to buy and which to sell. This is the basis of that third benefit, worry-free investing.

For many who chose that alternative the discretionary aspect of the service carries a hidden trap.

THE MANAGED MONEY TRAP

While attractive for peace-of-mind investing, discretionary money management lures investors with high returns during bull markets and disappoints with poor results during bear markets. This weakness causes many investors to give up on money management when markets are low, ensuring that they buy high and sell low. This trap is a version of the market timing trap.

Discretionary money management, although routine for the very wealthy, is invariably sought out by other investors only during the bull phase of the market. Historically high returns advertised by portfolio managers entice investors to sign a money management contract.

Eventually the portfolio's rate of return turns negative and trust and confidence in the manager diminish. Because of this, most investors who turn their money over to a third party for total control and discretion eventually lose confidence in that manager. Major reasons for this disillusionment are their lack of involvement in the investing process and the inevitability of a disappointment in the rate of return. The discretionary money manager's relationship with investors compares to that of a mutual fund salesperson. Annual reviews take place where the discussion centres on the rate of return achieved by the manager. If the rate of return dips too low, the investor fires the manager and moves back to something safer, such as money market instruments or bonds.

The discretionary portfolio management investor may become the victim of the same phenomenon that caused mutual fund holders to add money in bull markets and dump funds during bear market periods.

The third alternative that avoids both the involuntary market timing trap of mutual funds and the market timing trap of discretionary money management requires that you stay involved and keep control of your individual investment portfolio. By maintaining control you lower the probability of firing the manager during a difficult market period and you completely eliminate any chance of other investors' actions hurting your investments. You establish yourself as an independent investor.

You can invest directly in common stocks, bonds, and treasury bills. You can manage an investment portfolio of your own, with some help from professional advisors. You can choose to take a different path from the crowd.

Make a Decision to Take a More Independent Route

You have the choice as an individual investor. You can follow the crowd into that huge pool of money, looking for the questionable benefits of diversification, professional management, and worry-free investing. This chapter outlined how the last two benefits are more illusory than real.

Evidence clearly shows that the current popularity of actively managed mutual funds relates directly to the sales effort and advertising undertaken by fund companies. Much of the expansion of mutual fund holdings in Canada and the United States came at the expense of direct stock market holdings. Individuals sold their stock holdings and purchased mutual funds, and gave up their investing independence. This phenomenon accelerated dramatically around 1992, as fund advertising started to dominate the airwaves. People lost the desire or the confidence to own individual stocks directly.

The difficulties of direct stock ownership are as exaggerated in people's minds as the benefits of mutual funds. Shareholders of companies enjoy many privileges and few burdens. Brokerage accounts holding stock sit patiently, requiring only a little attention. Companies that pay dividends regularly deposit additional money into these accounts, without any effort on the part of the owner and without the shareholder paying any annual management fees.

Eventually, the investor comes to identify with each company held, realizing that the management and employees of those companies all are working for the shareholder. Annual reports show up in the mail, and the investor sneaks a look. Internet web sites provide copious amounts of information about each company, and the investor finds that curiosity draws his attention there.

You will see in the coming chapters that direct stock and bond ownership is much simpler than many think. There are some basic pitfalls that must be avoided to achieve success. These are outlined as well as the remedies. The advantages of maintaining your independence as an investor outweigh the small challenges associated with direct stock ownership. And, if you are willing to make a commitment to travel a different path from the crowd, you will feel a sense of accomplishment and contentment, and pride in achieving something worthwhile.

Two

Build Your Personal Investment Portfolio of Bonds and Stocks

Once you decide to take a more independent path, you need to make arrangements to meet the basic requirements for successful portfolio investing. When managing your portfolio you want to duplicate the good features of mutual funds and discretionary portfolio management, while avoiding the traps.

In chapter 1, I stated that mutual funds are sold by extolling three possible benefits: diversification, professional management, and worry-free investing.

When closely examined, the benefits of mutual funds can be reduced to one feature that deserves retention. This feature is diversification. Adequate diversification remains very important. Professional management and worry-free investing are more promise than reality.

The benefits of professional management are nebulous, at best. A mutual fund cannot provide professional management over an entire investment cycle. Nervous investors force fund managers to sell stocks near the bottom of a bear market and during the early stages of the next bull market, negating the influence of a manager. Fund managers find themselves confronting a flood of new money of tsunami proportions when stock prices reach their highest levels, again making professional management difficult, if not irrelevant. To be fair to mutual fund managers it needs to be said that this problem of dealing with a public that insists on buying high and selling low confronts all investment professionals, including investment advisors.

Worry-free investing or peace of mind also is impossible to achieve with mutual funds. Investors invariably find plenty to worry about when the occasional bear market arrives. The best that most investors could hope to find is a system that reduces their anxiety to a manageable level. This anxiety level must be kept low enough to avoid panic withdrawals. In later chapters I explain how this can be accomplished.

Successful investors find worry-reduced investing comes from personal control over their investments. You can find a measure of confidence in your investing with the help of professionals. Not the kind of professionals who say "trust me" and take over control of your money, but the type who work as coaches and advisors. Investors using professional advisors to help supervise their portfolios reach a level of comfort, even at stressful times. A degree of worry-free investing comes from knowledge, involvement, and control.

The knowledge level of investors working with professionals increases dramatically over time. In later chapters I will explain how best to use these professionals without giving up control and involvement.

The benefit advertised by mutual funds that holds up under close scrutiny is diversification. Most properly managed mutual funds provide instant diversification for any amount of money invested. This feature of mutual funds must be duplicated when a switch is made to independent portfolio investing. While diversifying a portfolio seems challenging at first, the effort required is very manageable.

DIVERSIFICATION IS IMPORTANT

For the individual who wants success with safety, diversification is essential. Adequate diversification holds the key to surviving in all markets, bull and bear. You must find a way to reach the minimum safe standard of diversification in your portfolio.

A look at the most successful investors might be useful in determining how much diversification is enough. Ironically, many very wealthy investors lack sufficient diversification in their investment portfolios. Their portfolios are not safe. Outstanding wealth results from extreme risk-taking. The most direct path to the top 100 list of wealthiest people is to put all your eggs in one basket. The well-known examples come to mind—Bill Gates of Microsoft; the Thomson family, owners of a Canadian-based information services and publishing empire; the Bronfmans, of the liquor dynasty; the owners of Netscape, and Amazon.com; and the list goes on. These individuals and many others like them concentrate their holdings in one company.

Less obvious examples are frequently found in your hometown—business owners who run one business and who leave an estate with several million dollars from that company. Undoubtedly, you know some of these people, or know of them. This approach to wealth creation will always be the most direct and rewarding. For most of us though, this approach carries too much risk and worry.

The list of the wealthiest people in the world who prospered without adequate diversification focuses on the survivors. Not included in this list and not recorded in any other list are those who tried to put all their eggs in one basket and failed. This list, if it existed, would be much longer. Millions and millions of people tried and failed to achieve exceptional wealth through aggressive risk-taking. Copying those few who succeeded against huge odds makes no sense for most of us.

A majority of investors prefer a more moderate path of seeking material comfort, if not wealth, without excessive risk. Moderation suits the average saver. For those of you who need a lower risk approach, diversification is like oxygen. Investors need it to survive.

Incidentally, not all mutual funds guarantee diversification. Many funds pursue performance by concentrating on one aspect or sector of the market. When spectacular returns push that fund to the top of the performance list, money rolls in. This concentration carries huge risk. When the performance reports glow, investment in these funds leads to an obvious buy high, sell low trap. When the sector that the fund is playing cools off, the performance drops to the bottom of the comparative charts, and most of the money exits the fund. These investors were really speculating more than investing. Many investment professionals categorize sectors as "hot" if they are performing well and "cold" if stocks in that sector are drifting lower or are flat.

Most financial planners who sell mutual funds use the diversification argument to disparage the independent path of portfolio management. Their scepticism about investors' ability to manage their own portfolio holds some justification. Mutual fund salespeople, as well as financial planners, witness the results of a portfolio's lack of diversification often. Planners see unsuccessful stock portfolios every day, brought to them by unhappy investors. A nearly universal observation about these portfolio disasters seen by financial planners is a lack of diversification.

These under-diversified portfolios usually consist of fewer than five stocks. When one or two of those stocks hits a rough patch in the road, or falls into a sinkhole and disappears altogether, the portfolio goes on the critical list. At this point, the investor heads for a different advisor, often a financial planner. This financial planner, who often specializes in mutual funds, sees the portfolio with a fresh eye, wondering who guided this investor onto the rocks. After exposure to a few problem portfolios, the planner decides that ownership of individual stocks is the culprit. The philosophy of individual stock holdings unfairly gets the blame for these bad results. The planners' concern is understandable, but based on a false assumption. The true culprit is a lack of diversification, not ownership of stocks.

The good news—you can build a portfolio that is sufficiently diversified with a surprisingly small amount of effort. You can do it for less cost than the median management fee on an equity mutual fund. The important point to remember is:

Diversification is essential to success in portfolio investing.

A DIVERSIFIED PORTFOLIO

Before you diversify the stock market holdings in the common stock portion of your portfolio, you need to look at the overall portfolio itself. This diversification at the portfolio level is easily accomplished.

The term diversified portfolio means a group of investment selections that is balanced for safety and growth. Proper portfolio diversification usually requires a balance of holdings between fixed income (safety) and common stocks (growth). Once this portfolio balance is achieved, a second type of diversification among the common stock holdings must be established.

Safety comes from the type of security held as well as the number and variety. A sense of protection comes from lowering the risk or volatility of the portfolio. Volatility measures the amount of fluctuation in the overall value of the portfolio of bonds and stocks.

For most investors, a balanced portfolio consists of government bonds and common stocks. The portfolio holds government bonds for safety and common stocks for growth. Balancing the portfolio between two different types of securities lowers the risk and volatility of the portfolio. In the investment game "different" investments means those that usually react in opposite ways.

For a balanced portfolio to work ideally, the two segments of the portfolio must move in different directions from each other during the various phases of the market cycle. Usually one section of the portfolio reacts less than the other in up and down markets.

You will find it easier to understand a balanced portfolio of bonds and stocks after an examination of the different characteristics of each type.

The easiest step in selecting actual investments comes with the bond section. The bond section of the portfolio gives you safety and income, with low volatility.

The Fixed Income (Bond) Section

A bond represents a loan to a corporation or government. That loan includes a promise to pay interest, usually every six months, and to repay the principal when the loan matures. When you as an individual investor purchase a bond you make a loan to the issuer. You must determine first if the borrower is worthy of your trust. You need that loan repayment as well as the interest.

Both governments and corporations issue bonds. Our diversification goal is to have a portion of the portfolio as safe as possible, so government bonds meet this need better than corporate bonds.

In Canada, government bonds are issued by the federal, provincial, and municipal governments. Since governments have their own taxing power, they command the highest credit ratings with agencies like Moody's, Standard and Poors, and Dominion Bond Rating Service (DBRS). According to a rule of the rating agencies, provincial governments' ratings cannot exceed the rating held by the federal government. Provincial government ratings are either lower or equal to federal ratings. This rating gap reflects a higher perceived risk for the provincial governments. Yet, provincial government bonds still qualify as safe havens for many institutional investors. This strong belief in provincial credit quality shows up in the narrow spread between federal and provincial bond yields. One meaning of the term "spread" refers to the difference in yield between federal and provincial bonds. Provincial bonds normally yield an interest rate less than 1% higher than federal bonds. A higher yield usually indicates a higher risk. Municipal bonds lack adequate liquidity and safety, features that are important at turning points in the cycle.

Factors affecting a credit rating for government bonds include population growth, industry diversification, overall tax levels, political stability, age of population, and any factor that affects that jurisdiction's ability to raise money. In North America, these factors usually vary only slightly. Outside of North America the judgement needed to recognize variations in credit quality becomes infinitely more difficult. You need to stick to Canadian bonds or U.S. bonds to keep things simple.

As long as safety goals are met, provincial bonds provide a slightly better income than federal government bonds. Both bond categories are much safer than corporate bonds.

All Canadian provinces issue bonds to finance their government operations. The small differences in risk level between provinces make diversification of a government bond portfolio less urgent. Large portfolios (greater than $1 000 000) usually diversify extensively, holding 5 or 10 different bond issues. For a smaller portfolio, this is not important as long as the bonds are safe—government issuers. Two or three different provinces such as Ontario, British Columbia, or Alberta provide sufficient safety.

Gouvernement de Québec bonds yield a slightly higher return due to concerns about political stability. Venturesome investors might consider purchasing these bonds, especially in light of the election results in November 1998. These elections seemed to show that Quebecers, while they like Lucien Bouchard and the Parti Quebecois government, prefer not to separate from Canada or vote in a referendum with that question. In spite of this political uncertainty, Quebec-based investment advisors recommend Quebec government bonds regularly. The probability that these bonds will act the same as Ontario or Alberta is high. Investors in these bonds enjoy a premium return for a bond that is likely as safe as Ontario.

The term to maturity of the bond affects the return and risk of the portfolio. Selecting the term to maturity carefully keeps the overall risk of the portfolio under control. Some time and care needs to be spent on selecting the date of maturity for each bond as this will have an impact on the returns as well. The term to maturity of a bond means the amount of time left until the bond expires. For example, a bond issued with a termination date of June 1, 2010 ceases to pay interest on that date. Bondholders turn in their certificates on that date to receive repayment of their original investment.

The original buyer of that bond often turns it over to others long before maturity. The bond market facilitates this turnover or trading. The ease of trading for a bond is known as liquidity. A bond that is frequently traded is "liquid." Less frequently traded bonds (or stocks) are called "illiquid." A well-known type of bond, the Canada Savings Bond, is always liquid since it can be redeemed at any time at the holder's option although it is non-transferable. Yields are usually higher for regular government bonds than Canada Savings Bonds because of this redemption option. Unless you need the benefit of this instant liquidity you will receive a better return with provincial or federal government bonds.

Most Government of Canada bonds trade frequently and readily. Some provincial government bonds are more liquid than others. For the individual investor, liquidity matters less than safety. Safety is of paramount importance in the fixed income section of the portfolio.

Once the bond is issued and trading in the bond market, the original term to maturity and yield change. As each day goes by, the bond has a shorter term to maturity. When a bond is re-sold, the yield is recalculated, to reflect the remaining term to maturity and current interest rates. A new bond buyer looks at the bond as if it began its life when re-purchased.

My experience with bond investors tells me that the concepts of term to maturity and yield present a difficulty. Investors find it challenging to distinguish between the yield at the time of issue and the yield at the time of purchase. Sometimes this quirk of investors meant I got more credit for selecting bonds than I deserved.

For example, in the early to middle years of the 1980s, Canadian bonds appeared with interest rates as high as 15%. One popular Government of Canada issue that many investors bought matures in 2007 with a 14% coupon.

The Government of Canada bond, paying 14%, traded actively for a few years. Investors buying this bond when interest rates were less than 14%, which was most of the time, paid a premium to the seller. A premium on this bond equalized interest rates for the new buyer. If the interest rate on current issues of similar bonds was 11%, then the buyer of a bond from the older issue, with a 14% rate, would pay a substantially higher price than the original price. The original price of a bond is known as "par value." A bond starts and ends its life at par value.

When subsequent buyers pay more than par value for a bond in the trading market the interest income (known as the coupon) is the same as original investors received. But because they paid more than par value for the bond, the yield is less. This premium price above "par value" makes the 14% coupon yield the current rate of interest or 11%.

Many buyers were convinced that they were getting 14% interest, even when they paid a premium to buy the bond. I know they bragged to their friends and spouses about the 14% bonds they found. I tried on many occasions to explain the difference between the 14% coupon and the 11% actual yield they received.

You will notice in the bond section of the newspaper that beside the bond description there are terms such as coupon, price, and yield. For example, a Government of Canada bond with a coupon of 10% due in 3.5 years carries a price of 116.25 and a yield of 4.77%. How could a 10% bond yield only 4.77%?

Let me try to explain it here for you.

Calculation of the Yield to Maturity

If a bond maturing in 2007 yields 14% (the coupon rate), a $100 000 bond pays $14 000 annually. If the buyer pays $100 000 (par value) for the bond, the yield is 14%. In this case the "yield" refers to both the "coupon rate" and the "yield to maturity," as they are equal. The coupon rate and the yield to maturity are equal only when the bond is trading exactly at par value.

If the older bond were sold today, the seller would first look at the rate of interest offered by similar bonds issued today. Let's say that similar new bonds are being sold with an interest rate of 8.9%. This means that the person selling the older bond should raise the price of his bond to the point where the buyer will receive an 8.9% return. Earning $14 000 income at 8.9% requires that a bond cost $127 272. How does $14 000 income on an investment of $127 272 equal a yield of 8.9%?

In the example here, the investor has paid $127 272 for a bond that matures at $100 000. If held to maturity, that bond produces a loss of $27 272 for the investor. This investor needs to consider that loss in the rate of return calculation. This is done by amortizing (spreading) the loss over the remaining term to maturity. A 2007 bond has seven years left to maturity in the year 2000. (In practice, the term to maturity calculates months and days as well.)

The approximate return on that bond to maturity includes a loss of $27 272 over seven years—$3896 each year. If you subtract that sum from the $14 000 of annual interest income, you get $10 104. This calculation gives the impression that the yield is just 7.9% (10 104 ÷ 127 272). There is one more quirk to calculating bond yields that brings the yield back to the 8.9% level.

Bond traders take into consideration the average capital invested before quoting the "yield to maturity." The actual yield to maturity assumes that the investor has an average amount of capital invested—the cost price ($127 272) and the maturity price ($100 000). The investor paid $127 272 and receives back $100 000 at maturity in 2007. By convention, the amount invested over the seven years is considered to be the average of the two numbers—$113 636.

The actual yield to maturity then is $10 104 divided by $113 636 times 100 = 8.89%. The bond used in this example would have the following information in the newspaper: a bond with a coupon of 14% due in 7 years carries a price of 127.27 and a yield of 8.89%.

Many investors believe they are getting an exceptionally good yield when they buy a bond like the 14% of 2007. In fact, if held to maturity the yield on that bond is much lower than it looks. By the time maturity arrives the investor may forget that $127 272 was invested originally.

One more important consideration deserves discussion in the bond yield calculation. The income tax impact of the two types of income involved matters a great deal to the taxable investor. If the bond is held in a Registered Retirement Savings Plan (RRSP) or Registered Retirement Income Fund (RRIF), the tax implications can be ignored.

Investors pay income tax annually on interest income received. The 14% income or $14 000 attracts taxation at the investor's highest marginal tax rate. On the other hand, the loss of $3896 per year can not be used as a deduction against income. This loss can be used only a deduction against capital gains at the time of sale or maturity. The deduction is allowed only if there is a capital gain to match it. In my experience, many bond portfolio investors find it difficult to use up this loss. Some investors miss using this loss for tax purposes because they forget to claim it. Others fail to use it because there are no capital gains to offset the loss. If full tax is paid on the income, and no deduction is claimed for the loss, the after-tax result for this 14% bond is much worse than a bond selling at par yielding 8.89%.

In practice, an investor who is taxable at high marginal rates is better off with a discount bond. A "discount" bond trades below par value because it has a lower coupon rate than the current rate of interest on comparable bonds. A lower coupon rate means lower interest income, which determines taxes payable. A bond with a face value of $100 000 trading at $90 000 is a discount bond. The owner of a discount bond is compensated for lower interest income with a capital gain at maturity or when the bond is sold. The tax advantage of a discount bond comes from the deferral of tax on the capital gain portion of the return. Since taxes are paid on current income only, the discount bond defers tax payable on the capital gain portion until the bond is sold or matures.

Discount bonds exist when a bond has a coupon rate that is lower than the market yield to maturity. For example, a bond with a coupon of 4% and the market yield to maturity of 5% sells at a discount. In the late years of the 1990s these discount bonds almost disappeared. Interest rates fell steadily for several years leaving the market full of bonds issued when interest rates were higher. Bonds with coupons higher than the market yields sell at a premium, and bonds with coupons lower than the market yield sell at a discount. The market yield to maturity fell to such low levels that virtually no bonds existed with coupon rates lower than market rates.

Volatility and Term to Maturity

The potential volatility of the portfolio increases with the term to maturity of the bond. In other words, a twenty-year bond will fluctuate in value much more than a five-year bond. Of course, in the end, the face value is paid at maturity regardless of the term. However, a rise in interest rates could depress the value of the bond portion of the portfolio. The longer the term to maturity remaining for the bond, the more severe the volatility when interest rates change. For example, if interest rates rose from 4.90% to 10%, a bond maturing in ten years would drop in value by 27.7%. For a bond with 27 years remaining, an increase in rates from 5.27% to 9% means a loss in value of 34.6%. While these kinds of interest rate increases seem far-fetched, the risk still remains. A portfolio with bonds with more than ten years to maturity represents a bigger risk than most investors realize.

Since the purpose of the bond section is to provide the portfolio with safety and stability, I prefer to hold shorter maturity bonds. Maturities up to ten years meet these needs adequately in most markets.

Between 1984 and 1997 most of my clients' portfolios held bonds of a long term maturity, i.e., longer than ten years. Often they held bonds with 20-year maturities. This worked well as the general level of interest rates drifted down. Capital gains accrued as bonds bought with coupons of 10% or higher moved up in price as rates fell to 8%, 7%, and even 5%. Those attractive 10% rates compensated investors for the additional risk of longer-term bonds. With the current (1999) rates of 5% to 6% for longer-term bonds, the slightly higher returns of the longer term do not justify the much higher risk, in my opinion.

Diversification in maturities provides additional safety. Your portfolio could include Treasury bills (less than one year), two- or three-year bonds, five-year bonds and some longer-term bonds.

Portfolios with a higher percentage exposure to the stock market need a shorter term to maturity in the bond section.

For example, if an investor maintains an exposure of 70% of the portfolio to equities, then his portfolio risk level is improved by holding bonds of maturities of less than five years. This is important because common stocks are essentially long-term investments. By holding shorter-term bonds to compensate, the average equivalent term to maturity of the portfolio shortens. The overall volatility of the portfolio declines, helping the investor through the difficult bear markets. Proper diversification means holding both short term and long term investments.

Once you have a few different government bonds with varying maturities the bond section of the portfolio is complete. There is no need to spend a lot of time on the bond holdings in the portfolio. When a bond matures, it is replaced. If the average term to maturity shortens as the years go by, a long-term bond purchase balances the portfolio.

Interest payments from bonds build up in the portfolio. These payments usually arrive every six months. For investors needing regular income I try to find bonds that pay in different months. For example, a bond with a December 1 maturity pays interest every December 1 and every June 1. A bond with a March 31 maturity pays on March 31 and also on September 30. It usually helps with cash flow considerations to stagger the maturities and therefore the payments so there is a regular cash flow around the calendar. Bond interest payments provide a good tool for re-balancing the portfolio, a concept discussed at length later.

This description of bonds and bond markets covers enough ground to allow the management of the bond portion of the portfolio. The help of a good "coach" or investment advisor completes the requirements for success.

The most important thing to remember about bonds is their purpose. Bonds provide safety and income. They are not likely to provide capital growth. For capital growth purchase ownership of corporations in the form of stocks. Bonds represent a loan to government. While they paid exceptional returns in the 15 years from 1982 to 1997, bonds normally produce mediocre returns. This is normal for a low-risk loan to a credit-worthy entity such as a government.

The really good returns are found in the stock market. I turn your attention now to the stock market portion of the portfolio, as 95% of your time will be spent there. The first consideration when building the common stock section of your portfolio is an understanding of the risks and rewards.

What is the Appropriate Level of Risk for You?

For most people the level of risk in their portfolio is directly proportional to the degree of involvement in common stocks. You must decide how much involvement you wish to have in the stock market. The decision carries significance for the outcome of your investment program since the stock market is potentially the most rewarding portion of the investment portfolio.

Rational investors seek to maximize their return and minimize their risk. Often when I ask a new client to describe their investment objectives the response is a version of the following statement: "I want the highest possible return without taking any risk." I feel better if they laugh a little after they say it. The ones that keep a straight face give me an urge to call my lawyer. Joking or not, these investors are expressing their feelings about investing honestly. At the deepest level of the human psyche all investors desire great economic gains without sacrifice. The fact that this is not possible does not deter many people. Otherwise lottery tickets, bingo halls, casinos, video lottery machines, and day trading on Internet stocks would not be such fast-growing activities. In the stock market investing game it helps if people take a more sensible attitude toward risk and reward. Most mature investors recognize that to get a reward a risk must be endured.

First, a quick short story will illustrate the importance of meanings of words like risk.

WHAT DOES "LOVE" MEAN TO YOU?

I participated in a seminar on communication skills once. The seminar leaders used a technique that you may have seen. Each of us was asked to write down 5 synonyms for the word "love," without consulting with anyone else. I dutifully wrote down my five, finding the task difficult and a little embarrassing. Among the eight people in my group we had about 35 words chosen to represent our interpretation of "love." (A few could not think of five words). I was amazed to discover that there were only one or two words overlapping among the 35 possibilities. To this day I would not believe it if I had not witnessed it firsthand. The seminar leader assured us that this result was normal; there was never much duplication. Obviously, the point the seminar leaders wished to drive home was that people have different meanings for important words.

Without any doubt, if the same exercise was performed with the word "risk" there would be 35 different interpretations of that word too.

Volatility

When investment experts say the word "risk" they usually mean volatility. Volatility means the degree of fluctuation in the investment(s) and determines the amount of risk of that investment. The more the value changes or fluctuates over a fixed time period, the riskier that investment. Experts use a statistical measurement technique called standard deviation to measure volatility.

I discovered over many years of listening that most investors have a different idea of risk from the experts. Most of them think of risk in terms of losing all their money. Frequently, novice and experienced investors alike say "I know that if I venture into the stock market I must be prepared to lose everything." Given that frame of mind, it is amazing that people still buy stocks.

Catastrophic Risk and Market Risk

These investors understand intuitively part of the story. They are right that any single stock could go to zero. This happens with some securities, usually speculative ones. Occasionally even "blue chip" companies like the former Royal Trustco also go under. This is called catastrophic or company-specific risk. There is also the risk of fluctuations in the overall level of the stock market prices. This is called market risk.

For any reasonable portfolio management technique the probability is zero that catastrophic risk will cause the whole portfolio to disappear, but both catastrophic and market risk still influence portfolio values. The risk that is most likely to torpedo an investment program is the possibility that wide fluctuations in value will cause an investor to cancel the investing program at a time when a poor return is made for that investor. The history of stock and bond markets shows that fluctuations in the rate of return of the portfolio diminish the longer the portfolio is held. Rates of return still may fluctuate widely in any one year. In other words the major risk of any investment program is getting caught in a buy high, sell low trap, as many investors do.

You can avoid this trap with the techniques described in this book. However, it is important to understand that the average investor succumbs to this risk frequently. This is the reason that studies show that investors, as a group, achieve much poorer returns than markets deliver.

In spite of the risks of the stock market as well as individual stocks going bankrupt, including common stocks in your portfolio is definitely worth the trouble.

Why Equities Are Important

The highest risk portfolio is one with all investable funds (100%) in the common stock market. This portfolio would also provide the opportunity to make the highest return over longer periods of time.

Jeremy Siegel, in his book *Stocks for the Long Run* (McGraw-Hill, 1994), produced a chart that shows the returns on bonds, stocks, and other investments from 1802 to 1997. As you can see he compared stocks to bonds, Treasury bills, gold, and the CPI (Consumer Price Index), a measure of inflation. You might be amazed to discover how much the returns in the stock market beat other investments. The investment of $1 in common stocks resulted in $7.47 million in 1997, an 8.4% annual compound return.

His analysis of past returns in the stock market required certain assumptions. One assumption that seems particularly important to note concerns dividends. Siegel assumed that all dividends paid by companies owned were reinvested in the stock market as received. For most of the 195-year period from 1802 to 1997 dividends made up a large portion of the return on common stocks. In fact, dividends on common stocks usually exceeded the interest paid on bonds. Only in the 1950s did bond interest pass the dividend return on stocks for the first time. Up until the last 50 years the rationale was that investors needed a higher dividend return on stocks to entice them to take the risk of owning a stock. So dividends were very important to the growth in the portfolio. The assumption of reinvesting dividends is unrealistic as there is no record of investors consistently reinvesting dividends over such a long period of time.

Returns on bonds, stocks, and other investments, 1802–1997

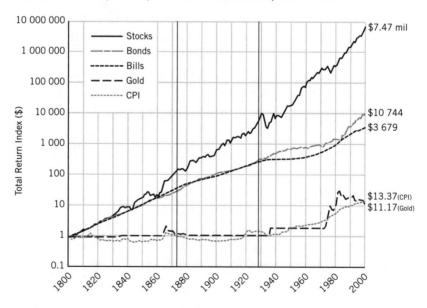

So $1 going to $7.5 million over 195 years is theoretically possible, but in practice, all investors eventually dip into the returns from their stocks, either for living expenses or to pay taxes. Siegel points out that $1 million invested in 1802 and reinvested throughout would be worth $7.5 trillion in 1997, about half the value of the entire U.S. stock market. Since a period of 195 years is only six or seven generations of human life it would be possible for a family to maintain a portfolio intact throughout such a period, but the necessity of taxes and living expenses would seriously erode the capital. As well, in the United States, but not in Canada, inheritance taxes on death would take a large chunk of the money even if dividends were reinvested. In Canada, capital gains taxes on death would force the sale of part of the portfolio just to pay taxes due, even if no shares were sold in the market.

The bond market return over the period was 4.7% annual compound return, not much different from bond returns of 1999. A 4.7% return meant $1 grew to a paltry $10 774. So the difference between 4.7% and 8.4% after 195 years is equivalent to the gap between $10 744 and $7.47 million. I know you will agree that this extra $7.459256 million is worth taking some trouble to capture. The rewards of taking the extra effort and risk of the stock market are substantial.

The Stock Market Section of the Portfolio

Stock market investments produce more excitement, anxiety, and reward than bond investments. You just saw that the return on common stock exceeds other alternatives by a huge margin, over time. Common stocks also carry more risk than bonds. Proper diversification reduces the risk of investing in the stock market.

The number of individual stocks held in a portfolio is the key element of diversification—the more different stocks the more the portfolio is diversified. But there is a limit as to how far you need to go. As an individual investor you cannot buy "the market," at least not with individual stocks. There are 500 stocks in the S&P 500, with over 3000 listed on the New York Stock Exchange. In Toronto there are 300 in the TSE 300 and several thousand companies listed on the exchange. No single individual has enough money to buy all the shares listed.

Some have diversified to extraordinary lengths as described in the book *The Money Masters* by John Train (Harper & Row, 1980). Sir John

Templeton, founder of the Templeton Group of mutual funds, bought stocks just before the start of the Second World War. He instructed his broker to purchase shares in all of the companies selling for $1 or less on the New York Stock Exchange and American Stock Exchange.

When his broker called back to say that he had spent $100 on every company that was not actually bankrupt, Templeton replied, "No, no, I want them all. Every last one, bankrupt or not." As all shares were very depressed due to the Depression of the 1930s, most of the approximately 100 companies he bought increased in value and he eventually sold the shares for $40 000, more than four times his cost.

One interesting aspect of this series of transactions is Templeton's insistence on buying all of the stocks that fit his criteria, not eliminating the ones in bankruptcy. This is one type of true diversification. He was not prejudging which of the stocks would turn out to be the best or the worst. While it is not reported, I expect that some of his biggest winners came from that group his broker wanted to exclude. Templeton knew also that he needed many different companies because of the risk associated with buying companies trading for less than $1. Presumably, even though the war provided a major shot in the arm for the American economy, many of those companies went broke. The winners sprinkled among the 100 stocks more than made up for those that failed completely.

This experience influenced his attitude toward investment in a lasting manner. His management style emphasized worldwide diversification. Portfolios managed by the Templeton Group, no longer owned or managed by John Templeton, still hold a large number of stocks relative to other funds in the same category. This extensive diversification helped the Templeton Growth Fund, founded in 1954, survive the 1960s and 1970s, when so many other funds disappeared.

Today Templeton's feat would be more unusual. There are so many more companies than in 1939. Transaction costs become a significant problem for any plan that involves a large number of different companies, unless you are an institutional investor. There is no need to copy Templeton's method exactly. You do need to find the minimum diversification for safety, however.

Safety and Diversification in Common Stocks

Since you cannot buy the whole stock market, you need to make a decision about how many stocks you wish to own. The goal of adequate diversification is to have enough stocks in a portfolio to ensure safety from a disastrous stock pick.

Genuine diversification requires additional care when making an individual stock purchase. The extra effort is worthwhile, however, as the benefits are huge.

The number of stocks in your portfolio makes a difference for performance and safety. Both too few stocks and too many stocks can be harmful. A portfolio with 50 or more stocks is overdiversified, which means it is erring on the side of safety but giving up performance potential. Some investors overdiversify out of necessity, not choice. For example, mutual funds hold more stocks than is optimal because they must invest too much money to cram into a few stocks. For performance reasons they would like to be able to buy fewer different companies, but they cannot.

As individuals, investors can pick one stock, two stocks, or a hundred. Investors, left to their own devices, are more likely to err on the side of too few stocks. However, I have seen some "collectors" who just keep adding more and more positions until the portfolio becomes an unmanageable mess.

Even if money did not limit you to holding fewer stocks, you would still find it best to limit the number of stocks. Apart from performance considerations, transaction costs go up dramatically with the number of stocks. The amount of time to follow, research, and analyze stocks increases exponentially as a large number of stocks are added to the portfolio. And time is limited. An excessively diversified portfolio becomes too difficult to follow, leading to confusion and neglect. Bookkeeping consumes too much time, leading to additional expense for accounting help.

There is a basic trade-off between performance and the number of stocks held. Performance tends toward mediocrity as the number of stocks increases. Eventually the performance of a portfolio with several hundred stocks will be the same as the market as a whole. Why spend a lot of time and money for stock selection to accomplish the average, at best?

The compelling reason for diversification is safety. Safety comes from minimizing the risk of owning one stock that gets into trouble. As mentioned above, this risk is called company-specific or catastrophic risk and can be stated as the risk of one company going bankrupt and the total loss of the investment in that company. Adding more stocks to the portfolio reduces the risk to the portfolio for this type of risk.

A second type of risk is the overall risk of the stock market itself. Even if your portfolio held all the stocks on the stock exchange, a bear market decline would reduce the value of your holdings by the amount of the stock market decline. This possibility is called "market risk." Adding stocks to a portfolio does not reduce "market risk."

A statistical method exists to determine the minimum number of stocks for safety without hurting performance. Several academic studies highlight the amount of risk versus the number of stocks. The table below, from *An Introduction to Risk and Return from Common Stocks* by R. A. Brealey (MIT Press, 1987), shows the risk associated with buying different numbers of stocks.

Risk of a portfolio that is evenly divided among a number of typical stocks

Number of holdings	Yearly variability	Reduction in variability as % of potential
1	40%	0%
2	32.2	43
3	29.2	60
4	27.6	69
5	26.5	75
6	25.8	78
7	25.3	81
8	24.9	83
9	24.6	85
10	24.3	87
15	23.6	91
20	23.2	93
50	22.4	97
100	22.2	98
All stocks	21.9	100

The yearly variability referred to in the table describes the average annual fluctuation of a group of typical stocks. Part of that fluctuation is due to the stock market itself and part is due to the individual stocks in the group.

The following graph shows how the risk or variability associated with a particular individual stock declines as the number of stocks in a portfolio increases. By looking closely at this data it becomes clear that a portfolio manager can lower the risk of owning any individual stock by adding

Risk and the Number of Holdings in a Portfolio

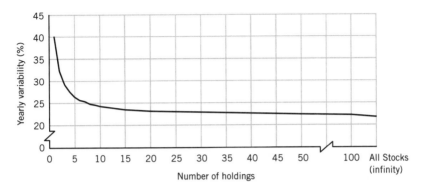

stocks to the portfolio. However, as the number of stocks held increases, adding one more stock to the portfolio lowers the total risk by a smaller and smaller amount. Smart investors look for the point where the marginal benefit of adding a stock is less than the additional cost or loss of performance.

The Law of Diminishing Returns

The amount of risk that can be removed by owning more stocks is limited by the risk of the stock market itself. In the graph this limit shows up on the bottom line that refers to all stocks. In other words, any investor can remove all of the "company-specific" risk by adding thousands of stocks. Adding all the stocks on the market cannot lower the total risk below 21.9%. Using a portfolio of 10 stocks removes 87% of the risk (leaves 13%) and choosing 15 stocks removes 91%. Adding five more stocks to a ten-stock portfolio, and making the portfolio 50% more complicated, only removes 4% of the variability in the portfolio. The more stocks added the less impact made on lowering variability. If going from a 15-stock portfolio to one of thousands of stocks only removes an additional 9% of the risk, the law of diminishing returns applies very severely here.

The good news is that portfolio risk is reduced by almost half by holding ten stocks instead of one stock. The variability of one stock is 40% and the variability of ten stocks is 24.3%. Since variability declines only slightly more by going to 100 stocks (22.2%), there is an insignificant additional benefit to adding 90 more stocks. This means that individual investors can achieve adequate diversification without adding a large number of stocks. This also means that the average mutual fund holds far too many stocks for optimal performance. An institutional money manager would need to hold less than 20 stocks to have a good chance of outperforming the stock market, using this statistical analysis. At 100 stocks, which many institutional portfolios hold, only 2% of the variability is due to individual stock selection while 98% is due to market fluctuation.

The advantages of choosing a small number of stocks are better potential performance and lower costs. A larger number of stocks lowers the chance of outperforming the market and increases the costs of managing that portfolio.

Owning a large number of stocks increases the time that must be spent to manage the portfolio. The time required to review the portfolio with an advisor increases dramatically with more stocks. Investors need more time to read annual reports and check for the latest news. Decision-making becomes so onerous that neglect often creeps in. Having too many stocks makes each decision less critical to the outcome of the portfolio. A certain type of laziness sets in when there are too many stocks.

A portfolio with neither too many nor too few stocks is ideal. Having a small number of stocks increases the pressure when choices are made. In this case some pressure is good, since it makes an investor pay attention. A good indicator of moderation is a portfolio where each stock involves enough money to get your attention, but not so much that you worry incessantly. A portfolio worth $100 000 invested in 100 stocks means each company represents only $1 000. This is not a large sum for anyone with $100 000 to invest in the first place! At the other end of the scale, another investor with $100 000 in only two stocks would need to commit $50 000 to each company. For me, this would be too much money in one stock. A portfolio of $100 000 spread over 10 stocks means investing $10 000 in each. This commitment is large enough to get our attention without being too frightening.

Warren Buffet has achieved fame due to his outstanding success in stock selection. He developed his incredible track record by owning a small number of companies and watching the basket carefully. Today Buffet holds the bulk of his fortune (U.S.$ 37 billion) in just seven companies: GEICO, General RE, American Express, Coca-Cola, Federal Home Loan Mortgage Corporation, Gillette, and the Washington Post.

Owning five or less companies may indeed be ideal for performance. However, I believe such a concentrated portfolio puts too much pressure on the ability of an investor and advisor to choose companies for investment. In my experience less than ten stocks is too few for most individual investors. Mr. Buffett is a very talented full-time investor, unlike most people who spend less than one hour a month on their stock portfolio. As a full-time investor, Buffet probably spent more than five hours per day on his portfolio. Who, other than a professional, wants to spend that much time on the stock market?

A very small list of holdings works well when investors can influence a company with their own expertise and control. Individuals such as Warren Buffet take an active role in the management of companies, usually serving on the board of directors. They take a hand in selecting managers, encouraging them to excel in their handling of the affairs of the company. If the company starts to run into trouble, these owners act to correct the problem. If the difficulties are insurmountable the company is often sold to outsiders before all is lost.

Your expertise probably lies in areas other than the stock market. As a portfolio investor in the stock market, you choose not to spend all your time on investing. By simply adding a sufficient number of stocks to your portfolio, your risk falls dramatically. You sleep more easily at night. If you can equal or better the performance of the stock market you will have an adequate return while still being able to forget about the stock market during most of your day.

Many investment advisors recommend too few stocks. Without a determined effort to expand the number of stocks, many clients and advisors tend to hold five stocks or less. The advisors watch these stocks very closely, recommending frequent changes to their clients if the stock rises or falls even by a small amount. In contrast, a properly diversified portfolio is usually the result of a positive decision to hold a specific number of stocks for a meaningful period of time, with careful monitoring and periodic review.

Another type of investment advisor, known as an investment counsellor, offers discretionary money management. Their clients often are wealthy individuals who have inherited money or sold a business. Many of these clients show little interest in the stock market. Some of these investment counsellors tend to hold large numbers of stocks, usually more than 30. They choose 25, 30, or 50 stocks or more and hold them in all the portfolios they manage for other people. They are trying to limit the impact of one bad stock. They are more concerned about losing an account due to bad performance than they are excited about trying to better the market.

These money managers know that the fastest way to lose a client is to have a large negative performance result in one year. Clients attracted to investment counsellors are not very tolerant of negative surprises. They accept mediocre returns more readily. Risk avoidance becomes very important for investment counsellors and their clients.

Using the graph as a measure of adequate diversification, you can see that a portfolio of 10 stocks gives reasonable safety. I suggest that you own between 10 and 15 stocks. This is all the diversification you need but if you are nervous about individual stocks, the peace of mind that comes with more stocks justifies the performance penalty of holding more stocks. For safety reasons, I prefer too many stocks in a portfolio over too few.

Clients holding less than 10 stocks make me nervous about the safety of their portfolio. One company getting into serious trouble causes serious damage to the performance of a portfolio with fewer than 10 stocks. I call this getting "torpedoed" by one stock.

Diversifying Internationally

Mutual fund companies spend a large amount of money on advertising in the media. One of the hottest sales topics in mutual fund circles in the last few years revolves around the idea of spreading your investment dollars around the world or at least outside of Canada. A concerted lobbying effort is underway to convince the government to lift the restriction of a maximum 20% foreign content for RRSPs and pension plans. The attraction for the fund companies comes from the perception by most investors that they lack the knowledge to invest directly in other stock markets.

Academic studies show that international diversification lowers the volatility of a portfolio, if the markets added to the portfolio are not highly correlated with the other stocks in the portfolio. Japan makes a good diversification for Canadian investors as the correlation between Canadian and Japanese stocks is low.

International diversification is not essential for success as an independent investor. Few of the really successful individual investors such as Buffet bought stocks outside of their home market. Knowledge and familiarity with companies is much more important than chasing the latest emerging market. After all, all we need is ten good companies.

Many Canadian companies are diversified worldwide in their revenues and profits. Companies such as Alcan Aluminum, Bombardier, Laidlaw, Nortel, and many others receive the bulk of their revenues and profits outside of Canada. Companies in the resource sector (such as oil, gas, nickel, copper, uranium, coal, and lumber) sell most of their product on the world markets. The Canadian companies operating in these markets have learned to work on a global basis. Any portfolio that includes these internationally oriented Canadian companies achieves a significant diversification without taking the risk of entering unknown markets.

If you are interested in investing in companies based in other countries a good starting place is the New York Stock Exchange, where foreign companies are listed as American Depositary Receipts (ADR). Of course all of the U.S. companies are readily accessible on the U.S. exchanges also. The ADR companies trade with ease on New York and represent the largest and most stable companies in their home countries. Several major Japanese and European companies trade as ADRs. Research on these companies may be available from your investment dealer or the Internet.

I believe it may be more folly than wisdom to move large amounts of money outside of Canada at this time. The Canadian market underperformed the rest of the world for the last ten years, the Canadian dollar is near record low levels and international portfolio managers have ignored Canada for several years. Canada as a sector would have to be considered "cold" meaning that there must be dozens of companies on the TSE that are bargains that would be difficult to find elsewhere. Unless Canada remains permanently out-of-favour, which is not likely, our own market represents a genuine opportunity for value investing in an out-of-favour sector. And there is more than enough diversity to allow adequate and genuine diversification within Canada.

Genuine Diversification—How to Get It

Proper diversification involves more than owning at least 10 companies. You need to pay attention to the type of company as well as the number. An easy way to ensure adequate diversity in the portfolio comes with the use of industry sectors. The stock market divides nicely into industry sectors. Choosing companies all from one sector would make an unsafe portfolio.

For example, ten companies in the oil and gas industry are just as vulnerable to a drop in the price of a barrel of oil as one company. In Alberta, where I live, the price of oil affects a lot of industrial activity. When oil prices plunged from $40 a barrel to $10 in the early 1980s, many investors discovered how concentrated their holdings were. Some of my clients at that time held shares in real estate and oil and gas companies. One told me that he only invested in companies where he knew the chief executive officer personally. When the dramatic slowdown in the oilpatch arrived, they learned that real estate companies depended as much as oil and gas producers on the price of oil. Alberta entrepreneurs who held several million dollars worth of common stock lost everything in the 1982 bear market. Invariably they held real estate personally, outside of the stock market. These holdings usually carried debt. The combined effect of the drop in real estate and stock market holdings wiped out several fortunes in the $10 million to $100 million range. The common mistake was concentration in holdings that were correlated to the same factor, the price of oil.

As a bull market progresses there is a tendency to purchase more and more companies in the sector that performs the best. This is detrimental to adequate diversification. Mutual fund investors do the same thing when they choose specialized sector funds based on historical performance. They are loading up on one sector trying to chase performance. This is much more risky than investors realize, as last year's winner is next year's dog.

Diversification involves owning companies in different industries and sectors that behave differently in the various stages of the market and business cycles.

This challenge may sound like a tall order but, in practice, achieving diversification is simple. It helps to know that the stock market is divided into sectors that, by definition, are diversified in nature. So the most direct way to get adequate diversification is to use the work already done for us by stock exchange statisticians.

In later chapters I describe how to use sectors and research analysts to achieve true diversification, without doing much work. You will discover how easily you can build a well-diversified stock market portfolio with adequate safety.

Part 2

The Individual Investor's
Edge Over the Professionals

Three

Avoid Playing the Professionals' Game

Imagine trying to beat a professional golfer in a game of golf. Even a scratch handicap player who wins the local club tournament most of the time has little chance to beat a pro consistently. The pro plays better under pressure, practices more often, has better coaching, and can afford better equipment.

No weekend golfer would expect to be able to compete with the professionals in a major tournament. Perversely however, weekend investors try all the time to win the professional investing game, perhaps without realizing they are playing. If investors knew the whole story about professional investing they would never dream of playing the game the professional way.

The good news is that individual investors have no need to compete directly with the professionals. Individuals can play their own game, a different game with much more favourable odds.

Professionals play more than one type of investment game. It is important for you to understand how some of these games work. By understanding the rules, you recognize when you are in a game you cannot win. Independent investors can avoid the trap of trying to beat the professionals at their game by not playing.

Some of you have seen the Japanese Sumo wrestlers on television. Even junior athletes weigh 300 pounds, while championship-class wrestlers top 600 pounds. Their competition consists of trying to push the other wrestler out of a small ring. Matches last a few seconds usually. You and I would never try to win a shoving match with one of these behemoths. If we had a choice of competitive event with a Sumo wrestler we would suggest a foot race or perhaps a shoelace-tying contest, as apparently none of them can reach their shoes, or even see them.

The individual investor occupies the same position with the professionals. You cannot win playing the pros' game but you outperform every time at some of the other investment challenges. First you must understand which games to avoid. In the next chapter I outline how to play a game more suited to the individual investor.

PROFESSIONALS' ADVANTAGES

Professional investors (sometimes called institutional investors) manage other people's money, usually in mutual funds or pension plans. They are responsible for the majority of trading and control of stocks in the world today. Managers of institutional money dominate the investment scene primarily due to the explosive growth in mutual fund assets.

Professional money managers try to beat each other constantly. Comparative performance records drive recognition and income for these "hired guns." Professionals as a group usually buy and sell the same group of stocks. The differences between them are in the quality of research, interpretation of facts, and the speed of information flow and decision-making.

The pros demand, and get, preferential treatment from institutional stock salespeople, individuals who make a living on commission sales in the stock market. The reality of the investment business dictates that an investor with an order for 200 000 shares will get a call before an investor with 200 shares. Even at the institutional rate of commission of 5 cents per share, a 200 000-share order yields $10 000 while the 200-share order might give $200 or $300 at most. Whom would you spend most of your time talking to if you made your money on commissions?

Instantaneous Information

Information becomes available to professionals instantly. Institutional salespeople compete to be first to call with significant breaking news. With the commissions involved, when news breaks professionals will get a call from the investment dealers before the individuals every time.

Individual investors, known as retail investors, operate at a disadvantage in the information game. Individuals must work very hard to keep up on the news flow in the stock market. With the Internet and other electronic means of information dispersion, individuals could receive news about the same time as professionals, in theory. In practice, however, individuals cannot watch their computer screens all day. Pros can study the market constantly, listening for any changes and watching every movement. A full-time investor will know more about the latest investment news than a part-time investor who has to earn a living in his "real life."

Quick Response Time

Even in a perfect world where individuals and professional investors receive information simultaneously, professionals would still have a major advantage. Professionals make quick decisions, executing trades often in seconds. If the latest high-flying Internet stock reports some setback on the news wire at 1:30 P.M., the pros can dump it by 1:32 P.M. before there is a big drop in price.

A LITTLE TOO TRIGGER-HAPPY

Most professional investors keep a "hot" button active on their computer keyboard that allows them to enter trades instantly. This fact came to light in a humorous but frightening way recently when a large number of trades were executed in the futures market for bonds. The bond futures contract is a derivative instrument that allows traders to buy or sell a contract equivalent to $100 000 or $1 000 000 of government bonds. The amount varies depending on the type of bond involved.

One day, a rookie trader leaned on the "hot" trade button, triggering a large number of sell orders in a rapid fashion. This cascade of sell orders disrupted the market dramatically for a few minutes, which is the reason the story appeared. *The Daily Telegraph* (November 14, 1998) reported that "a junior trader cost his employers an estimated 10 million British pounds yesterday after a training exercise went disastrously wrong and he ended up taking part in an 11.5 billion pound transaction." Screens flashed with the news that someone wanted to sell 130 000 German bond futures contracts. Traders are used to dealing in 10 000 lots. One said: "At first I thought it was a Rio trade, which is where someone makes a last-ditch attempt to recover losses by betting their bank, or, if that fails books a one-way ticket to Brazil." It is a little frightening to think of all the computers hooked directly to the trading floor with the power to move a market in a few seconds.

By contrast, an individual receiving the same information would like to think about what to do, talk to an advisor, talk to a spouse, and then call to execute the trade. These activities take anywhere from two hours to two days to complete for most people. Even an individual sitting at home, watching a screen and trading through the computer would probably take a few minutes to make a decision. And the stocks that are popular with professionals can move 10% or 20% in a few minutes. The reality is that professionals play the information game much better than amateurs. Individuals who do not accept this usually learn very expensive lessons trying to play the game.

GAMES PROFESSIONALS PLAY

The New Issue Game

Many investors make money occasionally through the purchase of new issues. Most investors would be better off completely avoiding these special offerings. As a rule the purchase of new issues is a professional game that individuals play at a significant disadvantage.

A type of issue, called an initial public offering, appears when a company is new to the stock exchange, issuing shares for the first time to the public. A different type of new issue involves the issue of additional shares from a company already trading on the stock exchange.

Companies issue shares on the stock exchange when it seems likely that the shares will fetch a premium price. The appetite of professional investment accounts for that type of stock is a key variable when looking at the timing of the offering. The company approaches two or three underwriters to explore the possibility of a new issue. The underwriters act as middlemen, and break up the new issue to sell to various investors. The underwriters (investment dealers) negotiate a price for the initial public offering of shares with the issuing company. The most common method of pricing new issues values the shares in comparison to similar publicly traded companies. Prices for new issues are also determined by looking at financial ratios such as price to earnings, price to cash flow, and price to book value.

Underwriters try to get the price of the stock down to the lowest acceptable level that will meet the expectations of the issuer. Price is important to the underwriter because the lower the price the easier it is to sell the issue. If the issuer is a sought-after company, competition among underwriters often bids the price higher. At the same time, underwriters must check with professional investors to make sure they do not bid too high and get stuck with an issue that is impossible to sell.

Occasionally, an underwriter prices a new issue at a very attractive price. If demand among the pros is good for companies in that sector the new issue will sell out immediately. When the issue sells out quickly, the stock price will usually rise in the market after the issue.

On the other hand, if the underwriters misjudge the market and price the issue too high then there is unsold stock remaining in the hands of the underwriter. This "overhang" of stock weighs heavily on the price of that stock for weeks after the new issue comes out. Each time the stock has a little rally the underwriter is there, selling stock and pushing the price back down.

Professional investors, keeping constantly in touch with the market, get to be very skilled at judging when a new issue is hot (lots of demand). When there is a hot new issue the pros are all over the salespeople demanding a bigger portion or "allotment" of that issue. Professional investors demand their share of the attractive new issues and they get taken care of. Once the new issue sells out there is no more stock available for other clients. For performance reasons each pro needs to get as much of a hot new issue as the next pro. If the issue goes to a premium in the market the competitive nature of fund performance dictates full participation in each such new issue.

In view of this feeding frenzy around new issues would it surprise you to learn that individual investors get a smaller share of the more sought-after new issues than the pros, if they get any share at all?

Occasionally the underwriter misjudges the market by pricing a new issue too high, or bringing it into a market that is not receptive to that type of company. This situation requires Herculean sales efforts from all of the underwriter's employees. New issues that move slowly become a problem for the underwriter. Salespeople make every effort to sell the new issue quickly. If the pros decide to "pass," or not purchase the shares, then other investors get a chance to buy more shares. New issues become available to individual investors after they are turned down by the pros, except for new issues that are more suitable to individual investors, often for tax reasons. These issues are not marketed to the pros and can be very good investments, if specifically designed for individual investors.

THE NEW ISSUE TRAP

Professional investors usually get first pick of promising new issues, leaving the less attractive issues for individual investors.

New issue offerings make sense for professional investors who manage mutual funds and other large pots of money. With new issues, the pros can purchase large amounts of stock without worrying about disrupting the market. The mutual fund avoids the transaction impact cost of acquiring a large block of stock in the market. Transaction impact occurs when buy orders move the price of a stock higher while it is being bought. Mutual fund managers in the late 1990s need to be careful when they place large amounts of money in the stock market. Many stocks trade thinly on the market making accumulating a position problematic. New issues help with this difficulty. As money rolls into a fund the manager needs to find new places to put money.

Salespeople find fund managers very receptive to new issues when the market is buoyant. In some cases fund managers instigate a a new issue by mentioning to an underwriter that they would like a position in a stock. The dealer then approaches the company, and the management of the company agrees to sell some shares.

While liquidity problems cause headaches every day for institutional investors, individuals seldom need to worry. Investors buy stocks in smaller blocks of 200 or 500 or 5000 shares. New issues offer no advantage to the average investor who needs to invest some money, other than the fact that the pricing of the new issue includes commissions.

The professionals have a major advantage when buying new issues. They get first pick of the issues and they get to pass when they think the issue is slow to sell. Individuals cannot overcome this discriminatory treatment unless they buy a large amount of new issue stock frequently, making them quasi-institutional. When new issues are involved, most investors would never qualify for the preferential treatment offered to the professionals. The good news for individuals is that they do not have to compete for new issue stock. Since all new issue stock is soon trading on the stock exchange, a retail investor can wait for a period of time and then buy the stock from the market.

The investor who avoids the new issue trap chooses his or her investments from the thousands of stocks trading on the exchange. The decision to buy a stock based on when a stock is inexpensive will yield a much better return than deciding to try to purchase a new issue. Since the timing of a new issue is determined by the company executives, the stock price will usually be at the high end of the range for that stock. Unless they are forced to by dire financial circumstances, the company managers will not sell their stock when the sector or the company is out of favour and the stock price is low. So buying new issue offerings usually means that the timing is good for the seller, which means the timing is poor for the buyer. The institutions buy because they have a lot of cash that they have to spend while you can pick your spots and buy when the price is right.

Why not let the professional investors compete for new issues with each other? The smart individual investor looks for areas of the market where the pros are not active. These sectors offer better bargains than those involved in the new issue game.

The Hot Sector Game

Professional investors worry a lot about performance. These hired guns know that their jobs depend on producing good numbers for quarterly and annual performance reports. Without good numbers, the job that pays several hundred thousand dollars a year, and a bonus, will go to someone else.

The pro faces the challenge of making profitable trades in the market regularly, without the luxury of waiting very long for the results. Mutual fund managers need to show performance numbers on a short-term horizon, not over three or five years. In the late 1990s very few investors have the patience to sit with an underperforming fund for that long.

Since performance means being competitive with other managers, the numbers that really matter are relative performance numbers. Mutual fund and pension plan consultants measure performance in relation to other funds and the index benchmarks. If the vast majority of funds are doing poorly then a manager need not worry about poor absolute performance. The trick is not to stand out from the crowd very much, especially on the down side.

In a strong bull market a manager needs numbers that show he or she is keeping up with the better-performing funds. If there is a hot sector or group of stocks outperforming the market a manager must purchase some of these stocks or run the risk of being left behind.

As the bull market ages, the pressure builds to conform to the hot sectors in the market. Being a contrarian fund manager carries more risk than reward. If the fund manager leaves out a hot sector and the rest of the funds hold that sector that manager can lose his job. On the other hand if all funds have that sector and there is a sudden drop the manager will keep his job even if the absolute performance is negative. The manager is safe because the relative performance (compared to other funds in the same category) is acceptable.

THE HOT SECTOR TRAP

Investors buy overpriced shares of companies in a "hot" sector to avoid missing potential profits. Professionals are forced to do this to maintain the relative performance of the fund, while individuals do this because they get excited about a sector showing quick profits.

This pressure leads to a situation where fund managers buy overpriced stocks in a hot sector. The managers know that these stocks are dangerous as speculative investments.

A good example of this occurred during the summer of 1997 when a speculative market in gold mining shares collapsed. Mutual funds shocked their shareholders when statements showed that the funds held shares in the most spectacular examples. Investors wondered why their supposedly conservative fund became involved in such risky ventures. On the other hand, if the market had continued to rise further and there was no fraud to halt the rise, these same consumers of investment products would express anger that their fund missed out on the profits. The pro's job is tough, at times.

Many of the investors who bought these funds failed to investigate the reasons behind such good performance, so the funds that avoided these risky stocks lost assets to their more aggressive rivals. In a perfect world, investors would have been aware that the better performance was due to the purchase of very risky stocks. Investors would reward the more prudent fund managers by staying with them, accepting the poorer relative performance numbers. In our world though, investors sometimes punish fund managers for doing the right thing, at least in the short run.

The fund managers know how the real world works. They might think that a stock is too risky for their fund but cannot afford to take the chance that a hot sector might get even hotter. So they do the pragmatic thing by purchasing a defensive position in a risky sector.

This scenario repeats over and over. Sectors become hot as investors get excited, and money pours in. The infatuation with a particular stock sector knows no limits. As profits multiply, more money arrives to get in on the game. Share prices surge higher, attracting even more money. Rising prices draw even more investors like moths to a flame.

Prudent investors watch the relative values of stocks in one sector compared to other sectors. When the sector shows signs of a mania, the cautious investors depart, leaving the final stage of the game to those who can afford the most risk. Some cautious investors depart too early, often leaving six months or a year before the sector burns out and becomes a falling star. For an individual this is merely an annoyance. The investor rationalizes that it is better to be early than late, and it is.

The professional who abandons a hot sector early runs the risk of falling behind in the relative performance game. At the final stages of a runaway speculative market the game becomes very dangerous. Each professional is watching the market very closely for a sign that the party is over. Nobody wants to be the last to leave the party—and not because they learned it is impolite. It is a matter of survival for these pros.

Eventually a bad piece of news emerges (such as a mining fraud), or a shift in the market arrives and it is time to depart. The fund managers try to leave as quickly as possible. Offering huge blocks of stock for sale, they show little regard for price. The faster the sale the better as they know that the sector will drop dramatically. Certainly the next quarterly statement of that fund must not show any shares in the sector that crashes. So the selling is vicious and the price declines are dramatic.

Once the players have moved on that sector will not recover for many months or even a couple of years. In the case of the gold sector collapse in 1997, more than two years have passed (to early 1999) without any recovery in that sector.

Professionals play this game because they must. Individual investors are under no such obligation to play the hot sector game. Investors operate at a disadvantage because of limited access to information and slower execution of trades. Trading hot sector stocks carries much more risk for individuals who get around to selling a few days after the pros are gone. Stocks can drop 10%, 20%, or 40% in just a few hours when the funds decide to depart.

The good news is that retail investors have no need to compete with the pros on this level. Other market sectors yield bargain stocks more easily. "Short-term performance anxiety" problems need not affect the individual investor.

A good rule for you—avoid purchasing stocks in a hot sector. Positions purchased long ago, before a sector became hot, can be held, if you feel strongly about a particular company. It is usually possible, however, to find an equally strong company at a much lower (and safer) price in another sector. Why not switch before the funds depart and turn a hot sector into a disaster zone?

The Index Game

The 1990–2000 period will be remembered by economic historians for the exponential growth in mutual fund assets and other managed investment products. A related important development in the investment world received less attention until very recently. The growth in popularity of index funds parallels the public interest in having someone else manage their money. In chapter 1 I described these funds briefly. To understand the professional investor game you need more information about these vehicles for investment.

An index measures the aggregate changes of some large collection of numbers. For example, the Consumer Price Index (CPI) purports to measure the degree of inflation or deflation that consumers experience. Every index measures such changes imperfectly.

Stock market indexes work the same way. The Toronto Stock Exchange 300 follows the movements of 300 stocks listed on that exchange. The TSE 300 represents the market for most people. When people ask "How did the market do today?" they usually mean the TSE 300.

Newspapers and television report the TSE 300 movements each day. In the United States, the Dow Jones Industrial Average follows the movement of only 30 stocks. The investing public considers the movement of the Dow to approximate the market as a whole. More sophisticated investors are aware that the S&P 500, which tracks 500 U.S. stocks, is a better approximation of what the market is doing.

Limitations of Indexes

In the case of the Dow, with only 30 stocks, most people can easily see the problem. How could only 30 of the largest companies accurately represent what happens with thousands of publicly listed companies? It would be foolish for anyone to rely solely on that index. Even so, things have improved as the Dow was founded in 1896 with just 12 stocks.

Indexes such as the S&P 500, which tracks many more stocks, still carry the difficulty of misrepresenting the broader markets. Understanding the problem with indexes involves a look at the weighting of the components of the index. Each stock in the index carries a weight based on the size of the capitalization of that company. Those who manage the stock index calculate the capitalization of a company by multiplying the number of outstanding shares times the price of those shares. For example, General Electric, (GE) is a large company with huge market capitalization. GE's capitalization was $325 billion in January 1999. GE traded at over $100 per share with 3.25 billion shares outstanding. The index gives much importance (weight) to share price movements in GE. The other company with an even greater capitalization is Microsoft (MSFT)— 2.46 billion shares at $165 (January 1999) per share—$413 billion. Together just these two made up more than 7% of the S&P 500 index at December 31, 1998. A situation where two observations out of 500 (0.4%) carry more than 7% of the weight is obviously very distorted. At the end of December 1998 the top 30 stocks in the S&P 500 accounted for more than 40% of the total weight in the index.

You can easily see that a price movement in General Electric or Microsoft is very important to the S&P 500 index. In 1998 the top 30 stocks contributed 46% of the increase in the value, with Microsoft alone accounting for 8% of the increase. The five leaders, Microsoft, General Electric, Wal-Mart, Intel, and Cisco deserve credit for a full 23% of the increase of the index. Just as the CPI is only an approximation of true inflation, the movement of the index is only an approximation of the real stock market. Only if an investor owns stocks in the same proportion as the index would the index represent the stock market for that individual.

Trying to Beat the Indexes

You saw earlier that the professional investment game revolves around relative short-term performance. Relative performance means comparisons to other professional investors. As you have seen, this comparison drives the behaviour of the pros in an important way. The relative performance of the professional investor compared to the index is also very important. The professional investor needs to beat the index to show that professional management works. If the pros cannot beat the S&P 500 or the TSE 300 why pay them an average of 2% to 2.5% to manage your money?

For several years in the early 1990s more than 75% of all U.S. money managers failed to match the S&P 500 in performance. Even at the best of times fewer than 50% of professionals were able to match the index. The last two years were disastrous for fund managers as more than 90% of them failed to match the S&P 500 index. In December 1998 *Business Week* reported that the average fund earned only 7% for the previous 12 months while the index gained 27%. Even more questionable results were reported by the *Wall Street Journal* in July 1998: "Only 90 out of 1022 actively managed U.S. diversified stock funds beat the returns of the S&P index in the five years through the end of June."

The main reason for this discrepancy comes from the split in returns between large-cap and small-cap stocks. Large-caps have capitalizations in the range of $10 billion or more while small-caps are worth less than U.S.$1 billion. According to *Business Week,* "the performance gap between large-cap and small-cap funds has reached historically high levels." The Russell 2000 index, a broad-based small cap index, actually declined in 1998 by 3.4% while the S&P 500 rose 27%. So any investor or fund manager wishing to match the index would have to buy over-priced large-cap stocks exclusively. And this becomes a factor in the market as institutions dump small-cap stocks and add more large-cap stocks, driving the gap ever wider.

As a result of the outperformance of the index relative to the average stock, many managers make it their goal just to match the relevant index. In order to match that index, the professional investor buys the stocks that are in the index, in the same proportions as the index weighting. Because of the weighting factor, the movement of the index tracks the stock prices of the largest companies more than smaller companies. In trying to duplicate the performance, the fund manager holds more shares of the larger companies than the smaller companies. As the weighting of a particular company increases, the fund manager must buy more shares of that company.

Funds marketed as matching the index are known as index funds while those that secretly try to match the index are known as closet indexers. The performance discrepancy means that most fund managers do some amount of closet indexing for reasons of survival. The main difference between closet indexers and indexers is the management fee. These fees average 1.5% to 3.0% for active managers and as low as 0.18% for indexers. You can see why some active managers stay in the closet when it comes to matching the index.

Two factors determine the weighting of a company in the index. Changes in the number of outstanding shares on the stock market affects the weighting. Increases in the number of shares outstanding result from secondary issues of common stock or option exercises by employees. A purchase by a company of its own stock reduces the number of shares outstanding, counterbalancing the continuous issuance of stock from employees exercising their stock options. This purchase of stock for cancellation is known as a share buyback. These two factors, offsetting each another, leave most companies with small changes in the numbers of shares outstanding.

The second weighting factor, a change in share price, makes a bigger impact on capitalization. When the stock prices of the larger companies increase, the weighting of that company grows in importance to the index. So the fund manager buys more stock in the largest companies as their share prices rise. The pro must do this if the goal is to match or beat the index. For example from September 1998 to January 1999 Microsoft's share price galloped ahead from $110 to $165, dramatically increasing the weighting in the index. All the indexers and closet-indexers scrambled to buy more Microsoft, pushing the price even higher.

Indexes and Large-Cap Stocks

As most professional investors follow this investment formula, buying pressure converges on the large companies that rise in price. Buying pressure forces prices higher, attracting more buying pressure, forcing prices higher and so it goes. Large-caps become relatively more expensive compared to small-caps and the average stock in the market.

The concentration of large company influence in the TSE 300 is just as important as in the S&P 500. The top 30 stocks in the TSE 300 represent almost 50% of the capitalization and weighting of the entire index. Professional investors concerned about relative performance must keep a large portion of their portfolio in these 30 stocks, mostly ignoring the other 270 companies.

A new index called the S&P/TSE 60, introduced in late 1998, has started to attract attention. This is a capitalization-weighted index also, with just as much concentration as the TSE 300. The top 11 companies by size in the new S&P/TSE 60 index make up more than 50% of the index weighting. These 11 companies are the five largest banks, CIBC, Royal Bank, Bank of Montreal, Bank of Nova Scotia, and Toronto Dominion; BCE and Northern Telecom (Nortel) in the communications sector; and Seagram, Canadian Pacific, Transcanada Pipeline, and Bombardier. The top seven companies—the banks plus BCE and Nortel—make up 40% of the S&P/TSE 60 index. Obviously, matching either index is a matter of owning a significant weighting in a small number of large-cap stocks.

This concentration in just a few companies makes it mandatory for professionals to own the large companies, unless they wish to risk falling behind the index. This happened in the period 1996 to 1999 to more than one large Canadian mutual fund company. In 1996 the share price of the bank stocks started to move higher. As the stock prices moved up, some professional investors bought more bank shares to match the index weighting in their portfolios. If they wanted to cover the risk of falling behind the index they had to buy more shares, even as the bank stock prices rose.

The cumulative buying pressure of all these professional investors resulted in a huge move upwards in the bank stocks. Simultaneously there was a large price increase in U.S. bank stock prices due to merger mania and similar capitalization increases. The combination of these pressures forced bank stock prices even higher leading to even more index buying.

By 1998 the average bank stock had doubled once and was well on the way to a second doubling. Bank stocks increased to a higher proportion of the index as other stock market sectors lagged behind. The metals and minerals index dropped to a weighting of less than 4%, oil and gas to 8.6%, and paper and forest products to 2.2%, while the financial services index moved above 22%. Fund managers shunned resource stocks and loaded up on more banks.

Chase the Index or Look for Value

The question that must be addressed relates to value. The buying pressure due to indexing really has nothing to do with the question of share price and values. Are these companies overpriced because of this involuntary index buying? One needs to pause for breath when the valuations of these companies are examined. Microsoft, Dell, Lucent, Pfizer (a pharmaceutical company that produces Viagra), and Wal-Mart made up 52% of the stock market gains in the S&P 500 in the first nine months of 1998. Their median performance was +75% while the rest of the S&P was down an average 6%! The cash flow multiples of these stocks are through the stratosphere with Microsoft trading at 55 times cash flow, Dell at 75 times cash flow and Pfizer at 53 times cash flow. Wal-Mart is trading at "only" 30 times cash flow. All these numbers at October 1998.

History shows us that this emphasis on just a few over-valued companies is dangerous. The so-called Nifty Fifty, introduced in Chapter 1, were a group of companies, including Xerox, IBM, Polaroid, and Coca-Cola, that became popular with institutional investors in the late 1960s during the last mutual fund boom. Most investors agreed that the Nifty Fifty were companies destined to be successful for decades to come. They were "one-decision" stocks that people believed were safe to "buy and hold" forever. Professional investors believed that growth in the businesses of these companies was assured so stock prices would steadily rise for many years to come. Since growth was assured it did not matter what price was paid for these shares. Price-earnings ratios rose to an unprecedented 100 times in some cases. Investors, mostly professionals, paid exorbitant prices for the shares of these companies in the early 1970s. Mutual funds and other market participants suffered huge losses when the share prices of these same companies collapsed during the severe bear market of 1973–74.

The Nifty Fifty mania came to be recognized as an institutional investor's mania. Individuals who owned mutual fund shares from the 1960s bore the brunt of the damage caused by that particular form of insanity. This collective temporary insanity, as some described it, proved that professionals are just as likely to get caught up in manias as individuals. A mania endorsed by professionals gives a cloak of respectability that makes the situation more seductive for all.

THE INDEX WEIGHTING TRAP

The drive to match an index leads investors to buy the companies most heavily weighted in the index. This interest alone inflates the price of the companies. A correction to the price of the shares may result in a loss from which it takes years to recover.

There is a striking similarity between today and the late 1960s. Institutional money pours into the largest companies on the exchange. Retail investors rely on the pros to know the "best" investments. If the investing public knew that the pros were only buying the large-caps to match the index, regardless of value or price, they might experience a feeling of nervous anxiety.

The involvement of a large number of professionals managing other people's money allows these manias to grab hold. There would never be a group of individual investors willing to load up on the largest companies in their portfolio excessively and then buy more shares as the price rises. The natural instinct for the individual is to sell when a profit appears. Only by purchasing a managed product, such as a mutual fund or other index-related product, would an individual investor fall into the trap of playing the index game.

Individuals tempted by the attraction of the current index fund mania need to examine this history and pause. What happens if the flow of money is reversed so that index funds lose assets? The largest companies will bear the brunt of the heaviest selling since the index contains inordinately larger amounts of the biggest companies. So loading up on those companies at these inflated values could result in a 25-year or longer wait until valuations came back into line, as it did when the Nifty Fifty mania ended in 1972.

The real bargains in the stock market today exist outside of the 20 largest capitalization companies in the United States and Canada. These bargains often trade at cash flow multiples of 10 to 15 times, price-earnings ratios of 17 to 25 times, and have greater growth prospects because they are smaller. The larger a company, the more difficult it is to maintain a rapid growth rate. Many of these smaller companies were devastated in the correction in the fall of 1998.

In the next chapter I show how easy it is for an individual to beat the professionals by changing the rules of the game. The constraints faced by the pros do not apply to individuals. There is no "short-term performance anxiety" for individuals, unless it is self-imposed. There is no need to match the index or to follow the crowd into dangerous waters filled with over-priced shares. The individual investor sets his own course through the investment world, buying when stocks are inexpensive and selling those companies that become overvalued.

Four

The Natural Advantages of the Individual Investor

Wise investors know that patience is one of the rarest of virtues. Patience in the emotional world of money and investing pays off. While a manager of institutional money, mutual funds, or pension plans cannot afford to wait for good results, a retail investor has adequate time to follow a strategy of patient investing.

You saw in the last chapter how the short-term orientation of mutual fund buyers affects the behaviour of the investment professional. The professional must live with this reality while individuals who invest directly in equities can ignore short-term performance discrepancies. Time pressures of a different sort apply to the individual.

For the individual, the main time constraint is retirement. Even then, investments often are held to retirement and beyond. Many investors leave estates holding common shares for beneficiaries. Some beneficiaries continue to hold common shares long after the death of the original purchaser.

Most huge fortunes grew over decades of ownership. Unlike the average investor, these creators of large family fortunes arrange their affairs so these investments pass on to the next generation and continue to grow. In Canada fortunes pass from one generation to another after the payment of capital gains tax. Some wealthy families use trusts to leave share investments to the next generation. The rewards for patience are substantial.

For most of us who are not involved in creating a huge family inheritance, the goal is to build a portfolio that can generate some income during retirement. Beyond that goal, if the money lasts, some investors wish to leave an estate for their children. These two goals are representative of 90% of the clients that come to me for investment advice.

Investors accomplish these objectives if they exercise good judgement and patience with their investments. You have seen that building a diversified portfolio that includes common stocks helps to accomplish these goals. To ensure success you also need to select investments that will perform well over time.

EXPLOITING YOUR ADVANTAGES

The fundamental basis of successful investing is to buy low and sell high. One method to accomplish this feat is to buy and hold forever. Because of the tendency of stock markets to rise over time, shares of successful companies that were bought long ago will eventually rise to higher levels. Most investors wish to speed up the process a little by buying low and selling high.

The markets fluctuate in cycles that last from hours to decades. Within these cycles, there is ample opportunity theoretically to buy low and sell high. You are competing against a large number of professional investors in this activity however, so you need some kind of an edge.

Patience

One technique available to all investors is to buy a stock or sector that is out-of-favour. Since the stock market moves in a way similar to fashion cycles we can buy the equivalent of short skirts when the fashion is for long skirts and wait until the short skirts come back in fashion. Another old-fashioned saying encourages us to buy straw hats in January. This is the strategy of the contrarian investor. To be successful with this strategy investors need an adequate supply of patience.

Patience is a luxury the institutional investor cannot afford. The pressures of performance comparisons to index funds and other fund managers make the strategy of buying and waiting unavailable to most fund managers and other professionals. On the other hand, the individual can afford to wait. The only pressure for short-term results on the individual is self-imposed or spouse-imposed. Since the use of time and patience is not practical for a mutual fund manager, the individual has a natural competitive advantage. In addition, the patient independent investor carries an advantage over other individuals—and they are the majority—who lack patience.

Individuals have the potential to be far more successful investors than professionals if they refrain from playing the professional game. Instead, individuals need to use their natural advantages. An individual can choose to wait for a longer period of time before an investment works out. There is no board of directors criticizing a selection that has not made a profit after three months or six months or two years. It is important to exploit this advantage. All successful individual investors in public or private markets use this natural advantage.

It helps to think about stock market investing in a way similar to the private business owner. The main difference between private business and the stock market is the ease of buying and selling. A private business owner often has no alternative but to use patience and take the long view. A private business owner may own the business for 30 or 40 years. At different times in the business cycle that business probably earned little or no profits. Perhaps there were losses for a couple of years. The business, if it could have been sold, would have yielded very little capital. Often there were moments when the owner would have given the business back to the bank if he could. Since the owner found it easier to keep on than to quit he persevered, more from stubbornness than rational decision-making. After many years the business became established and the cycles less severe. If that owner had had the ability to sell the business with one phone call, as we do in the stock market, he might not have stayed in long enough to own the valuable business he eventually ended up with. There are more than a few very surprised multi-millionaires in the ranks of older owner-managers of businesses. After they get over their shock at discovering their business is worth a lot of money, they usually adjust quickly to their new-found fortunes.

Investors in the stock market own businesses. Unfortunately, in most cases, they do not think about their stocks as companies, they think of them as stocks. The owner of a common share in a company is the owner of the business. All of the people working for that company are working for the owners. If you can think of yourself as an owner of businesses you might find the patience to stay around long enough to reap the rewards.

Take a Different Path

In my opinion, the investment philosophy that works best for an individual investor is to buy stocks of good companies that are out-of-favour and wait until they come back in favour. When these stocks become popular you can sell them and move to other stocks that are out-of-favour. In this way you can take advantage of your natural edge over the professionals. The main attributes required on your part are patience and the fortitude to stand apart from the crowd.

"Out-of-favour" stocks are those that are unpopular with other investors, including the professionals. Increasingly, as you have seen, the market is driven by the actions of the professionals, especially the mutual fund managers. These managers tend to be of the same type, usually younger than 35, educated to a graduate degree level, and very bright. They are in a hurry to prove themselves and very competitive with each other. As a group the exercise of patience would not come naturally to them. Think of your attitude to the world when you were in your early years. This age group lacks the characteristic of patience, although there are many exceptions.

These professionals also lack experience as investors due to their age and employment history. Rapid growth in the mutual fund industry in the last ten years determines that most professionals are relatively new to the stock market business. Most of these managers were in their early to middle twenties when the 1987 crash occurred. When the 1981–82 bear gripped the markets these portfolio managers graced the halls of junior and senior high schools. A limited amount of experience with bull and bear markets leads to a lack of appreciation for the magic that time works for a portfolio.

Contrarian Investing Without Time Pressure

The absence of external time pressure is the biggest single natural advantage available to the individual. Other than a spouse who disagrees with an investment program, no person holds the power to force an investor to divest a particular investment because it has not yet performed. When a couple agree on an investment approach it is possible to stick to that strategy in the face of short-term setbacks. The longer the time horizon, the more certainty of success an investment program holds.

If an investor has patience, one of the best strategies for investing is contrarian investing. Contrarian investing means buying common stocks when others are selling and selling when others are buying. Since buying pressure and selling pressure of the crowd determines the relative value of stocks, contrarians buy when investments are inexpensive and sell when investments are expensive. In other words, they buy low and sell high. If you wish to follow a contrarian approach you need a method to identify when it is time to buy low and when to sell high. A method that takes advantage of differences in value between sectors is called sector rotation.

THE SECTOR ROTATION TECHNIQUE

Stock Market Sectors

The stock markets of the world are classified into sectors and sub-sectors. Companies are grouped together, sometimes arbitrarily, into classifications based on their type of business or industry. Each sector contains several companies that are similar in the nature of their business. Usually, the stock prices of companies in the same sector rise and fall together. Statisticians say they are highly correlated, which means that fluctuations in the stock prices of that group show a history of moving in the same direction.

An example is the oil and gas sector. This sector is made up of different sub-sectors such as integrated companies, small producers, and large producers. If the oil price or natural gas price declines most stock prices in that sector fall also. A company's stock price varies in the degree of rising and falling due to special factors unique to that company, but the overall trend for all stock prices in that sector is consistent.

Special Categories

Sectors normally refer to categories based on industrial classifications. Other subcategories of the market can be used. Stocks can be divided into groups by size, called market capitalization. This size category can be applied within a sector to choose individual stocks. In chapter 3 I outlined the current discrepancy between large-cap and small-cap stocks. If these categories are considered to be market sectors then you would consider the small-cap sector as attractive relative to the large-cap sector. The small-cap sector is definitely out-of-favour compared to other categories. Since most Canadian stocks fall into the small-cap definition the whole Canadian market is an out-of-favour sector if small-caps are out of favour.

Using Sectors to Get Diversification

Balanced investors use the division of the market into these categories as a natural way to ensure diversification and to filter the choice of stocks. As there are 14 sectors in the TSE 300, it is easy to pick a few stocks from each sector to narrow your choices. This filtering process yields a manageable list of companies to examine more closely. This approach ensures adequate diversification since stocks in different sectors usually are not highly correlated with each other.

For example, the huge drop in oil prices in the mid 1980s devastated the oil and gas sector but had little effect on the computer stocks, and was a positive event for the many industries where energy costs are a substantial portion of total costs. The Japanese stock markets rose because oil prices are a cost to most industries in that country, which does not produce any oil of its own. Canadian stock markets sagged since oil and gas companies made up a significant portion of the TSE 300. These differences in the makeup of the Canadian and Japanese markets show up in stock price movements. The correlation between stock market returns in Japan and Canada was low (with a correlation of 0.20) between 1967 and 1980. By contrast, the U.S. and Canadian markets were correlated at 0.70, a high value indicating close linkages of movements in stock prices. So true diversification for a Canadian investor may require the addition of Japanese stocks rather than U.S. stocks. This is an interesting idea since today Japan suffers from the effects of a nine-year bear market where the index is 60% lower today than the 1989 peak. The Japanese market is truly an out-of-favour sector.

Weighting the Sectors

Returning to the 14 sectors that comprise the TSE, each sector holds a percentage of the total index. This percentage is known as a weighting, as discussed in the previous chapter. Many portfolio managers match the percentage of the total index in the portfolios they manage. This is called "market weighting." They can "underweight" or "overweight" sectors they like or dislike. Professional investors often strive for sector neutrality, meaning that they own stocks in roughly the same proportion (weighting) as they occur in the index. As an independent investor you can do better by emphasizing sectors that are inexpensive and avoiding sectors that are overpriced.

All of the 300 companies that are included in the TSE Composite Index are allocated to a sector. The sector categories vary in size depending on the size of the companies included. For example, the financial services sector, consisting of banking stocks and a few others, is one of the largest, at 22.6%, because the banks are very large companies, with huge stock market capitalizations. The real estate sector, on the other hand, is very small, with a 2% weighting.

If you pick one stock from each of the sectors in the TSE 300 you achieve a diversification roughly equivalent to that of the TSE 300. You could easily match the weighting of the index in the TSE 300 in the portfolio by purchasing more or fewer shares of each chosen stock.

The TSE 300 sectors

Sector	Percentage weighting Dec. 31 1998
Communications & Media	3.9
Conglomerates	3.5
Consumer Products	7.3
Financial Services	22.6
Gold & Precious Minerals	5.0
Industrial Products	18.8
Merchandising	3.5
Mines and Minerals	3.8
Oil and Gas	8.6
Paper & Forest Products	2.2
Pipelines	3.5
Real Estate	2.0
Transport/Environment	2.6
Utilities	12.7

The reader may notice some interesting anomalies in these sectors. For example, the weighting in just three sectors—financial services, industrial products, and utilities—make up 54% of the index. All sectors obviously are not equal.

The task of building a portfolio is simplified by thinking of the TSE as made up of these sectors. Most brokerage firms can send out a monthly or quarterly portfolio report that shows your portfolio with the companies reported under their sectors. Examining this report will you a quick check on the diversification of your portfolio. Portfolio reporting with sectors helps to determine if there is enough diversification. If four or five stocks out of a 10-stock portfolio come from one sector more work needs to be done on proper diversification.

Some sectors are more homogenous than others. For example, the financial services sector includes five major bank stocks and a few others. If the five banks are owned in a portfolio of 10 stocks there is a high probability that all five stocks would move together after certain market events, such as a large change in interest rates. Owning the five banks is roughly the same as owning one bank five times over. The industrial products sector, however, contains many diverse companies. If the five companies are from the industrial products sector, and each from a different industry sub-group, then the portfolio might still meet the principles of proper diversity, since industrial companies can be more dissimilar to each other than banks. The industrial products sector is probably the only sector that provides this diversity from within a sector. In any case, it makes sense to spread your choices among at least five of the fourteen sectors.

"Bonds In Drag"

The interest-sensitive sectors deserve special mention. The interest-sensitive sectors are financial services, pipelines, and utilities, making up 38.8% of the index weighting. To some degree all stocks respond to changes in the general level of interest rates but these sectors comprise companies that are especially sensitive to interest rate changes. Investors with diversified portfolios that include government bonds need to pay special attention to this fact as government bonds are also interest-sensitive. Since the companies in these sectors act like bonds in most market conditions I call them "bonds in drag" or bonds in disguise. Many investors lack the awareness to know when they are loading up excessively on interest-sensitive issues by purchasing these stocks in addition to the securities in the bond sections of their portfolio. This is similar to over-weighting a sector, especially if the bond portion of your portfolio is substantial. If you decide to keep a sizeable portion of your portfolio in the bond section, such as more than 50%, then the sensible approach is to choose common stocks that are not interest-sensitive. The other 11 sectors not considered interest-sensitive provide many choices that will give you better diversification.

Both investors and brokers fall into a bad habit of picking stocks in the hot part of the market, since those stocks are outperforming the market. They want to return to an area giving quick profits and a good feeling. If you buy one stock and it goes up then you might buy another stock in the same category, looking for that same success. This can be a major mistake that results in holding a group of stocks in a sector that is topping out and heading for a long period of underperformance. Instead investors do well if they look for a new stock in an out-of-favour sector after selling a stock from a hot sector. Using sectors to check on adequate diversification of a portfolio helps to achieve proper sector weighting.

USING SECTOR ROTATION TO BUY LOW AND SELL HIGH

Sector rotation investing involves moving from one sector of the market to another as the relative prospects for that sector become more or less attractive. This method is a natural one for individuals who are using the filter of industry sectors to narrow their choice of stocks. Institutional investors also use this technique but the main difference for the pros is their short-term view. Sector rotation yields more consistent results if a longer-term approach is taken.

Identifying an Out-of-Favour Sector

When contrarian investors buy companies in a sector they look to buy when prices are low. One easy way to do this is to look for an out-of-favour sector. Research analysts who follow a sector can usually tell us quickly whether their sector is in-favour or out-of-favour. Their paycheque fluctuates according to the amount of activity in their sector in the form of commissions and underwriting fees. This means that a conversation with an analyst whose sector is in the doldrums is usually depressing. Punctuated by long pauses and frequent sighs, the conversation holds as much excitement as a wrong number. During a spell of inactivity, it is even difficult to reach such an analyst on the telephone. Often, he is reluctant to answer as most incoming callers are worried brokers and irate investors who feel they should have been warned about the crash in that sector. Frequently analysts are fired or change firms during a down cycle in their sector, so a good indicator of bottoming in a sector occurs when analyst coverage is "temporarily interrupted." The investment firm is slow to replace an analyst in an out-of-favour sector due to a lack of commissions and inactivity.

The opposite situation occurs when a sector is attractive and most investors are fully participating. Few bargains turn up at such times. Analysts in those sectors are riding high, giving interviews to an adoring press and fielding calls from grateful investors who are looking for the next winning stock. Enthusiastic, upbeat analysts give me cause for concern, as analysts generally are cautious and only reluctantly promotional. After all, they chose an analytical career, not a sales job. Only an outstanding series of months or years in their assigned sector will cause such a personality change in most analysts. Analysts, just like brokers and investors, become too pessimistic toward the bottom and too optimistic toward the top of the cycle for their sector. As an independent investor you can use this quirk to your advantage.

Mathematical methods of assessing the relative popularity of a sector exist too. Stock exchange statisticians keep records of the relative strength of each sector compared to the index. This information is available in the monthly publication *The Toronto Stock Exchange Review* and these numbers are easily obtained by asking an investment advisor/coach to provide them. In a few minutes of work any broker can find out which sectors are underperforming and which are outperforming the index. The hard part of this method comes when trying to determine if a sector is likely to continue to outperform or underperform. And of course, investors buy shares in companies, not sectors.

When to Exit A Hot Sector

A different approach is needed when examining common shares held in the portfolio that have risen in value. While those sectors that have outperformed are likely to fall back at some point as the law of "regression to the mean," or return to the average, kicks in, investment performance suffers if investors are too quick to exit a stock just because it has increased in price. I wish to emphasize that the idea of exiting a hot sector applies only when a sector becomes seriously overvalued. This is rarely the case. Most sectors fluctuate between mildly warm and cool for years, never becoming really hot. In chapter 9 I explain why it is important not to be in a hurry to sell a good company just because the price has risen. This is one of the most damaging mistakes when investing in common shares.

It bears repeating that periods of outperformance and underperformance can last longer than expected. Since you are likely to have at least five sectors represented in your portfolio you will have sectors in most stages from cold to hot and all the phases in between. The idea is not to be perfect in timing the moves from hot to cool. It is more of an evolutionary development. As portfolio changes are contemplated, look for out-of-favour companies to replace those that have run up to unsustainable levels.

Sector Rotation in Summary

The sector rotation method of stock selection can be summarized as the attempt to buy companies in sectors that are cool and sell companies when the sector is hot. If a sector is completely out-of-favour you want to wait for a sign that things are starting to warm up a little before taking a position in that sector. The usual start of a period when a sector is out-of-favour comes from a massive selling of stocks due to an unfavourable fundamental event, such as commodity prices dropping or the demand for a product collapsing. This triggers a rush for the exits on the part of professional money managers. When institutional investors exit a sector en masse, as they often do, it is usually a long time before they will re-enter the field. The fundamental factors need to turn around, which takes time.

In addition, the portfolio managers are human, with pet likes and dislikes. Portfolio managers have an emotional reason to dislike any sector that hurt their performance, especially if they sold at a loss. This emotional factor will keep many individuals and fund managers from coming back to that sector soon. It is best for the contrarian investor to wait until the hurt feelings are a distant memory, which can take several months or even a year or two.

To repeat, the key advantage for the individual investor is the ability to use patience. But there is a limit to patience. No one wants to buy into a sector that is years away from heating up again. You want to catch the turn just a few months before the rest of the world. Any individual forced to wait for years in a cold sector gets impatient and frustrated. So the goal is to catch a sector just when it is coming out of the penalty box and back into play. The bad news is that this timing can be difficult. The good news is that the risks are not great if you get it wrong. If a mistake is made, and the wait turns into a couple of years rather than months, no serious harm is done as long as the company is solid and the sector eventually turns.

After a few months or years a sector will warm up again. Everyone will be playing in this sector, with large price gains in the share prices of companies. Stocks that could not find takers at $20 will be trading at $40 and higher. New share issues by the companies will be frequent, so investment firms will be writing research reports portraying the companies as favourable and assigning a "buy" rating. Business for companies in a hot industry sector is usually outstanding with earnings and revenue growth beyond expectations. The demand for these shares will be strong due to the publicity and the good results of the businesses involved. Price-earnings ratios will expand to a level higher than the average for the market. Another good indicator of a hot sector is unusually high trading volumes in the stocks of that sector.

THE HOT SECTOR CONCENTRATION TRAP

Investors take a profit on gains they make in a sector and then turn around and buy more high-priced stock in the same sector, losing an opportunity to diversify and find a less expensive investment.

Investors may have large gains in stocks they hold in a sector, but when they decide to sell and take a profit they will often turn around and buy another high-priced stock in the same sector. This buying and selling within a hot sector makes little sense because the investors will give back most or all of their profits when the sector turns cold.

For the individual investor using the sector rotation method, the characteristics of a hot market can signal a time to sell out. It is more profitable to look for opportunities in a cool sector where bargains are easily found. The practitioner of sector rotation tries to guess where the professional or institutional money will go next and get there ahead of the pros. I prefer not to be left behind in a hot sector when the fund managers decide to exit.

This requires the discipline to leave the party when the guests are still laughing and talking, the champagne is still flowing and there are no signs of the festivities ending. A few hours later, the party mood will be very different. Only a few people will remain, everyone is asleep or drunk, and all that is left for the next morning is to clean up the mess.

Measures of value such as price-earnings ratios and book values can be used to decide when a sector is hot or cold. Often it is enough to examine the sector performance compared to the TSE 300 over a two or three year period. Those that have underperformed are out-of-favour and worth a look. When establishing a new position in a stock why not look for an undervalued situation?

SECTOR ROTATION IS NOT THE SAME AS MARKET TIMING

There is a lot of confusion between sector rotation and market timing. As will be discussed in chapter 7, it is impossible to time the ups and downs of the stock market itself. Market-timers try to jump in and out of the stock market altogether, treating the whole stock market as a sector. This carries the risk of missing major market gains. A mistake in market timing is just too costly. Sector rotation, on the other hand, is quite feasible and practical. To make changes in portfolios based first on the sectors within the market and second on the relative values of different companies provides a challenge that is manageable. Timing the relative strengths and weaknesses of sectors in the market is easier than trying to time the stock market itself. The consequences of missing a sector's turnaround are minor compared to the damage caused by sitting out of the stock market when a bull market starts to kick in.

Of necessity, independent investors must exit a hot sector earlier than the professionals to avoid playing the professional game where instant decisions and action are required. And individuals can afford to enter a cool sector at an earlier stage and exercise the luxury of patience that professionals cannot afford.

ADVANCED TECHNIQUES FOR SECTOR ROTATION

A sophisticated form of sector rotation involves timing the purchase of stocks in sectors based on the stage of the bull or bear market. Study of past cycles demonstrates that certain categories of stocks do better at different stages of the bull market. There are many different forms of this sector rotation technique, none of which are perfect, primarily because there are substantial variances from one bull market to the next in the sectors that move earlier and later.

Sector Rotation Shifts As Bull Markets Age

Financial Services	early recovery
Electric and Gas Utilities	early recovery
Large-Capitalization	early recovery
Utilities	early recovery
Consumer Products	early to mid recovery
Transportation / Environment	early to mid recovery
Industrial Products	mid recovery
Technology	mid to late recovery
Communications & Media	late recovery
Paper & Forest Products	late recovery
IPOs	late recovery
Junior Mines	late recovery
Mines and Minerals	late recovery
Oil and Gas	late recovery
Small-Capitalization	late recovery

These categorizations are imprecise and variable from one bull market to the next. In fact, some analysts would disagree with some of the categories I have listed. It depends on their personal experience with bull and bear markets.

The Canadian stock market is unique in the world stock markets in having a preponderance of late cycle companies. This is due to the emphasis of resource stocks and economically sensitive companies, as well as the small-cap nature of the market. Canadian stocks do very well when an economic recovery is well entrenched and global economic growth is positive, especially the United States economy. When economies overheat as they sometimes do near the end of a cycle, Canadian resource companies prosper. Commodity prices rise due to shortages that develop and profits soar. Examples of Canadian sectors that often excel in the late recovery period are Mines and Minerals, Junior Mines, Paper and Forest Products, Small Capitalization, and Oil and Gas.

One example of this type of stock market can be seen in the 1979–81 period. Canadian stock markets moved to a substantial premium to the U.S. markets during a period of inflation and rapid economic growth. The cycle ended with 18% interest rates choking off economic growth and a deep recession ensued. Will the Canadian market provide another period of outperformance with late-cycle companies? So far in the 1990s the Canadian market dramatically underperformed the U.S. stock market and even government bonds. According to Siegel as discussed in chapter 2, this is a very unusual trend that has occurred only rarely in the last 200 years. If the economic strength in the United States is followed by European growth and Asian recovery the Canadian market will recover and shine. Only the most patient investors will enjoy the benefits of such a surge, if it comes, since by 1999 most had given up on the Canadian market. From such a humble start the best and most powerful bull markets are born.

Early Bull Market

In general, with exceptions, it can be stated that the earlier recovery period of the new bull market is led by interest-sensitive and blue chip stocks. The more substantial and established a company is, the more likely the frightened investor is to risk a purchase. At the end of a major bear market every investor is frightened and cautious.

Early in the bull market investors act with caution. Higher quality sectors are emphasized at this stage. By higher quality I mean companies with good dividends and businesses that are reliable. Utilities, for example, provide a product that is stable in demand, sometimes with monopoly power. As the bull market progresses and investors get more confident they are willing to take more risk, which leads to movement in the more cyclical and growth stocks. More cyclical stocks are found where profits and losses depend on the business cycle, such as mines and forest products.

Late Bull Market

Near the end of a long bull market the more speculative, newer, and smaller companies are popular because they provide the quickest gains to the speculative-minded investor. For example, the mania for Internet stocks would never happen at the end of a bear market or early in a new bull market.

As the bull market progresses investors lose their fear, becoming more and more adventurous, either in buying stocks directly or in the type of mutual fund they seek out. So at the end of a bull market portfolios are overloaded with speculative stocks and missing many of the blue chip names that were held earlier on.

Now, if you will think back for a minute to the discussion about mutual funds and the problems that arise when redemptions are heavy during a bear market you will perhaps see a strategy that takes advantage of the professionals who manage funds and their unfortunate mutual fund investors.

Taking Advantage of Professional Investors

The mutual fund managers sell their blue chip companies at some point in the bear market due to the redemptions forced on them by panicky mutual fund investors. Since shares of the major companies are the only ones the funds can sell quickly at this stage in the bear market, they will dump them on the market. If you, as an independent investor, are ready you can buy blue chip companies at bargain prices. The fund managers will be selling the stocks that will be the first to warm up in the next bull market.

Actions of fund managers will be the determining factor for the start of the new bull market. Once most of the funds have sold their blue chips the recovery can begin. This is true because, after the funds are through, the selling will end, allowing a rebound in the most heavily-sold sector. Past turning points in the market show that an absence of sellers is of itself sufficient to cause a major upward move, without a large amount of new buyers. Prices of stocks are marked up each day by holders unwilling to sell at the current prices. This upward price movement of blue chip stocks attracts investors back into the market, starting the new bull market.

Buying When the Pros Are Selling

Unlike the mutual funds, which have difficulties with liquidity, independent investors caught with speculative stocks at the end of the bull market can adjust their portfolio to include the blue chip sector. This is easier for the independent investor because of the small number of shares held. It is not possible for the mutual fund managers because of the huge positions they hold as discussed in chapter 1 in the section "They Held the Wrong Stocks." In the past, popular or speculative stock sectors stayed cold for many months and even years, as the fund managers, hungry for liquidity, continued to sell some shares each time the stocks rose a little in price. The period from 1970 to 1980 saw funds disposing of the Nifty Fifty stocks continuously as redemptions continued to plague them.

This ability to realign portfolios to take advantage of a shift in sectors is a major advantage for the independent investor over the professional mutual fund or institutional investor. The power of this advantage shows up more in the bear markets than bull markets because limited liquidity is more problematic in a bear market. Individuals still need to find the discipline to sell some of their positions in formerly hot sectors, even at a loss, to take advantage of the blue chip sales by fund companies.

Independent investors using sector rotation and a knowledge of the type of portfolios held by mutual fund managers will be able to take advantage of opportunities created by the forced liquidation of quality companies in the next bear market.

Using the natural advantages of patience, sector rotation, and independent decision-making, individuals will find investing rewarding. There are opportunities at every stage of the market cycle for investors who make use of their natural advantages. At times the road will be difficult, especially when others are making quick and easy profits chasing the latest overvalued, hot stocks. The feeling of accomplishment that comes from patiently following an independent path to success lasts much longer than the fleeting surge of pleasure that follows a quick speculative venture.

When discussing the need to avoid the mutual fund traps, most investors state that they find it difficult to imagine having the time and expertise to invest directly in the stock market. They implicitly assume they would be on their own, picking stocks and deciding when to sell. Investors can use help that is available from qualified investment advisors and research analysts who do most of this work for the independent investor.

The challenge is to find the right kind of help, in an investment world with more and more contradictory information. Part 3 of this book simplifies those choices for you as you establish your independence as an investor.

Part 3

Finding the Right Advisor
to Be Your Guide

Five

Avoid the Consumer / Seller Trap

Once you commit to the idea of investing in the stock market and move beyond guaranteed investments only, you need help. Few investors venture into the dangerous waters of equity investing without seeking advice, usually professional advice. Most observers agree that as an independent investor you need to get professional help in managing your portfolio. All investors could use competent help with stock selection, maintaining balance, knowing when to sell, record keeping, and avoiding big mistakes. The trick is to find the kind of help that will get you to where you need to go.

Investors benefit from assistance provided by various types of professionals. Research analysts play a big role in discerning the better companies from the mediocre. In a chapter 10 I will show you how to use research to your advantage. Accountants give useful advice in minimizing taxation on gains and income. Lawyers specializing in estate planning provide useful advice when investments are large enough to cause worries about estate succession.

However, the person who directs your choice of stock market investments makes the biggest impact on your investment future. Your choice of advisor influences the amount of success and peace of mind you achieve in the investment process. Unfortunately, you may find out that you chose an unsuitable advisor only years later. Happily, there are ways to increase the chances of making a good selection, even if you are very inexperienced in investing.

COMPENSATION METHODS MATTER

In making a choice about advisors, investors find it useful to have as much information as possible. Questions to ask include: How is the person motivated to behave? What are the financial arrangements that constrain your salesperson? Is the advisor in a position to give independent, unbiased advice? Where are the traps?

I heard a statement a few years ago when I was branch manager that clarified the situation. A manager commented in one of our regular meetings that "what gets rewarded, gets done." Tortured syntax aside, he was saying that people act if they get compensated and refuse to act if there is no financial reward. It is important then to know what sort of things your salesperson gets paid for doing. Is your advisor simply a salesperson selling an investment product or does your advisor get paid to provide independent, unbiased advice?

There are several different payment models for investment salespeople. In most cases salespeople get paid for transactions. Sometimes, in addition, salespeople receive an ongoing trailer fee as part of an annual management fee of a mutual fund or managed portfolio account. On rare occasions, advisors get paid for spending a certain amount of time with an investor, similar to a lawyer who bills by the hour. This is very unusual because investors are unwilling to pay up front for financial advice that seems to be available for "free" elsewhere.

In most cases a top salesperson earns substantial income by making sales of some service or product. Investment sales is no exception. In a bull market, a career in investment sales is one of the most financially rewarding activities on the planet, for those who are not talented enough to make it as a professional athlete. Even athletes often become investment salespeople after their knees give out. In a bear market, contrary to popular belief, investment salespeople do very poorly.

Hidden Fees Help Make the Sale

One popular method of paying investment salespeople in Canada is the deferred sales charge (DSC), or rear-end load, attached to many mutual funds today. The deferred sales charge arrived in 1987, introduced by MacKenzie Financial. This type of charge allowed consumers to believe that they were getting the fund purchase free, as long as they held the fund for a minimum number of years. The sales charge declines each year the fund is held, reaching zero after five or six years. Salespeople find buyers of these rear-end load funds with the pitch that there is no commission paid. Since there is an element of truth to this if the fund is held for several years, investors find it attractive. "Just hang on for the long term" is the rallying cry. Prior to 1987 funds were sold with a front-end load, which varied between 9% on small purchases and 2% on larger ones.

The obvious question is: How does the salesperson get paid if the charge is deferred? The sales commission, usually 5%, is paid to the salesperson up front by a third party, usually the mutual fund company or a limited partnership designed solely for the purpose of financing up-front fees. The cost of that commission is then recovered by charging a higher annual management fee. The investor pays the commission in the end, just in a different form. Since management fees are paid every year as a percentage of the total investment, they form a large part of the cost of owning the fund. But they are more hidden than an up-front commission. Management fees are taken out of the money in the fund, before the performance of the fund is reported.

Many salespeople gloss over the fact that the annual management fees are higher for DSC funds than regular funds because of the need to recover deferred sales charges. Buyers of these products get the impression that they are getting something for nothing.

According to the book *The Wealthy Boomer—Life after Mutual Funds*, there have been changes in the annual management fees for mutual funds since the deferred sales charges were introduced. In the 1980s, prior to the introduction of DSC funds, the yearly management fee was usually 1% or less. To pay for the cost of rear-end loads, management fees (also known as a management expense ratio or MER) increased. A portion of the management fee is used to reimburse those who put up the cash to pay the salesperson his commission. Today these management fees average over 2% for Canadian equity funds and 2.4% for international funds. A portion of this fee, usually 0.25% to 0.50%, goes to the asset-gatherer as a trailer fee, as compensation or inducement to leave the assets with that fund.

Over 80% of all load fund sales in Canada are of the deferred sales charge type. Since an annual management fee is charged as long as the fund is owned, and is calculated on the current value of the assets, the old front end load charge sales model was less costly for consumers. For example, if the value of a holding in a fund increased from $20 000 to $80 000 over 15 years, a 10% annual return, the annual management fee difference between front end load and rear end load of 1% would represent $800. This means that a consumer could have saved the equivalent of one year's management fee increase by paying an upfront commission. The difference is that the higher MER is paid each and every year and increases with the assets, while the front end load is paid just once, based on the original capital. So consumers are paying a much higher cost with a deferred-sales-charge fund and its higher MER than they were with an up-front fee and a lower MER. The advantage to the salespeople is that the fee structure is often never discussed. The advantage to the consumer is the appearance of getting something for nothing.

Mutual fund companies were innovative in setting up deferred sales charges for mutual funds. They were giving mutual fund buyers what they wanted. If the salesperson could make the sale more easily with deferred charge funds then more of those funds would be sold. And it worked—assets soared as more funds were sold following the 1987 change in sales charges.

Deferred sales charge funds make another difference for consumers of mutual fund products. It costs money to withdraw from these funds during the first six to nine years of ownership. This fact makes a large withdrawal of money from these funds unlikely since investors hate paying these charges. This reluctance to pay rear-end load fees will keep many investors in funds longer during the initial phase of the next bear market. Most will sell out eventually anyway, just at a later time when stock prices are even lower. In the last mutual fund popularity cycle of the 1960s all funds were sold with an up-front fee. Investors paid no exit fee to depart the fund when things turned sour. This time the withdrawals will be more gradual and mutual fund companies will continue to collect their annual management fees for many years.

No-Load Funds

No-load funds operate on a similar misconception. While there is no upfront commission or rear end load fee there is still the annual management fee or MER, often a hefty one that goes entirely to the mutual fund company. Many consumers of investment products are attracted to no load funds because of the lack of a fee to invest. Apart from the ongoing nature of the MER these consumers are also forgoing the assistance of an investment professional. It is important to pick an investment that ensures that your advisor has a reason to stay involved in your investment program.

THE ASSET-GATHERER

New financial salespeople in the world of the 1990s are encouraged by their training programs to "gather assets." Trainers actively discourage them from trying to manage money or select stocks for their clients. The asset-gatherer salesperson turns over the responsibility for managing money to others, freeing up time to gather assets. Gathering assets means attracting investors to open accounts and deposit or transfer in their investment funds from other brokers or banks. Many of the salespeople who started in the investment business in the 1990s see themselves primarily as asset-gatherers, not portfolio managers or stock pickers.

An Asset-Gatherer Is a Salesperson

The asset-gatherer type of advisor specializes in the business of bringing in investment dollars and then turning them over to be managed by a third party. Usually this third party is a mutual fund company or an investment counsellor. The mutual fund can be offered by the advisor's own firm (an in-house product) or it can be offered by an independent company. In each case neither the investment advisor nor the client involve themselves in the purchase and sale decisions that are made for that account. The advisor gets paid an initial commission to place the money and usually an ongoing fee as long as the money remains with the fund or counsellor. The salesperson who deals directly with the public gets paid for signing the client and delivering the assets. Many investors insist on being sold on their investment choices, an attitude that puts a premium on sales skills for people in the investment sales business.

The asset-gatherer becomes an expert about various rates of return of the funds and the management styles of the money managers. The mutual fund companies and investment dealers encourage this type of salesperson as they bring in a lot of money for mutual funds and/or in-house managed products. These products are sold to investors who prefer not to take the time to make choices and stay involved on an ongoing basis. This type of investor becomes more a consumer of investment products than an investor.

In her 1998 report *Investment Funds in Canada and Consumer Protection—Strategies for the Millennium* (Industry Canada, 1998), Glorianne Stromberg, former member of the Ontario Securities Commission, addressed this issue. She reported that:

> Several industry participants made comments to the effect that the "securities model" is no longer working and that we need to think in terms of building a consumer model. They observed that people who are buying investment funds (and in particular mutual funds) have the mindset of a consumer and not . . . an investor.

This trend toward salespeople who recommend the products of other professionals is an important development of the 1990s. The relationship between investor (consumer) and advisor (salesperson) changes materially with this new paradigm. One major difference is the number of clients or consumers that can be handled by one salesperson. Prior to the late 1980s, an advisor might have from 50 up to 200 good clients. This limit arose naturally because of the necessity for the advisor to be part salesperson, part portfolio manager. Today, under the asset-gatherer paradigm, salespeople handling 1000 or more clients (purchasers) are found in most offices. The asset-gathering salesperson handles more buyers as he has less ongoing work to do with each client. The asset-gatherer spends time gathering assets rather than managing them. Under the previous paradigm, investment advisors with stock selection and portfolio management responsibilities spent more time with each client, as part of the portfolio management process.

Limited Involvement with the "Customer"

The asset-gatherer relationship is sold on a financial planning model. At the beginning of the relationship, the salesperson gathers information at an interview. Then, after reviewing the individual's situation, the advisor recommends a particular group of managed products that meet the needs of the client. If the investor agrees to the recommendations, the products are purchased for the client. The mutual fund salesperson receives a commission. Once a product is selected the salesperson has very little additional work to perform. There are limited opportunities for ongoing involvement between the investor and the salesperson. An occasional sales call from the advisor to see if there is additional money to be invested becomes the norm for these relationships.

Clients find few opportunities to assess the competence of the salesperson in this kind of relationship. The initial interview and the rate of return on the products purchased at the beginning remain the focus of any assessment. What was the rate of return last year? The last three quarters? Any judgement of the advisor must be based on the historical rate of return of the products selected.

Any ongoing assessments are based again on investment performance. When recent performance is good the asset-gatherer calls to see if more money is available. If the client feels good about the salesperson money is added to the account because performance is good. In addition to these calls for more money, many competent asset-gatherers do an excellent job of annual reviews, providing information to the client. Again, these annual reviews centre on performance. Asset gatherers realize that they have few opportunities for significant client involvement and try to make up for that with birthday cards, informative seminars on topics such as estate planning, notes in the mail, and client appreciation events. As long as the performance of the investment product is good, the relationship stays warm and friendly.

Asset-Gatherers Offer Convenience

The asset-gatherers seem likely to last for at least a few years as people find convenience in buying an investment product. The minimal involvement aspect of this service fits well for two-career families who are at the height of their involvement with their professions, their children, and their ageing parents. Their belief that there is not enough time to manage an investment portfolio is reinforced by fund advertising and individual sales pitches. Managed products, especially mutual funds, appear ideal to these investors, many of whom are baby-boomers.

The busy baby boomer might ask: If the asset gatherer can place my money in a managed product (mutual fund) and achieve a good return and I do not have to spend much time at it, why would I consider anything else? Where is the trap in this type of relationship? Many investment consumers see few of the vulnerabilities of the consumer/sales relationship evolving in the 1990s investment game. Stromberg reports:

> Intermediaries commonly portray themselves as providing financial planning and investment advisory services, but in reality are often only selling product. Compensation is linked to product sales, and the consumer/investor often fails to understand the implications of the situation. Knowledge gaps leave consumer/investors vulnerable.

WEAKNESSES OF THE CONSUMER/SELLER MODEL

The fundamental weakness in the salesperson/consumer relationship is the lack of client involvement in the investing process. Related problems follow from the method used to make the sale. The asset gatherer extracts a commitment from the customer by talking primarily about the rate of return on the investment. The sales pitch revolves around comparisons of past rates of return on various instruments and products. By impressing the potential buyer with high historical returns the salesperson cements the sale but also prepares the ground for future problems of a market timing trap nature.

Salespeople seldom talk about funds or products that have horrible rates of return. Prospects would not listen to them if they did. Presentations focus on the positive features and benefits of the products, since this approach facilitates the sale. The most prominent feature of an investment product, whether mutual fund or managed portfolio account, is its rate of return. Measurement services such as Bell Charts, Morningstar, and Lipper distinguish among the funds using track records as the major variable. Consumers that purchase funds invariably give the fund's performance the most weight in their final decision.

In an ideal world investors would find a way to assess other factors along with performance. The quality of the managers, their length of time in the business, the type of common stocks held by the fund, the management fees charged, the amount of risk taken by the fund to reach a performance level, and the amount of trading in the fund are just some of the factors that would be considered.

To their credit, many product salespeople try to discuss these features with clients. However, assessments of such intangibles are difficult, if not impossible. Even if these factors could be measured they often change with time and with managers. The managers with the best performance seem to move from one fund company to another frequently.

Quality issues often are overlooked in favour of quantity issues simply because quantity can be measured and quality cannot. This is a good example of the difficulty of measuring the important things in life. In a mutual fund how would investors measure the integrity of the managers? How does an investor distinguish among the various styles of investment management? How else can an investor choose other than by performance records? So the product salesperson and the buyer focus on performance. Once the selection is made the buyer watches the investments with varying degrees of attention. If the investment does well attention turns to other matters. The promise of "worry-free" investing arrives.

A Bull Market Fosters False Expectations

This carefree period lasts as long as the bull market climbs steadily higher. Of course, there may be times of nervousness or disenchantment when the consumer identifies other products that are doing better. Brief discussions initiated by the concerned consumer are held, ending with an admonition by the salesperson to remember that the investment was purchased for the long term. As long as the investment does reasonably well the investor stays with it.

If the rate of return is exceptionally good the happy consumer often discovers more money to add to the original stake. The salesperson suggests adding more money to the products that have the best returns, as this is the path of least resistance. Imagine how poor a salesperson would be who always talked about the product with the worst track record!

You are probably seeing the *buy high* nature of this activity. All discussions centre on good performance. Money is added when markets are good. The most money is committed when past performance looks the best. As a consumer the buyer is relegated to the role of shopper, looking for the best product with the feature of highest historical return for its category.

Problems Emerge During a Bear Market

Real, but hidden, problems in the seller-consumer relationship only emerge when the market goes into a slump and the product track record is minus 10% or worse. Now the consumer is worried. He calls the salesperson to find out what is going on. This call is a challenge for the managed-product salesperson with hundreds of clients. The lack of contact between the customer and salesperson since the initial interview means there is little rapport between them. Since that one meeting was a sales presentation, the seller highlighted mostly the positive attributes of the investment. The rapport that was established at that time was founded on the idea that this salesperson knew how to get a better rate of return than their previous advisor, or their bank.

During that meeting, the purchaser of the investment heard only good things about the proposed investment. After a downturn the fundamental basis of the relationship shifts. The spoken (or unspoken) promise of high returns has been broken. The trust level drops dramatically. The investor questions the salesperson closely. How did you select this investment? How much risk is there? Does the salesperson really know what is going on? Since the consumer sees the investment as a product, the investment looks defective when the best feature, its return, is broken. But there is no warranty.

This client is only one of hundreds for the asset-gathering type salesperson. The salesperson gives only a small amount of time to the worried client, whose name he might not have recognized when the phone call came in. After all, there has been very little direct contact between them. The customer begins to feel a complete lack of commitment to the investment as well as the seller. The salesperson and the product have failed to deliver. It is only a matter of time until the product is sold, at a loss, and the salesperson is replaced.

A fundamental problem is the weak commitment from the client to the investment process. The buy high, sell low trap that the asset-gatherer and his customers entered was set and baited with the premise that the salesperson has a product with such a great return that success is guaranteed with minimal involvement or effort by the consumer. The consumer took little responsibility for the choices made and expected an excellent result.

Once the inevitable bear market appeared the client panicked. By initially trusting the salesperson and the product too much, the investor created unreasonable expectations. Once the expectations were not met, the investor reacted by selling the product.

THE INVESTMENT "CONSUMER" TRAP

Investors treat their investments as if they were interchangeable consumer products. Buy decisions are based on unreasonable expectations fostered by the initial sales method. Investors are not prepared for bear markets.

The investor was committed only as long as the results were positive. Without a strong relationship with the client the salesperson lost any chance to influence the investor once the rate of return turned seriously negative. Since the rate of return was the only significant factor in the decision to buy the product it makes sense for the investor to cancel the arrangement when that factor turns negative. The investor felt little or no commitment to the process used to select the investment or to the advisor who recommended the product. The *sell low* ending of this scenario comes about as the investor bails out at or near the market bottom.

Of course, the scenario often varies a little from the straight *buy high, sell low* one described. One variation involves switching products and salespersons. As one product fails to meet expectations the various funds are screened for one that has a better rate of return. The buyer/investor jumps from one to the other, often several times. Along with the change in product there is frequently a change in salesperson. As long as the process involves primarily rate of return and purchasing a product the buyer will continue his downward spiral of buying high and selling low.

The commission paid up front to the asset-gatherer pulls him on to find new clients. Most of his time must be spent looking for new clients. There is little money to be made from the existing clients, other than the trailer fee paid by the mutual fund. The real gravy comes with a new client. So the asset-gatherer does what an asset-gatherer does best—gathers assets. Once the sale is made the product salesperson no longer is responsible for the portfolio. That responsibility shifts entirely to the consumer and the product manager. The salesperson's commission is received and safe. The missing link is commitment and involvement.

Investments are sold, not bought, says the old adage. With the muscle of the megamillion-dollar marketing budgets, investment product pitches make serious inroads into our daily lives. Television advertising by mutual funds, rare just five years ago, dominate the prime-time and sports shows. Newspapers are full of advertisements for funds, augmented by investment columnists who cheerfully promote the investment products of their paper's biggest advertising customers.

Stromberg reports: "Where once portfolio management skills were the most sought after skills for mutual fund management companies, marketing skills are now perceived as an even more essential asset."

A sobering thought: If the salespeople are concentrating on sales and the mutual fund companies are focusing on marketing skills, who is worrying about the quality of the investments?

THE STOCK JOCKEY

Many investment salespeople make a living selling individual stocks rather than investment products, although this type is much rarer today than in the previous decade. Some call this sales type the stock jockey.

As long as there are investors who like to be "sold" on a stock before they commit to a purchase these brokers will survive. This salesperson presents a particular stock pick as the "must buy" choice of the day. Some call this sales model the "stock du jour" method. Quoting the research department of his firm or "inside" information, the sales presentation focuses on the short-term prospects for the future price of a single stock. Knowing that the investor needs to have a compelling reason to take action the salesperson draws the investor's attention to reasons why the stock should rise sharply in the near future. Often this pitch is oriented toward a short time frame.

Stock jockeys spend some time looking for new clients, offering a hot stock idea as the lure to the prospective client. The target of the stock jockey takes little or no responsibility for the investment process when agreeing to purchase stocks one at a time. It is easy to walk away, blaming either the stock market or the stock jockey for the bad results.

There are similarities between the asset-gatherer and the stock jockey. Each of them holds out the return on investment as the primary decision-making factor. In the case of the stock jockey the future rate of return holds centre place in the discussion. This discussion about the future differentiates the stock jockey from the asset-gatherer. Another difference between the stock jockey and the asset-gatherer is the amount of contact. A client who is willing to listen to a pitch about a stock may receive daily calls from his stock jockey broker, encouraging him to move quickly. This ongoing and frequent contact helps the client stay involved in the market, at least as long as the bull market and the money lasts.

THE STOCK JOCKEY TRAP

A stock salesperson pitches clients to buy stocks with a short time frame in mind. The portfolio grows into an incoherent collection of poor investments, as performing investments are sold for a profit and declining investments are held in hope of improvement.

The portfolio grows into a hodge-podge collection of hot picks that the stock salesperson sold to the client. Those picks that go up are sold for a profit and those that go down are often held, hoping for an improvement. A client's relationship with a stock jockey depends on stock-picking success, and breaks down depending on the skill and luck of the broker. Because of the short-term nature of the trades the relationship is often short-lived as well.

Although the broker must call each time before the purchase is made, the client takes little responsibility for the choice of stocks. The broker is the one who pushes the client into the choice, hoping that more winners are found than losers. Clients who use stock jockeys for their investment activities often hold accounts at several brokers. Spreading the assets around also helps the client avoid responsibility for the results from the accounts. Clients move between brokers as well, although frequently a genuine friendship develops between the client and the broker.

The stock du jour salesperson needs frequent trading to make a living as the clientele attracted to this type is not large. The stock jockey type broker suffers today from serious losses of clients to the electronic trading systems on the Internet. It is normal for these salespeople to deal with less than 50 people, actively trading most of the time. Unlike the asset-gatherer, stock jockeys know their clients very well. The type of stock market determines the success or failure of these salespeople. While an active market in junior or speculative stocks is ideal, blue chip markets work less well.

In this model, the stock jockey takes a lot of responsibility for the success of his recommendations. When his picks are doing well, he is on top of the world. When his stocks are down, so is his mood. Stock jockeys often become depressed about their stocks during a stretch of bad luck or bad markets. On the positive side, brokers of this type sometimes develop a genuine ability to sense market trends and stock cycles. Their survival depends on it, just as the asset-gatherer needs exceptional selling skills. Stock jockeys like living on the edge. Often their clients are cut from the same cloth. Trading of this nature is often primarily entertainment for the investor.

In my role as branch manager I was required to review all client trading activities on a daily basis, especially actively traded accounts of a speculative nature, to protect clients from overly aggressive brokers. Once I received a shock in reviewing the account of one of the most prominent members of our legal community, who sat on several boards of major companies. His account with the firm was full of stocks apparently collected by the "stock du jour" method. When confronted, the broker insisted that the client loved taking a plunge and would invariably agree to a suggestion of the "stock du jour" type.

THE KEY IS COMMITMENT

These two types of salespersons, the stock jockey and the asset-gatherer, cover the extreme ends of the spectrum in investment sales. But there is a common denominator that causes trouble for their clients. The link is the lack of responsibility taken by the client (buyer) and the advisor (seller) for the investing process.

In each case the advisor usually takes the initiative to sell the client on an investment. The investor sits back and waits to be told what to buy with their savings. The advisor is put in the role of salesperson and the client plays the role of customer. The product is the investment or stock. The warranty is non-existent. The evidence of whether the product works is performance. Once the sale is made and the commission is collected the salesperson loses a sense of commitment. A salesperson's job is to make the sale. A relationship is a bonus, if it happens. Many investment salespersons are paid in such a way that spending their time to develop a relationship is not sufficiently rewarded. What gets rewarded, gets done.

With all this advertising and sales pressure it would be surprising if potential investors managed to break free of the consumer mold. And yet, savers must break out of the consumer/buyer mold to become successful independent investors. Investors place money into companies as owners of that company, not buyers of an investment product. Smart investors hire professionals to assist them in their search for decent companies to own. Any individual who really wants to be an investor avoids salespeople of the types described, because there is no opportunity for involvement, learning, and control. The investor who wishes to escape from the consumer/seller trap seeks commitment from his advisor and himself. The key to commitment is involvement, from both sides of the relationship.

THE IMPORTANCE OF INVOLVEMENT

I remember hearing a story early in my working career that made a deep impression on me. The story took place in a large, corporate organization. A recently promoted Vice President was asked to prepare a report for the CEO. As a junior person he wanted to make a good impression, sensing a rare opportunity for exposure that would be career-enhancing or career-limiting.

After working for many hours he finished the report and went to the CEO's office. While he was waiting he struck up a conversation with the elderly assistant who had worked for the CEO for many years. She asked to look at his report.

After quickly scanning the document and making some notes she called the nervous subordinate to her desk. She told him to take the report back and make some changes as she had marked. When he looked at the report he saw that she had suggested cosmetic changes that introduced spelling mistakes, poor syntax, and clumsy construction. None of the changes altered the basic thrust of the report, but they lowered the quality of the finished product. He protested, but after some reassurances from her he went back and made the changes. By the time he had finished he was confused and scared.

Back at the office he was ushered in and presented his report. Standing silently while the boss read the report, he saw the "old man" take out a red felt pen. He proceeded to pore over the paper, making a dozen or more comments in the margin. The VP's mind raced as he prepared himself for two years of duty in Greenland. The CEO spoke up.

"This is a good report but it needs some more work. Go back and make some corrections where I've indicated and then you'll have an acceptable proposal."

As the junior man passed the desk of the elderly assistant, he stopped to thank her. He remained perplexed but sensed that things had gone much better than he could have dreamed. She gave him some advice.

"The CEO didn't get a chance for as much schooling as most, so he taught himself. He loves to demonstrate his knowledge of English grammar. When he made those corrections to your paper, the proposal became his as well as yours. Now he has a stake in it, too. There won't be any problem getting his approval now. And he will sell it to the others on your behalf."

I saw the wisdom in that advice. Over the years I realized how important it is to make everyone a party to the process if you want buy-in to the result.

While it is possible to find a salesperson who wants involvement in your investment program, it is unlikely to happen by accident. Most salespeople are too busy selling to make the kind of ongoing commitment that you need. The way to find a relationship with an advisor of the type you need is to look for a coach, not a salesperson. A coach wants to become involved in your investment program and in the selection of the individual securities. In the next chapter I will describe the characteristics of the "coach" model of investment advisor. Every investor who wants to take responsibility for their investment needs a coach, not a salesperson. A coach gives advice, provides information, and takes time to teach the investment process.

The investor finds that, by taking a little responsibility for the process, the investment world becomes a more rewarding and more comfortable place. The nervousness of the customer/salesperson relationship is replaced by a feeling of confidence in the process and the advisor, even when a bear market causes a setback in returns.

An investment program that relies on outstanding returns alone cannot survive for long. A relationship that is based on a promise of steady growth in assets without involvement or risk lasts only as long as the bull market. And when the bear market comes, and the salesperson no longer engenders trust, the investor loses heart and sells out of the market. This is the trap inherent in dealing with a salesperson that must be avoided if you wish to be a successful investor.

Six

Use a Coach as Your Advisor

Your choice of an advisor affects the success of your investment program perhaps more than any other decision. This choice is more important than the selection of any individual stock or bond or investment firm. You enhance your chances of investment success materially if an advisor is found who adds value to the quality of investment decisions.

The investment books give some suggestions about picking a good advisor. Interviewing several advisors before making a choice is frequently mentioned. Most financial planning books prefer the referral method as the best source of advisor. If a friend is happy with an advisor these books recommend giving a lot of importance to their endorsement. I know from my personal experience that referrals are the best method of finding new clients. Prospective new clients come to the first meeting pre-sold on me as their advisor, as their friends have spent some time talking about me.

There are several potential weaknesses in picking a friend's advisor, no matter how highly recommended. Is the friend recommending that advisor because the market is high and he is happy about how well his investments are doing? Is the friend's comfort level affected by a positive rate of return on investment, ignoring other factors? Is the friend in the consumer/seller paradigm in his investment program? What kind of a plan for investing does the advisor use? And, most importantly, is the advisor a coach or salesperson? You need to examine the quality of the advisor on a deeper level than just the current state of a friend's portfolio. Some serious probing is necessary to reveal the true nature of that advisor. The last thing you need is to enter into a seller/consumer relationship.

HOW TO TELL A COACH FROM A SALESPERSON

A coach reveals himself in his actions, as well as his words. While an investment advisor coach has to have some sales skills to survive, the coach usually excels in other areas. A coach may not be as polished in the sales process as a salesperson, but his or her other skills are much more important in helping you with your investments. The sales skills of the salesperson help him make more money, not you. The investment management skills of a coach make more money for you.

An asset-gatherer type spends more time on selling new prospects than studying the stock market. The large number of clients dictates that client contact and prospecting are the main activities. Time for studying the market seldom appears in the busy schedule of an asset-gatherer. And, since the plan is to turn over all assets to a third-party manager, there is little interest in the quirks and opportunities of the stock market.

On the other hand, a coach studies the stock market. A coach who specializes in stocks and bonds retains most of the responsibility for choosing individual investments. That coach must become informed enough to help people decide if stock A is preferable to stock B.

While continuing to study the market, a coach teaches as well. A coach makes time to explain how the stock market works to a new investor. A coach expects that the client will be involved in investment decisions. For this reason, the coach needs to educate the investor in the philosophy and approach that will be used if they are to work together. Initially the coach may implement a plan for the investor who understands only a small part of the investing process. A good coach works from the beginning to educate the investor and draw him into the portfolio management decisions.

Coaching begins with information. Information about the plan, the process, and the philosophy are as important as specific stocks or investments. Investors will notice that a coach talks about an approach to investing rather than investment products. Education of the investor helps the coach perform. The more knowledgeable the investor becomes, the easier the coach's job is.

Most coaches avoid managed products or mutual funds. This choice helps the coach as much as the investor because a managed product takes both the coach and the client out of the investment process. Coaches prefer to remain involved in the decisions about investments, along with the investor. Together they implement the investment plan. Involvement and learning are key for both the coach and investor.

A Simple Plan

An advisor needs to have a comprehensive, understandable approach to the investment challenge. This plan must also be concise and easily communicated to any investor in five minutes or less.

"TRUST ME" ISN'T GOOD ENOUGH

Several years ago I attended an awards presentation for one of the top financial salespersons in Canada. This individual made a short presentation to the gathering after receiving his award. He stated that his investment process was "too complicated" to explain to clients. His career goal was to make $1 million in commissions in one day! While I was shocked by the nature of his career goal, I shuddered to think of his clients being told that they were not smart enough or sophisticated enough to understand his investment methods. It obviously worked for him with a large number of people since he was successful enough to receive the award. This "reverse psychology" sales approach works on people who are nervous and unsure of themselves. As you have heard already, many people wish to be told what to do.

This award-winning salesperson used the "trust me" method of selling. This attitude is a sign that the advisor lacks a plan that will nurture and educate the client. This advisor wants a docile client who is easily manipulated to agree to his suggestions without questions. Without a knowledge of the plan to fall back on, when the tough times come, consumers will have little confidence in this type of salesperson. One of the uses of the plan is to assess whether the type of investing is on track or not. When the going gets tough, the market is down, and the portfolio is underperforming the market, the plan is a touchstone that allows both parties to evaluate if the fault is in the process or just a temporary aberration.

The investor needs the plan as a measure of the quality of the advisor's advice. The advisor needs a plan as a tool to educate and retain clients when adversity appears. The best plans are simple. The basic elements of an investment philosophy describe what actions will be taken in a bull and bear market.

A good plan contains a description of the stock selection process. A good plan allows the investor to understand when to sell stocks and when to buy stocks. This plan needs to be easily understood even by a novice investor.

This book outlines a plan that is understandable and easy to follow. Hundreds of investors use this plan today. However, advisors do not need to write an entire book to have an investment plan. Any advisor who is of the "coach" type will be able to draw a description of her plan on one sheet of paper. Advisors who have a plan will be able to show it in the first meeting, and evidence will be easily produced that the plan is implemented with clients. The best proof of a good plan is in the client's portfolios. Investors who are selecting advisors can ask to see some client statements. These statements of actual clients' holdings will demonstrate whether the advisor implements the plan. Of course, the names are blanked out from the statements before they are photocopied.

Usually the advisor/coach invests for his own account. Why not ask to see a copy of that statement also? Does the statement reflect the plan presented? A coach who believes in an investment approach will be consistent by using that approach in personal investments. Setting an example is one of the strongest forms of leadership available. If the advisor recommends ten to fifteen good quality companies for the stock portion of the portfolio, these companies will be in his personal portfolio also. This makes the choice of common stocks more meaningful to the advisor, especially when the time comes to sell one and buy another.

HOW DOES A COACH GET PAID?

Your advisor needs to be compensated for the work performed. Every sensible investor will accept this fact, understanding that someone who is proficient at their job will make a good income in the investment business. The coach with a good reputation who works hard for her clients will have enough business already. These coaches often take clients primarily through referrals.

Some consumers who operate on the product purchase model shop around for the best deal. Invariably these product buyers either get taken in by hidden charges or they find a broker who undervalues himself, and is willing to discount his services to meet their demand. Some consumers still expect a discount, since the shopping world emphasizes bargains so much these days. These hard-bargainers often end up without an advisor to help them.

A Coach Prefers Full Disclosure

A good coach who deals directly in the stock and bond market prefers that investors receive direct notification of all charges or commissions at the time of each charge. In the stock market commissions are usually attached to each trade, and noted on the contract. This is visible to the client, separate from the cost of the stock itself.

Some investors who invest directly in the stock market with the help of a coach prefer to pay commissions on each transaction. This could be called the "pay-as-you-go" method. The investor approves each transaction prior to execution. The cost of operating a portfolio of this type remains in the control of the investor. In a 10-stock portfolio where there are two trades per year the costs average about 1% depending on the commission level charged. One percent is about half of the average 2% management fee charged by mutual fund companies. By paying a coach just 1% a year on the stock market portion of your portfolio you receive personal portfolio management, keep control, learn constantly about the investment process, and save money over managed products. The advantage of the pay-as-you-go method is that you control the costs of your investment portfolio.

It may happen that some commission-based accounts feel the advisor is calling with too many suggestions for changes. These investors are aware that each time a trade is made there is a cost. Sometimes trades that would help the portfolio are rejected by the client, who wishes to avoid the commissions. Clients who reject trades because of the commission costs or to punish the advisor for an investment that did not work out are hurting themselves as much as the advisor.

As an alternative to commissions, advisors more and more frequently offer the option of a fixed management fee as a percentage of the portfolio. This fee usually allows unlimited trading of stocks. These charges also compare favourably to mutual fund fees since there is no deferred sales charge. Charges are negotiable for larger accounts, usually averaging about 2% for equity portfolios and less for bond portfolios. An advantage of these fees is that they may be tax-deductible.

Annual management fee arrangements have another advantage—there is no incentive for the advisor to suggest more trades than necessary. Investors worried about their inability to say no to a stockbroker/advisor find this arrangement comfortable.

The disadvantage of the management fee method is that an advisor may pay less attention to clients paying by this method because the payment is not tied directly to his or her actions. Often the investor with the management fee arrangement feels that the advisor does not do enough trades.

I feel that either method works well if the relationship is based on a plan. With a coach as an advisor the investor will understand the reasons for each trade. With a commission-based account most clients can keep their costs low and their coach happy. When transactions are paid for with an annual fee clients know their costs in advance and can concentrate on following their plan.

Investors whose main goal is to minimize their costs are missing the point. The value of a coach must exceed the cost for the relationship to make sense. Any good coach can add more than enough value to justify charges of 1% to 2% per year. Inexperienced clients fail to appreciate that during a bear market a coach may be worth a great deal to the investor, even though the market is down. Smart clients want their coach to stay interested in their account during good markets and bad.

The main problem with compensation derives from a misunderstanding over what services are needed. Those consumers who like to be told what to do, or to be pushed into taking action are paying a salesperson a lot of money without receiving any coaching in return. It does not make sense to pay a salesperson 2% to 3% per year if there is no coaching provided. Simply introducing an investor to a product that could be bought directly from a bank or mutual fund company is not enough to warrant those charges. Additional time and services from the advisor must be available. Most salespersons in the investment field know this and work hard to provide extra services. Your challenge as an investor is to find a coach who provides valuable services that are useful to your investment program.

THE REAL ADVANTAGES OF A COACH

Experience

A coach helps an investor by sharing information and experience. No investor will live long enough to have the equivalent experience of a qualified coach and investment advisor. The daily activities of a coach expose him or her to many different situations and investments. Each investment advisor deals with hundreds of different families and investors. Each situation that the advisor sees is slightly different. By doing their job for 10 or 20 years or more the investment advisor experiences investment challenges from all periods of an investor's life cycle. From a youth given a gift of stock to an elderly couple planning their retirement needs, the advisor actively participates in thousands of investment decisions each year. If the advisor is coaching, not selling, these experiences teach lessons that can be applied to other investors.

Each investor only gets one chance to go through each stage of an investment life. Early in life the emphasis is on paying off the mortgage and raising the children. Later, there is money available for investing. Most investors are 45 or 50 years old when the mortgage is paid off and savings are substantial enough to allow them to get serious about investing. Each of us hits this prime investing age when the stock market is in a different stage of the cycle. Some reach the prime investing years when there is a bear market underway. Others find themselves with some investment dollars in the middle of a raging bull market.

There are perhaps 15 to 20 years of investing between the time savings are first available and retirement begins. Once retirement arrives investors need to draw on their savings to live, which limits, but does not eliminate, their investment options.

During those critical 15 years of investing the investment cycle does what it is going to do. Nothing the investor can do will change a bear market environment into a bull market. Investors form their opinions about investing in the first few years of their investing experience. Their experience only starts when they have significant dollars at risk.

There is little time for the investor to learn hard lessons from experience. Often a lesson takes five years to unfold and the investor realizes belatedly that a particular approach was a mistake, perhaps a costly one.

At this point only ten years remain for that investor to recover and apply the lesson to a new approach. With retirement ten years away, some investors give up and lose the chance to apply the lessons they learned. It's no mystery that many investors give up on investing and head back to government bonds and savings certificates after a few bad experiences.

Without the benefit of the experience of living through an investment cycle or two, investors will feel great fear and uncertainty during a bad market. And this results too often in the sellout of a portfolio and a retreat from the markets just before the cycle turns.

A good coach brings the experience of previous cycles and hundreds of different situations to the relationship. An experienced coach gives the investor confidence that times will improve when things look the darkest. An investor expects a coach to restrain his greed when the bull market is flying high and temptation is strong to take a risky plunge.

Education

The coach-investor relationship works well when there is time to discuss investments. The investor needs access to the time of the professional advisor to take advantage of the experience and wisdom accumulated in previous cycles. The investor must be receptive to taking advice as well. Often humans are determined to do it their way, trying to emulate Frank Sinatra's message in his most famous song, "I did it my way." In investing, nothing could be more expensive and dangerous!

Personal Meetings

I meet with prospective investors frequently. Investors have a chance to decide if they want to hire me as their coach. I assess whether the investor is one that I expect to be able to help. After a discussion of philosophy and plan, I like to close the meeting with what I believe is the biggest advantage of hiring someone like me.

Simply put, a coach offers access to his or her time. An investor who commits to a relationship with a coach can expect to phone the advisor and receive advice. The advisor gives his assessment of the situation, using experience and knowledge of many investors in previous cycles faced with comparable circumstances. This access is valuable. When investors realize the cost is less than a typical rear-end load mutual fund management fee the decision to hire a coach as an advisor makes sense.

The access to learning and research is more valuable than most investors realize. A coach can give valuable insights to the stock market and investing. Most coaches give access to research on individual stocks that help in building a portfolio.

The biggest bonus to the relationship comes when the investor realizes that he or she is not alone. The availability of the coach when difficult decisions need to be made becomes very important to most investors.

Seminars

Many top coaches provide seminars free of charge to prospective investors. These seminars save time for the coach as investors get a look at her philosophy and approach in a setting of 15 to 20 people or more. This means that the advisor gets access to many more people than is possible in a one-on-one environment. If the investor then wishes to meet one-on-one to discuss becoming a client, the advisor has saved valuable time that otherwise would have to be used to explain fundamental ideas.

Since many seminars are organized purely to sell mutual funds there needs to be caution here. As the Stromberg report points out, many salespeople hire a "shill" as a headliner for a seminar. Their job is to lure potential consumers to the seminar for the salesperson to sign up. These speakers must have celebrity status so they can draw big crowds. Usually the audiences for these seminars number in the hundreds. This type of seminar may provide little in the way of useful information. The normal format is to offer some financial planning tips surrounded by encouragement to use mutual funds, with some praise for the local salesperson sprinkled on top. But the celebrity will not be handling your account, the local salesperson will.

You need to find a coach who provides a seminar for a small group, and who uses the opportunity to reveal a plan and philosophy. A coach may provide information through the use of expert speakers at seminars, and that makes sense.

In a seminar situation or in a meeting the investor who is looking for a coach learns a lot by asking questions. The coach who has a plan that works will never be embarrassed or upset by a question. The questioner should feel that the coach attempted to answer the question honestly. I know from experience that a feeling of inadequacy or being put-down after asking a question is a very bad sign. In university, I asked a question once in a macroeconomics class. The professor proceeded to berate me for asking that question, and never explained his answer. His attitude was that I was too stupid or lazy to understand his lecture. I certainly never asked a question in that class again. Later, in graduate school in economics, I learned that the professor in question had a reputation for not understanding some of the material himself. He was covering up his inadequate preparation by attacking the questioner.

A good coach will answer any question without making the investor feel stupid for asking. Any attempt to embarrass or ridicule the questioner reveals that the salesperson either does not know his material or is deliberately trying to conceal information from the questioner. This attitude does not contribute to a good coach/investor relationship.

Model Portfolio

Some coaches who specialize in portfolio management will keep track of a model portfolio. This model will capture all of their recommendations, including the date and price. They track the value of the portfolio on a monthly basis, measuring the rate of return achieved. This is a sure sign that you have found a coach oriented toward portfolio management. The most interesting aspect of the portfolio is not the rate of return, which will vary with the market and other factors. You will learn more by asking to see the transactions (the buys and sells) in the portfolio. You can see what frequency of trading the coach likes. By asking questions about particular trades you will learn what factors the coach uses to make buy and sell recommendations. The coach will provide you with the cost of making the average number of trades for that portfolio, pointing out that your portfolio will never be identical to such a model. The portfolio reveals how much risk the coach likes when suggesting stocks.

By examining a portfolio statement you see how much diversification the coach uses. Are all the stock positions similar in size? Are there several industry groups represented? Are the names of the stocks household names? Picking a stock at random, ask the coach for a two-minute assessment. Does the coach sound as if he knows all about the company? Has the coach phoned the company to speak to the investor relations department? What is the research analyst's opinion on each stock in the portfolio? Are there more than one or two stocks in the portfolio that the research analyst does not like? This could be a sign that the coach is a frustrated research analyst who likes to prove the analysts wrong by betting against them. This is not a good sign. You want to see a coach who knows how to work with research analysts to manage your portfolio.

In chapter 10 I discuss how to use both research analysts and coaches to help get the best possible portfolio.

Involvement

Since a coach is trying to assist you to achieve your investment objectives while keeping you involved in the process, you can expect to be asked to make choices. If several common stocks are recommended, the smart coach will give you more than you need for proper diversification to choose from. This forces you to get involved, at least a bit. Once you make a choice between company X and company Y the portfolio becomes a little more yours and a little less the coach's. Since this feeling of ownership is very important to your chances of continuing in the investment game, you need a coach who encourages this type of participation. A salesperson who presents one stock or a set portfolio and suggests that this and only this choice will work is not really working in your interest. While this take-it-or-leave-it approach saves time initially, it leaves the investor feeling left out. A much better approach is to offer alternatives and choices among several companies, all of which would make good additions to the portfolio.

The opportunity to learn about investing through personal involvement in the selection process is an intangible benefit. Many investors see their involvement as a negative initially. They see their time being used up in the investment process. Later, after an experience with more difficult markets, investors understand that the time spent with a coach pays off many times over in the form of a reduced anxiety level. Investors with a healthy coach relationship discover that investing can be fun and a learning experience.

In chapter 10 I show how little time the process needs to take. The coach does the bulk of the work, always under your direction. The essential element is simplicity. Complicated approaches make you more dependent on others and usually cost more in fees.

So find a coach that shares your values and has an understandable and straightforward plan that works. Stay involved in your investment program and have some fun while learning.

Part 4

Using Balance and Re-balance
to Buy Low and Sell High

Seven
The Buy High, Sell Low Trap

By now you have enough information to recognize that a diversified portfolio of stocks and bonds and the help of an advisor/coach gives all that is needed for success in investing. Once investors accept that idea they are well on their way to a profitable experience. There are, however, a few more traps or difficulties that investors find along the path to success. One of the most tempting pitfalls is the idea that investors can beat the market by predicting the future directions of stock and bond prices.

THE MARKET TIMING TRAP

Market timers try to know when to be in the stock market and when to be out. Timers make wholesale jumps out of the market and back depending on their, or someone else's, view of the future direction of the stock market.

WHAT MAKES MARKET TIMERS TICK

These investors or traders (or, most likely, speculators) arm themselves with statistics proving that one needs to be in the stock market only for the upswings. For some, the computer tells when to get out and when to get back in.

Professional market timers use patented indicator variables that trigger buy and sell signals. Many market timers offer their opinions through newsletters and asset allocation mutual funds. Individual traders use economic and business news, advice from friends or business associates, recommendations from brokers and financial planners, or just a gut feeling to decide when to jump in or out.

Market timing is seductive because it plays on our natural human impatience. The market timing bug bites all investors eventually. The markets, both stock and bond, can idle along for long periods without much movement in either direction. The attraction of market timing rests on the premise that a trader gets in when the market is rising and gets out before the fall, and profits are enormous. Market timing, if it worked, would speed up the process of getting rich and avoid a lot of the pain.

There have been many periods in this century when markets have fallen drastically. The stock markets of 1987, 1981–82, 1973–74, and of course the one everybody has heard of, 1929–32, were all free falls that lasted from two months to three years. Any investor who experienced them would love to have missed those horrible times.

TYPES OF MARKET TIMING

For those long-suffering investors who stayed with the markets during these difficult times a market timing program looks appealing. The best time to offer these schemes to the investing public would be just after a major market setback. Not surprisingly, this is exactly what happens.

Asset Allocation Timing

After the downdraft in 1987, computerized formulas purporting to predict the stock market cycle popped up by the dozens. These formulas divided portfolios into cash, stocks, and bonds according to the expected return on each. This process is called asset allocation timing. Several U.S. and Canadian companies offered this service in the early 1990s. Most of these schemes, offered by mutual fund companies, died out when their returns failed to match the indexes.

Asset allocation services apportion money between the various types of investments. The computers depend on a predictive formula that decides the best time to be in a particular asset or type of investment. For example, if the stock market is expensive, the computer decides it is better to move to bonds or cash. If interest rates are about to rise it is best to avoid bonds because bonds fall in price as interest rates rise. If the stock market is bargain-priced then it is best to move out of cash or bonds and into a fully invested position.

Unfortunately, the human mind has not devised a reliable method of predicting the future in matters of the stock market, the weather, or politics! All of the asset allocation methods predict the future based on a theoretical model. Computers build these models by testing different formulas on historical data. They try to discover a predictive formula that would have worked in the past, if it had been used. Eventually they stumble across a mathematical model that seems to react properly to the swings in past markets. The formula has been "backtested." This procedure of finding a mathematical relationship by testing data from the past is called "curve-fitting."

Switching in and out of the stock market at the right moment in the past, the computerized asset allocation return surpasses normal stock market performance. Advertising these theoretical returns, promoters sell a new fund, always including the required phrase "past performance is not indicative of future results." These asset allocation funds collect management fees at a higher rate than normal.

These services attract people based on the lure of higher returns. Many such claims work for a time, building a large following of happy investors. All of these schemes eventually fail, because the future never repeats the past exactly.

Contrarian Timing

The fundamental premise of this renegade strategy is that the crowd is always wrong. For example, if the crowd likes the stock market then this strategy assumes the stock market is headed for trouble and a bear market. This method is known as contrarian investing. If the majority is buying the stock market, contrarians sell and if the majority of investors are sellers, these contrarians are buyers. At specific stages in the cycle, contrarian investing becomes popular and a large number of investors claim that they are contrarian investors. In the middle of a bull market most contrarians suffer huge losses by trying to go against a crowd that is fully invested and a market that continues to rise. After the start of the next bear market the contrarians reappear, coming out of their caves into the daylight.

This contrarian method is useful when choosing individual stocks and sectors as you saw above. This approach of buying stocks when others are selling is necessary for success in stock selection. But contrarian investing presents insurmountable difficulties when used to try to time the stock market.

Contrarian investing as a successful market-timing method requires knowledge of what the crowd is actually doing. One of the first challenges is to determine who is in the crowd. The investment scene is never homogenous. Some investors may be going into bonds while others like stocks. Others may be buying gold stocks while many like fast food restaurants.

Once the crowd is identified, a contrarian market timer needs to determine what the crowd is doing. Investors are notorious for saying one thing and doing something else. After the 1987 crash, for example, there were thousands of market timers and pundits who claimed to have sold before the crash. Few of them went public about their intentions before the crash, if they had actually sold. Many were rewriting history in their claim of being out of the market. I remember a very humourous article in *Barron's* by Alan Abelson shortly after the 1987 crash. He sarcastically pointed out that he must be a very wealthy man because when he added up all the billions of dollars sold by all the pundits claiming to be out of the market, he concluded that he, Alan, must own all the stocks on the New York Stock Exchange.

Individuals are also reluctant to disclose their actual involvement in the stock market, except when it makes them look good. An interesting exercise that is easy to perform helps to understand this tendency. The next time you are talking to an acquaintance bring up the stock market in the conversation. Ask them simply what their opinion is of the future direction of stock market prices. What do you think the market will do this year? Within 30 seconds you will know whether that person is invested in the stock market or not. If so, and the market is doing well, they will probably tell you what kind of stocks or mutual funds they own. If they are not in the stock market, and the market is hitting new highs, brace yourself for a negative blast about the risks of the market and the certainty of a collapse in the near future.

For contrarians to be contrary, they need this investment information about the public as a whole. This is difficult to obtain, although public participation in mutual funds is a good proxy. Statistics show that the public holds about 35% of its financial assets in the stock market, approximately the level reached in the 1960s. The trouble with contrarian investing comes in deciding if that level is the peak. Perhaps the crowd will reach 40% or even 50% participation before this "end of the millennium" bull market dies.

Timing methods that depend on predicting the future or where the crowd is going are difficult to implement. The enormous amount of research it would take just to determine what the crowd is doing in the stock market is out of reach of the individual investor.

Professional investors attempting to time the markets fail just as miserably as the individual investor. This fact is demonstrated by a look at headlines when the great crash of 1929 was not far off. Even a week before the crash many experts were predicting a strong economy and stock market in the newspaper.

One famous voice of contrarian wisdom in 1929, Roger Babson, a statistician, economist, and philosopher, spoke to the Annual National Business Conference as quoted in *The Commercial and Financial Chronicle,* September 7, 1929, stating that "sooner or later a crash is coming, and it may be terrific. Factories will shut down. Men will be thrown out of work. The vicious circle will get in full swing and the result will be a serious business depression."

Reacting to Babson's remarks, an editorial in *Barron's* said "he should not be taken seriously by anyone acquainted with the notorious inaccuracy of his past statements."

Timing the Economy

Jeremy Siegel, in his book *Stocks for the Long Run,* reports that "Billions of dollars of resources are spent trying to forecast the business cycle. It is not surprising that Wall Street employs so many economists desperately trying to predict the next recession or upturn. But the record of predicting exact business-cycle turning points is extremely poor." Examining the turning points he notes that official notification (by way of a declaration by government economists) of the start of a recession usually arrives several months after the actual start. This illustrates clearly the difficulties of gathering information. Business trends run in different patterns and directions, creating confusion in the numbers. Even experts paid to work full time on the problem succeed only after a significant lag time.

Siegel also examines the reaction of the stock market to recessions. Siegel found that the stock market declined before the actual start of the recession. In every case except two the stock market *anticipated* the economic recession, doing so by an average of 5.6 months. Three of the most severe North American recessions occurred in 1970, 1973–75, and 1981–82. The stock market anticipated these recessions by 13 months, 11 months, and 8 months respectively. These recessions were associated with the most severe stock market declines as well. In the 1968 bear market the level of stock prices dropped 25.5% of maximum decline over a 12-month period. In the 1972–74 bear market the index fell 40.1%, and in the 1980–82 bear market prices fell 14.2% in the United States.

The stock market anticipated the most severe recessions by an average of more than 10 months, a longer lead time than the average 5.6 months mentioned above. When it would be most important to know in advance of a recession, because of the severity of the decline, the bear market starts with an even greater lead time ahead of the recession.

In other words the economic news reporting is several months late and the stock market moves from five to ten months early. This means that the public reads newspaper reports of a recession beginning on average one year after the stock market decline begins. Since the average bear market lasts less than one year and the longest bear market in North America lasted three years, a one year delay means that most bear markets would be over by the time the public realized that a recession had started. And yet, if you examine the financial newspapers for quotes from experts and non-experts alike, you will see comments linking the future of the stock market to the current state of the economy. Could there be a more definitive reason for abandoning the attempt to time the market based on economic news reports?

Home-Grown Methods

Many investors have a home-grown method where they try to guess the direction of the market based on the news published in the newspaper and seen on television. The majority of investors and brokers entering the market for the first time use this "system." Certainly the general mood of the public and friends affects an individual's investment decisions.

As we have seen, news about the current state of the economy predicts the future level of the stock market very poorly but it does have a big influence on the feelings of investors.

YOU CAN'T ALWAYS TRUST YOUR FEELINGS

I applied for a job as a stockbroker in early 1975. Even though I had a full-time, challenging job, my evenings revolved around reading about the markets, poring over the financial papers and studying for the Canadian Securities Course, which qualified one for a job as a broker. My dream was to be a stockbroker, watching the stock market all day and handing out advice.

As I attended the interviews with an investment dealer it became clear that my opportunity had come. A final meeting over lunch was arranged, just confirming my decision to accept their offer.

I entered a large room full of empty desks with phones. The Trans Lux ticker tape scrolled across the front wall, up high where everyone could see it. A few men were standing at the front chatting quietly. As we approached them I asked my host where all the brokers were. Perhaps they were all at lunch, I ventured. His answer was vague and only became clear later. The desks were empty because the brokers had left the business. The boom years of the sixties had led to a gradual but serious slide in the number of brokers during the first half of the seventies. Many brokers, unable to earn enough on commissions, left the industry to sell real estate or pursue other careers. A recession had taken a further toll, and the major bear market from January 1973 to December 1974 had convinced most of the rest to leave.

As I chatted with my assigned companion for the "closing" lunch, my enthusiasm waned. How could I enter an industry that so many others had left? The broker who took me for lunch admitted that things were grim. His commissions were down to a mere fraction of previous levels. He confided that he, formerly a teacher, had been seduced by the mutual fund boom in the late 1960s. By the time his decision was made to enter the brokerage business the boom had ended. His experience in the 1970s was difficult as fewer investors were active. I suspected that he wished he had kept his teaching job, with a steady salary and decent pension. I started to think more positively toward my position with a major corporation, salary, and pension. Maybe a move to a commission-based, risky sales job like stockbroker wasn't such a good idea.

The feeling that developed was one of gloom. There was a pervasive mood of negative energy in the big room with the empty desks and the former teacher who was unable to convince himself he had made the right decision to enter the brokerage industry. We were unaware that as we chatted over lunch one of the most impressive bull market runs was already underway.

Within six months of December 1974 the Dow had increased by 50%. The negative climate in the investment industry that had overwhelmed my feelings was old news. By the time the newspapers, the brokers, and investors realized that the bull market had started, it was at least six months old.

The mood of the time influenced me greatly, causing a decision to walk away from the opportunity to pursue a lifelong dream. Because of my high motivation to do so, I eventually joined the investment business three years later, but the decision to try to time my entry into the stock-brokerage business was a costly one. The brokers who stayed with the business from 1975 to 1978 held a huge advantage over me, with their established client base when the truly great years of 1979, 1980, and 1981 arrived. By hesitating, I had acted similarly to an investor who waits for solid evidence from friends and the media that the stock market is the place to invest.

EVERY CYCLE IS DIFFERENT

The downfall of all market timing schemes comes from the inevitable change in the nature of cycles. A cycle never repeats exactly the same way. For example, in the 1974–81 period interest rates rose. During the same period the stock market increased in value, doubling the Dow.

Unlike the 1974–81 period, in the latter part of the 1980s and all of the 1990s, the stock market declined almost every time interest rates rose. Rates moved higher usually because of the U.S. Federal Reserve hiking them to slow the economy and restrain inflationary forces. To a degree, this relationship still exists. Each the time the interest rates are lowered the stock market rises. But there is no rule that says stock markets always rise when interest rates fall.

If you believe that the stock market must go up if interest rates are low or going lower, you must examine Japan. Interest rates declined for years, eventually reaching 1% or lower on long-term bonds in early 1998. Most North American investors would guess that the stock market must be in the stratosphere if rates were that low. The amazing fact about the last nine years in Japan is the stock market moved downward consistently throughout that period of falling interest rates. In 1998 the market traded as low as 1/3 of the peak in 1989. The Nikkei Index reached less than 13 000 after trading at 40 000 at the end of the 1980s. So falling interest rates are no guarantee.

In early 1999 the newspaper contained many experts commenting that the U.S. bull market must continue to move higher since the Federal Reserve would probably lower interest rates to fight off a global depression. In January 1999, the *Financial Post* reported one mutual fund manager saying: "the good news is the disinflationary environment is increasing the possibility of further reductions in North American interest rates that will mean that the North American equity market is unlikely to experience any protracted bear phase." To understand how ridiculous these opinions are, you need only to look at Japan, the second largest economy in the world.

A Unique Example: Japan's Bear Market 1989–98

The curious reader might wonder what happened to the mutual fund industry in Japan during that nine-year bear market. According to the *Nikeii Weekly*, November 28, 1999, in late 1998 Japanese savers held financial assets of approximately 1230 trillion yen or U.S.$10 trillion. Of that total, 60% was held in savings accounts. Savings accounts paid interest rates of 0.10% to 0.15% annually. No, that is not a misprint or a misplaced decimal. Japanese savers are more than a little gun-shy. They would rather take 10 years to earn 1% interest than risk their money in funds or stocks.

Investment trusts (mutual funds) accounted for a very small portion of that $10 trillion total in savings. Japanese investors were net sellers of investment trusts every year since 1990. In 1998, stock market investment trusts held just 11.71 trillion yen or about U.S.$100 billion, about a quarter of the total amount invested in investment trusts and just 1% of the total household financial assets. In 1989 the total in stock market investment trusts was four times higher. The stock market investment trust participation in Japan suffered a 75% decline in nine years.

The Japanese public is not involved in the stock market outside of investment trusts either. Individual stock trading activity on the Japanese stock exchanges measured 10.4%, a record low, at the end of 1998, down from 25% in 1991. At the end of an unusually long bear market, investors were not attracted to the stock market.

You can see that a market timing formula that simplistically compared stock market valuations to the level of interest rates to determine the correct allocation of stocks versus bonds would fail miserably if the Japanese attitude spread to North America. Yet even the Federal Reserve Bank in the U.S. uses a valuation model that compares interest rates to the earnings return on common stocks.

Why Mathematical Formulae Don't Work

The mathematical formula that worked for the 1974–81 market, where interest rates rose with the markets, would not have predicted the 1981–98 result properly. A formula based on the two periods taken together, if it could be found, may forecast the next decade or it may not.

Exogenous Factors

These market timing formulas cannot work over lengthy periods because relationships between the key variables shift unpredictably at times. These shifts are the result of exogenous factors. Computers cannot allow for exogenous variables. Exogenous, from the Greek root exo, means coming from the outside. Every formula must assume some exogenous variables to be fixed. These are the variables that are shown to have cause and effect relationships to each other, other factors remaining the same. Once one of the variables that were assumed to remain constant shifts, the old relationships between the remaining variables are invalid and useless for forecasting purposes.

For example, the outbreak of a world war would cause a shift of some exogenous factors. All the formulas that previously could predict the market based on a relationship between certain variables such as interest rates, earnings, dividends, and expectations among investors would become invalid. Computers would have to be reprogrammed to predict new relationships between these variables.

In another example, an exogenous variable that might be assumed constant is that investors have stable investment alternatives in Japan—

that interest rates in Japan remain the same. What happens then if the U.S. market continues as before but Japanese interest rates are at 1% for some period of time? What if a whole flood of Japanese money were to arrive in the United States because the interest rates in Japan had gone to 1% and rates in the United States were much higher? The U.S. bond market would explode upwards due to the influx of Japanese investors looking for higher interest rates. The computer could not allow for this possibility since the level of interest rates in Japan is an exogenous factor, assumed to be constant. This scenario actually played out in the 1990s, with over $400 billion in U.S. government bonds held by Japanese investors. What happens to the U.S. bond market if interest rates rise in Japan, as they have been for several months in 1999, and the Japanese decide to pull money out of the United States and back into their own stock and bond markets?

MARKET TIMING ADVICE

Investors who purchase market timing advice and asset allocation services are wasting their money. That money applied to the investments of their choice will yield a better return than money paid to a newsletter or mutual fund pushing a market timing formula.

The largest amount of damage done to investment programs is a result of individuals trying, either consciously or unconsciously, to time the market themselves. Most investors are closet market timers without realizing it. I often ask new clients what they expect from me when the next bear market hits. A disturbingly large percentage expect me to phone them before the bear market arrives so they can sell. In other words they expect me to be their market timing guru.

WHICH ADVISOR DO YOU BELIEVE?

The basic problem with expert opinions remains the impossibility of knowing which expert to follow. At any juncture in the stock market there are some experts on one side and many others opposing. Each transaction in the bond or stock market is a mixture of two conflicting views on the market as the seller and buyer obviously disagree. Many of these sellers and buyers are professionals such as money managers and mutual fund managers. One expert money manager is selling while the other is buying. Which one is right?

You, as an individual investor, must learn to listen for information but make your own decisions. Even better than trying to decide who is right is to find a method that allows you to ignore the various opinions and market trends completely. In chapter 8 I describe such a method.

A proliferation of newsletter advisory services gives forecasts of the likelihood of the market rising or falling. *Barron's* summarizes the various expert predictions available through these news services. Invariably the quotes contain a mixture of positive, negative, and neutral forecasts for the stock and bond markets. Each service presumably has some track record of success in guessing the direction of markets, but on any particular week it is impossible to know which of the differing opinions are correct and therefore valuable. In fact many contrarians use these expert predictors as a contrary indicator. If the percentage of bullish opinions rises, they argue, the market is due for a fall. If the advisors become universally bearish, history shows that the market usually rises soon after. Ironically, this reverse indicator based on expert opinion is one of the more popular contrarian market timing indicators.

WHY MARKET TIMING FAILS

The nervous investor becomes manic-depressive in his attitude toward the market. The market validates or crushes his feeling of worth on a daily basis. Periods of elation and depression alternate as the cycles go around.

Studies show that the typical investor engages in market timing and fails miserably. *The Global Strategy Investment Funds* newsletter (Fall, 1998) published a study by the U.S. research firm DALBAR, called the Quantitative Analysis of Investor Behavior (QAIB) Study. DALBAR examined data for the period 1984 to 1997, a very good period for U.S. stocks.

The report concluded that "investors are not holding their investments any longer than they did 13 years ago, and investors continue to act contrary to [their] own interests by chasing hot sectors, and dumping losing investments at the wrong time. When investors do not earn the returns that are published by mutual fund companies, they tend to blame the funds, instead of looking to their own behaviour and how it directly affects their real returns. Investors jump on the bandwagon too late, and switch in and out of funds trying to time the market."

The findings of the study are sobering. While the stock market returned an average 17% per year over the period, the average investor gained only 7%.

When this return of 7% is compared to the risk-free return on U.S. government bonds, the true nature of this disaster for individual investors becomes clear. U.S. government bonds returned an annual compound rate of 13.4% from 1982 to 1997. So the risk-free return was over 13%, the stock market return was over 17% and investors actually received 7%, because they tried, unsuccessfully, to time the market.

How could these investors manage to do so poorly in such a good stock and bond market? The answer lies in the psychology that determines decision-making under stress. Deep psychological forces affect human behaviour when it comes to an emotional activity such as managing money. Experts agree that two of the strongest emotions are fear and greed. At the top of the market the investor feels greed, upset that he is missing out.

Greed at the Top

The following fictional scene represents a typical conversation with a client at a point in the cycle close to the top of the market.

NEAR THE TOP OF THE MARKET

John sounded quite excited. "How's the market doing today?"

"The market is up a bunch today, John. Lots of foreign buying and new money from mutual funds showing up."

"Look's like things are going to stay hot for a while, don't you think?"

"I don't know John, it could go on forever or it could end tomorrow, who knows?"

"Everything I read in the newspapers and everyone I talk to tells me the market is going a lot higher. I want to get more involved. I was thinking about cashing in some bonds and getting more money into stocks."

"You are in the stock market. You've got 40% of your retirement plan into the stock market, already."

"I know that but I feel like I'm missing out on a lot of opportunities. I keep hearing about stocks that are doubling and tripling."

I could feel myself getting defensive. While John had done reasonably well in the market he had been very nervous a few years ago at the start of this wonderful bull market. At each mild correction that came along he complained loudly, going over each stock that declined as if it were a personal affront, a plot hatched by me to scuttle his dream of getting rich. In the last downturn he had pressured me to change the portfolio to the most conservative stocks available. Now these weren't going up fast enough for him and he was making me feel as if I had let him down.

"Those stocks that are doubling are usually the riskier stocks. They move most quickly just at the end of the bull market, trapping a lot of people. You've stayed with the more conservative stocks since the last downturn when you decided to adopt a low-risk strategy."

"Yes, I know, but you've been telling me to stay with a low-risk strategy for over a year and the market keeps going higher. My portfolio is just coasting along. I want to take a more aggressive stance."

"What happened to your concern about the next market crash?"

"Well, I talked things over with my wife. The only way we'll have enough for a comfortable retirement is to make our investments grow faster. We think we can put more money into the stock market now and take advantage of the opportunities in the bull market. We're not blaming you, it's just that we realize now that the market is not as risky as we thought. We've got more experience now."

"John, you have experience in a bull market. Real experience comes in a bear market. Whatever commitment you make now you need to stay with through the next bear market. Forty-percent exposure through a bear market is more than most will be able to handle. Do you really think you can live with more risk?"

"You keep trying to scare me with the next bear market. And it never comes. I keep losing money by being too cautious."

"Well, John, it's your money. You and your wife are the ones who have to live with whatever you decide to do."

While this is a fictional account, the conversation could happen between many stockbrokers and their clients during a strong bull market. Greed will lead that investor to be fully invested near the top of the bull market. That same investor would likely sell out late in the next bear market, after prices had fallen an average of 20% to 40%.

Family Pressures

Greed is only one factor of many that can affect decision-making. A spouse who lacks involvement in the investment process will influence your ability to resist the tendency to try and time the market. In a down market the spouse often becomes nervous and wants to sell out. In an up market the spouse may be happy and say nothing. An investment program that wins the confidence of a spouse only in rising markets is dangerous. Obviously when the market turns down and continues down for a time spousal pressure to sell out increases. This pressure reaches a peak often at market bottoms.

The uncommitted and uninvolved spouse presents a major risk to long term success. Lack of involvement leads to lack of confidence. A lack of confidence engenders fear in a bear market. Fear becomes panic and a sell-out of the portfolio inevitably follows.

An investment program can be threatened by a spouse who sits back, with arms crossed, waiting for proof that the stock market is "too risky" and the opportunity to say "I told you so." The sceptical spouse is bound to assert himself or herself just at the time when selling out would be a permanent loss for the portfolio.

Factors that play on the emotions exacerbate this tendency to extreme mood swings with investors. One such factor is the length of time until the money invested in the stock market is needed for some other purpose.

This Money is Saved for Our Children's Education!

If the family has an identified need for money in the near future, such as retirement income or a new house, there is little chance the portfolio can survive the next downturn. One spouse or the other will point out that the money being lost on the stock market would be better spent on the other family priority. Usually this discussion takes place toward the end of the downturn in the market, at a low point in the market cycle. So the stocks are sold to avoid any further loss. One use for money that causes particularly strong emotions is the fund for university education for children. Any downturn in the stock market will cause emotional pain and feelings of guilt if the money is earmarked for children.

This common experience frequently forms the basis for the belief that the stock market is a place where it is difficult or impossible to make money. Periods of involvement when the market "looks good" follow long periods of disinterest. The pendulum swings and the investors come and go. An examination of mutual fund money inflows and outflows leads to the conclusion that the large flows come into the stock market near the top and leave near the bottom.

Mutual fund advisors quote the QAIB survey to convince investors of the need to invest for the long term. This lecture on the requirement of going against human nature will not be enough for many of these investors to make it through the next bull and bear markets. The more sensible way to look at the QAIB survey is to recognize that we need as much help as we can get as well as a rock-solid plan to avoid the market timing trap.

Fear at the Bottom

Turning points near the bottom of the market decline are invariably accompanied by a climate of negative news. Most psychologists agree that fear is the strongest of our basic emotions. Humans are programmed to respond to fear immediately, without delay or thought. When there is a life or death situation that demands our attention, reacting quickly to fear makes sense. In the stock market, responding to fear usually means selling good-quality investments at ridiculously low prices.

NEAR THE BOTTOM OF THE MARKET

Thoughts about the meeting scheduled to start in a few minutes nagged at me. I had been awake several hours in the middle of the night, worrying about this meeting. A husband and wife were coming to see me, and they were unhappy.

The receptionist announced their arrival. I went out to greet them, hoping to improve the tone of what would come. I took it as a bad sign when they declined the offer of coffee or tea. They looked grim and businesslike.

"We want to talk to you about our portfolio. We are concerned about the drop in value over the last six months." The husband, Sean, an engineer, had opened the conversation. No small talk this time. Our relationship had become distant and strained, as the market and their portfolio moved lower and lower.

His wife hadn't been involved much before. I knew she was less excited about the stock market and had been happy before with guaranteed invest-ments when the rates were higher. Sean usually made the decisions, and I talked to him when changes were made. It seemed ominous that she had come to the meeting.

"I know that you and Sharon have been unhappy with the performance of your portfolio for some time now. It may be little comfort, but your portfolio has actually outperformed the TSE 300 by a small margin. The TSE is down about 24% and your portfolio is down 20%, or a little less. It looks like the bear mar-ket started about 11 months ago, last May. The average bear lasts about 9 months, and declines about 30%, so this one is longer and milder than aver-age, so far. It's more of a slow, drawn out affair, which is very hard on the emo-tions, I know."

Sharon spoke up; "Our accounts are worth less than they were two years ago. We can't afford to lose this money, we need it for retirement."

"I take a long term view of the markets. If you can hang in there, the mar-ket will eventually recover what it has lost and move higher. This has happened in every market cycle in the last 200 years. Sometimes it takes a lot of patience to make it through the bear markets."

"You said the same thing two months ago, and the market is down another 15%. We could have saved a lot of money by selling then and waiting to buy back in at lower levels."

"Well, you can do that if you want, but I don't recommend it. I know from experience in three previous bear markets that those who sell out never get back in near the bottom. They wait until the market recovers before jumping back in. So they miss that initial surge that lifts the market after a bottom, giv-ing the best performance of the next cycle. Everybody misses out except the few who stay in."

Sean continued his argument, with Sharon nodding agreement. "I know we said we were going to hold on for the long term when we got started with you. Now we are four years older, and the recession is bad. I may be forced out of my job into early retirement. Sharon's part-time job at the hospital isn't paying that well, since she gets fewer hours with the cutbacks. There are a lot of nurses com-ing back to work because they need the work. There's talk of another wage cut."

Sharon jumped in. "I'm really worried. I'm losing some sleep wondering about how things will work out. I just feel that if we could stop the losses in the retirement funds I would feel a lot better about our future."

I realized that they were close to pulling out. If they sold out now they wouldn't be back for a long time, if ever. This was the fourth or fifth time they had told me they were worried, so I knew they wanted to make a decision. I couldn't decide for them, but I really hated to see them give up.

"I can't tell you what to do. I know you've lost confidence in the stock market. It's just part of the market, it's not the whole story. Nobody has ever made money in the stock market over longer periods of time without going through some pain in a bear market. It wouldn't be real if there wasn't some pain to go along with the joy, would it?"

"We're not blaming you. You warned us about this happening. We didn't know that it would feel this bad. We are thinking that maybe we are just not cut out for the stock market."

"I think you have a better chance to make it through this than most other investors. At least you are talking to me about how you feel and not burying your head in the sand. You're not blaming everybody else for your losses, as some would. I wish I could guarantee you that it would turn around soon, but I can't. All we know for sure is that the bear market will end sometime, usually after most of the other investors give up. I hope that you decide to be among the few that stay with it for the next up market."

One problem with that meeting was the fact that I was being viewed as wrong about the market. By the time such meetings occur, usually investors and stockbrokers have talked two or three times on the telephone. During each phone call the investors demand reassurance that they are doing the right thing by staying with a declining market. Each time the broker reassures them, and they hold on and experience more pain. The broker loses credibility each time the market fails to recover. Usually by the time they sell out they are not asking for advice any more. Their minds are made up.

Looking back on interviews with clients near the bottom I remember the desperation of the people in that situation. They were in a lot of pain. The temptation to tell those clients to get out and "wait for the market to settle down" is strong. At the very least I wouldn't have to listen to them complaining about the bear market any more. But I know that most investors that give up at that point don't come back until the market recovers, and they usually change stockbrokers as well.

Every few years a time arrives when the stock market loses a large portion of the active investors. These investors leave because of a lack of determination or belief in the investing process. It's as if a giant comes along and shakes the investing tree. Those investors hanging on tightly remain while the rest fall to the ground, bruised and dejected. Your goal must be to find a way to hang on through all the cycles. It's essential to your long-term success.

These two fictional but representative examples of the emotions near the top and the bottom of a market cycle describe clearly how those investors in the QAIB study managed to make just 7% when 17% was made by the market. This is the norm, not the exception. As an individual investor you must find a way to avoid the buy high, sell low trap of trying to time the market. In chapter 8 I show exactly how the emotions can be removed from market timing decisions.

PERSPECTIVE AND PATIENCE LEAD
TO GREATER CONVICTION

The difficult thing about being in Sean and Sharon's situation is their lack of perspective. The historical trends mean very little when people experience that degree of distress. Your ability to achieve some perspective on your investment program is important. Perspective gives us options beyond an emotional reaction to current events.

In an interview in the *Financial Times of Canada* (January 1994), the retired mutual fund manager Peter Lynch responded to the question: What is your outlook for the U.S. market?

> No one has ever been able to predict the market. It's a total waste of time. The important thing to know is the volatility in the market. There have been 93 years in this century. Fifty times the market has declined 10% or more. So about once every two years, the market falls 10%. Of those 50 declines, 15 have been 25% or more. So that's 15 in 93 years, or about once every six years. Now, the first one would be called a correction, and the second would be called a bear market. This (volatility) is part of the market, and you just have to deal with it. Or you shouldn't own stocks or equity funds.

As arguably the most successful mutual fund manager of all time, Peter Lynch gives extremely good advice in his admonition to resign ourselves to fluctuations and volatility. Since the markets, especially stock markets, rise more than they fall over longer periods the good news is that we cannot be hurt by these fluctuations. You can only be damaged if you put yourself in the position of deciding to sell when the market is weak, or having to sell when the market is low.

You must also avoid putting yourself in a partnership with other investors who will get invested near the top and sell out when the market is low. As discussed in chapter 1, if you wish to achieve independence as an investor you must avoid mutual funds.

Another famous investor, successful beyond all others, confirms Lynch's statements. Warren Buffett, the richest man in North America before Bill Gates came along, made his money primarily by stock market investing. Buffett concentrates on owning individual stocks. He is quoted in the *Toronto Star* on July 17, 1993 as saying: "When we own businesses with outstanding managers our favourite holding period is forever."

Patience comes from conviction. And conviction grows with understanding and control. An investor who is undecided and unsure will almost certainly sell out at a loss, at the worst possible time. It is important to develop conviction in your investment program.

The rule is: If you are ever in the stock market, always be in the stock market.

You must make a decision to be a stock market investor. Not a market timer, not a speculator, but an investor. An investor is a person who holds stocks through the bull and bear markets. After all, someone has to own those good quality, blue chip companies when the mutual funds are dumping them.

This decision means that you forget about trying to do the impossible. By accepting this premise you have simplified your task enormously.

I propose that you make a decision to maintain a position in the stock market at all times.

Once made, this decision is not questioned or revisited. You decide to become an investor in the stock market for your lifetime. Your estate will contain a nice, sizeable portfolio of stocks and bonds for your heirs to fight over. Perhaps because of your example they too will decide to become investors in the stock market.

This may seem radical to you. Maintaining a position in all market cycles means that you will have to hold stocks through some terrible times. Others will be saying: Why not get out and wait for a better market? The answer is simply that enduring the pain of staying in stocks during a bear market is easier than trying to time the market cycles by getting in and out.

I am not advocating that you put all of your investment capital in stocks. No investor I have met in over 20 years has the temperament, experience, and patience to endure a bear market fully invested in stocks. I suggest only that you place a portion in common stocks with the goal of maintaining that percentage for the foreseeable future. In chapter 8, I discuss how to work this balanced approach to stock market investing.

Think of the freedom that comes from this decision. No sleepless nights wondering if the market has gone too high. No panicked calls to the stockbroker looking for reassurance when some political news looks bad.

Even the best stock market experts only try to pick stocks, not time the market. These individuals possess an ability to separate the wheat from the chaff, the better companies from the poorer ones. Like Peter Lynch though, they do not make the mistake of trying to time the market as well as pick stocks.

My suggestion to you is that you forget about trying to do the impossible. Let go of the belief that you can get in and out of markets at the "right time." Decide that if you are ever going to be in the stock market you will always be in. This decision is one of the most liberating you can make. The energy released can be used to pick companies for investment, work in the garden, ski, sail, travel, golf, or read books.

In the next chapter I will describe a method that allows you to be in the stock market all the time, without taking too much risk or losing sleep at night.

Eight

Keeping Your Balance

Market timing is an investment trap you must avoid to achieve success and investing independence. A method that ensures you can escape the negative consequences of the market timing trap is available to every investor. This approach, which I call balance and re-balance investing, is also known as policy asset allocation. The first step in this method is finding the level of exposure to common stocks that is right for you.

CHOOSING THE BALANCE
THAT IS RIGHT FOR YOU

The probability that an investor will cancel an investment program increases directly with the range of fluctuation in the value of the portfolio. The greater the fluctuations, especially on the downside, the more likely the investor is to give up, usually at a low point in the value. Once the investor does this, the loss is made permanent and the damage is done.

Your chosen degree of involvement in the stock market is the most important factor that determines the volatility of your investment portfolio. So the higher the level of equities in your portfolio, the greater the fluctuations in value, the larger the potential reward and the more likely it is that you will give up during a bear market, springing the buy high, sell low trap.

Most investors start a new investment program unaware of this risk. New portfolios are often put in place during a bull market, after several years of good markets. At such an exciting and optimistic time why would a new investor or investment salesperson want to emphasize the risk of selling a portfolio at a loss when the market is down? Naturally, the discussion at the beginning of an investment program centres on the potential upside, and on which investments offer the best return.

A lack of appreciation for the downside leads to unrealistic expectations. Investors expect a steadily rising portfolio, without major breaks. This attitude makes the inevitable downward fluctuations harder to accept.

Frequently this frame of mind leads investors to choose a level of participation in equities (common stocks) that is beyond their ability to sustain throughout the bull and bear markets in their investing future. Their focus is on how much they can make, not how much they might lose. And investors are correct in their assessment that equities are the place to be to make the most money; they just underestimate their ability to sustain stock market exposure over long periods.

Impatience and Fear Are the Greatest Risks

Failure in stock market investing most often occurs when the individual lacks the tenacity to stick around long enough to get these returns. The market does not fail the investor. It is usually the investor who fails the investment program. The risk is that the investor will pull the pin before the market works its magic. Based on my observation of hundreds of investors over several cycles, I believe that impatience and fear are the major risks facing investors. The impatience lurking in all of us defeats many potentially successful investment plans.

The risk of stock market fluctuations poses a relatively minor problem for the individual investor. His or her own temperament and emotional nature present the biggest risk. Can an investor stay calm enough in a crisis to follow a planned course of action? Can an investor resist the temptations of greed when the silly season arrives and most people are throwing caution to the wind? And most important, can an investor overcome the fear that urges him to get out of the market, even when prices are the lowest?

Since few can overcome their human nature, even with the strongest of wills, the investment program chosen must provide a remedy for this tendency toward impulsive actions.

The questions to be answered are: What is the risk level that the investor can sustain through all markets? At what level of risk does an investor start to worry to the point of not being able to sleep? At what level of caution do investors get frustrated with being left behind in a roaring bull market? In answering these questions investors set their level of comfort with exposure to risk and the stock market. The level of stock market involvement must be carefully chosen to reflect the personality of the investor. Your advisor cannot know the proper level of risk for you, at the initial meetings. For an investment professional to make such a judgement takes experience with a particular investor under stressful market conditions. As an inexperienced investor, an individual cannot know his proper level of risk either. Until the investor keeps money in the market for one or two up and down cycles he cannot know for certain his threshold of tolerance for fluctuations. The good news is that you do not have to know in advance your optimum level of risk to get started.

All you need to do is choose an initial level that approximates the highest level that can maintained through all market cycles.

Despite the irrefutable evidence assembled by Siegel and others that common stocks provide a vastly superior return, there will be times in your investing career when you wish you had never heard of the stock market. Market declines of 50% in the period from 1969 to 1974 or 80% from 1929 to 1932 were impossible for the majority of investors to handle.

Your actions during similar periods of stock market declines as well as during runaway bull markets will determine your success. Most people experience great pressures during major market declines or speculative booms. Some investor also find it impossible to deal with long periods of boring, static markets when nothing happens.

Almost anyone can make money in the stock market when a major bull market is in full stride. The differences among investors show up in the difficult periods between bull markets. The good news is that these periods are shorter.

The Importance of Temperament

The current direction of the market is not the important factor for determining your optimum level of equities. The overriding factor is your temperament. Other important factors are experience in investing, length of time until the funds are needed, and your spouse's attitude toward investing.

The temperament of the investor can determine success or failure in the investment game. Some investors panic when the market has been falling for some time and they take their losses and get out. This is the most common method of losing money. The market declines, the investor cannot stand the pressure of losing money and sells out the portfolio. The investor then sits on the sidelines, waiting for the market to go lower. During the period when this investor is out of the market his friends and family listen to a lengthy list of reasons why the market is going much lower. All investors who are out of the market adopt a negative attitude toward stocks. They hold this view to justify their decision to sell out.

Many investors active during the 1990s have not yet tested their panic level. The 1987 decline did not last long enough for many people to get spooked to the point where they phoned up their broker and said "Get me out, I can't stand it any more." This kind of desperation usually comes after a prolonged decline. Similar declines in 1990 and 1994 tested investors only slightly. The major stock market wobble of the fall of 1998 caught the attention of many. One could feel a collective holding of breath, especially when Asia, Latin America, and Russia all seemed to collapse at once. The subsequent recovery came quickly enough to reinforce the notion that such difficult periods are short in duration.

A serious bear market declines by an average 30%, which was experienced briefly in Canada in 1998. The United States experienced a milder 19.9% drop, measured by the S&P 500. Other broader indexes such as the Russell 2000 fell more sharply. During such a drop, the investor feels fear, wishing he had kept his money in Treasury bills. The pain of losing money becomes overwhelming. Nothing can be more difficult to cope with. A point is reached after a serious decline in the value of the equity portfolio that is the most dangerous for long term performance. I call this the moment of maximum despair.

An exit at this point is usually terminal for the investment career of that individual. The sold-out investor seldom re-enters the market before the market has made a long recovery. That investor usually will only try the market again at much more comfortable levels. Investors reach their comfort zone only after the market has risen for a sufficient period of time that it feels "safe" again. This type of investor cannot help but lose money. Unfortunately, this is a common experience.

YOUR EXPOSURE IS YOUR DECISION

You must find a way to avoid becoming captive to your emotions and feelings about the stock market. The only way I know to overcome the problem of temperament and emotion is the use of a technique that helps you do the right thing at the right time. Such an external discipline comes with the policy asset allocation method, or balance and re-balance. You commit a portion of your portfolio to the common stock market, described as a percentage of your total portfolio value, and try to keep this level roughly constant throughout your investing career. Of course, when life circumstances change as in retirement, an adjustment is made to allow for income needs. Adjustments in your commitment level can be made at other times, if you discover you made an error in your initial level.

By setting this exposure to the stock market you find a balance for you and the market. You balance your desire for a higher return with a healthy respect for the volatility of the market and your powerful emotions of fear and greed. Where you set the level of exposure is your decision. As the investor you are the one who will have to live with the consequences. For this method to work well, you, not anyone else, must make the decision about your percentage exposure to the stock market.

New Investors

If you are just starting out in investing or have little experience with bear markets, considering setting the exposure level to stocks at a low percentage of funds available for investment. A low level of exposure for most people would be 10% to 35%. A word of warning: once the level is set do not increase it in a rising market. Your greed will talk to you incessantly about missing out but you must resist. You will only compound your difficulties in the ensuing bear market if your equity level is raised late in a bull market.

The Effect of the Market Cycle

You might be starting out in a bull market that has risen for some time. As this is written in 1999, the stock market rise extends back to 1990

with few major breaks. The serious bear market in 1982 was more difficult and prolonged than the breaks of 1987, 1990, 1994, and 1998. The
1982 bear market included an experience with interest rates at 20%. Not
one investor could think of a reason to invest in common stocks when
Treasury bills were paying 18%. The irony is that common stocks were
seldom a better buy! When interest rates were above 15% it was the best
time in two decades to purchase stocks. Returns on stocks in the U.S.
market from that time far exceeded what was earned on bonds or Treasury bills. At the time, though, investors who were willing to invest in
common stocks were few and far between.

Setting Your Exposure During a Bull Market

Human nature dictates that you are more likely to be reading this book
when markets are comfortable. Investment books are more popular in
bull markets. You are more likely to be starting out in stock market
investing for the first time after a sustained rise in the markets. During the
1982 and 1988 bear markets, I had very few new clients interested in the
stock market. The few that started then have done very well. So if you are
considering getting involved for the first time in investing, take a look
around you. Has the market had a long, sustained rise without a major
break? Are investment books very popular? Does your local newspaper
run a separate business section with columnists writing about the latest
fad in investing? If so, recognize that you are perhaps in a later stage of a
bull market and consider setting your initial exposure at a restrained
level, one you can live with if a sharp break in the market occurs .

> **Set your equity exposure at the highest level that you think you can
> maintain in all markets.**

The good news is that the level you choose initially is not the critical
factor in your success. What is important, however, is that you choose a
level and stick to it throughout the cycle.

When you pick a percentage exposure to the stock market, ideally you
commit to maintain that level through all markets. You renounce the
game of continually reviewing, reneging, or recommitting to your participation, twisting continually to and fro on advice of friends, brokers, the
newspaper experts, economists, and investment gurus.

THE UNDEREXPOSURE TRAP

Investors are tempted to increase their stock market exposure during a bull market, continuing to throw money into the pot until a crash occurs.

A common mistake is starting with a percentage that is low in a new bull market. Investors are naturally too cautious at the end of a bear market but as the market action heats up the investor wants to get more involved. Usually after much delay and procrastination, the investor with too low an exposure moves further into the stock market.

As the bull market hits full stride it is normal for more speculative stocks to double or quadruple in a few months. This is the most risky period in the bull market cycle. The irony is that it feels safe and exciting to the investor. By now the market has been rising for a few years and everyone involved in the market has experienced some success. The investor who started with too low a percentage comes under immense pressure to increase that exposure. This is just the wrong time to be adding fuel to the fire. The cautious investor finds it hard to resist the desire to get more involved. He continuously calculates profits that might have been if only more money had been committed to the market earlier.

For this reason I advise all clients who are beginning during the bull phase to pick a level that is high enough to satisfy their greed factor. Then I suggest that they hold that percentage exposure level steady throughout the bull market until the next bear market comes. Many investors find this rule confining during a bull market. What if a genuine mistake is made with the initial level of stock market exposure?

The remedy is to find the patience to wait until the next bear market arrives. A bear market signals its arrival by a downturn in the market of 20% from the previous peak or in a twelve-month interval. In other words, the next time the stock market is 20% lower than its level one year ago, or the market index is 20% below a major top, the green light switches on to increase your stock market exposure. Since bear markets arrive on average every six years this rule of thumb dictates a possible multi-year delay in putting more funds into the market. This restraint avoids the likelihood of throwing more money into the pot just before a crash.

Never increase your percentage exposure to common stocks above the target level during a bull market. Wait for a 20% decline in the stock market before increasing your policy target percentage.

You can see how the selection of a very low percentage level at the beginning of a major multi-year bull market could severely test your patience. So pick a percentage that is high enough to give you a genuine chance to benefit from a bull market.

THE OVEREXPOSURE TRAP

An investor picks too high a percentage exposure before having his or her risk tolerance tested by a bear market. The investor eventually succumbs to fear and sells during the bear market.

The other common problem occurs when an investor picks too high a percentage exposure. This overexposed state usually happens in the late stages of a bull market—the most dangerous time. By then the fear of stock market investing leaves the investor, novice and experienced alike. Without the fear to hold her back, the first-time investor, or even the experienced investor, makes the mistake of substantially increasing her exposure to equity markets. She picks a percentage level of 60%, 70%, or even 100% of funds available for investing. While these levels may not be too high for some, the majority get very uncomfortable at such elevated exposures.

The investor with too large a commitment becomes very nervous as the bull market rolls over. Constant thoughts about the safety of Treasury bills invade the thoughts of this formerly daring investor. The pressure of a bear market decline of 30% or more is too great and the investor sells out either part or all of her position. She moves into the camp of those crying "the sky is falling" for the next few months or years as the market "gets back to normal." A very common phrase heard at this time is "I'll just sit on the sidelines until the market settles down." If you have ever uttered these words, you probably know what the pressure of a bear market feels like.

Investors must avoid the trap of selling some or all of their equities in a bear market. To avoid this trap I suggest another rule of thumb:

Never lower your target percentage of equity exposure until the stock market is up 30% from a recent low or over a twelve month period.

This guideline makes the panic sale unlikely. At least the sale of equities will not be completed during a major bottom. Most investors who follow this rule find that by the time the 30% rise is complete, the urge to get out has passed.

Setting Your Exposure During a Bear Market

I examined the past bear market periods and calculated what would happen to investors with their investment funds at different exposure levels. I found that the reality of stock market volatility is acceptable with a reasonably low degree of involvement in stocks. At a 30% level of stocks and 70% in bonds most investors I know would be able to handle the fluctuation in their portfolio, even through a major decline as was experienced from 1929 to 1932.

Zero Exposure Is Not Advantageous

The ultimate safety level is zero exposure to the stock market. This has two disadvantages even at a late stage in a bull market. First, the investor would miss out on some part of the bull market. Since there is no way of knowing how high is high, a bull market that seems mature could go substantially higher, leaving the investor out entirely. More importantly, the investor would fail to experience the bear market and therefore have no learning opportunity.

A level of zero percent exposure to the common stock market provides little opportunity for testing your temperament in adversity. The bear market cycle would not test the ability to withstand pain. The uninvolved investor loses interest in the market, which ensures that good opportunities are missed as the market approaches a bottom. I never suggest zero involvement, even to the most nervous investor.

As my grandfather, who was a stockbroker in the late 1920s in Winnipeg, Manitoba told me: "You don't learn anything about the markets until you have your own money at risk."

A Revolving Door

By the end of a bull market almost all of those who set their equity exposure level at zero earlier in the cycle have been drawn into the markets. They move their exposure up as the market cycle develops, sometimes reaching very high levels of risk just before the bear market starts. One of the major accomplishments of every substantial bull market is to draw most of the investing public into the market, with most of their money.

I am reminded of a few clients who, selling their common stocks in the bear market of 1990, felt that savings bonds and Treasury bills were the only acceptable investments. Interest rates in 1990 reached 13% so their attitude was widespread among investors. For several years after 1990 the market rose and fell, as an inebriated man making his way home, with two steps forward and one back. During this period I had little contact with those who sold back in 1990. By 1995 the stock market index had gained more than a thousand points from its 1990 level. As 1996 arrived I started to get telephone calls from some of these same people, expressing an interest in getting involved in the stock market again. They had missed out on some very substantial gains in the stock market, but they could not stand watching from the sidelines anymore. As they got involved in the bull market after a six-year absence I wondered what their reaction would be when the next bear market arrived. Would they sell out after a 20% decline in the value of their portfolio? I remembered, perhaps better than they, how upset they were with the 1990 bear market. These people were caught in a classic buy high, sell low trap, making decisions on their stock market involvement based on their emotions and the recent performance trends of the market.

Most beginning investors can pick a level that allows some exposure to risk without going overboard. Percentages such as 20%, 25%, 30%, or even 40% equities can be managed through bear markets and bull markets by many people, even the most nervous and excitable

A Pension Helps

A pension plan can make a big difference in your planning. One of my clients receives a modest pension from her years working for the government. A pension represents a fixed income, which is very similar to the bond or fixed income section of an investment portfolio. A quick calculation shows that a pension of $2000 per month represents $400 000 of government bonds at 6% interest rates. The pension is usually guaranteed for the life of the recipient and if married, for their survivor, often at a reduced level. If you have a pension or are a member of a plan that guarantees you a pension consider this as part of your portfolio. I consider it as part of the fixed income portion, as the equivalent of government bonds. The psychological effect is considerable. I have noticed clients with pensions are more likely to have patience in a bear market. A steady source of income from a pension or annuity can be a great comfort.

This analysis only applies to defined benefit plans. Such a plan guarantees a fixed monthly income in retirement, regardless of market conditions. A major shift occurred during the 1990s as many pension plans changed from a defined benefit plan to defined contribution plan. The defined benefit model meant that the company took the risk of providing a fixed amount of pension for its employees. For many years this was the only model. The newer, defined contribution model means the company is committed only to contributing a fixed amount of money each year, usually matching an employee contribution. In the defined contribution model the company takes no risk with respect to results. The employee carries all the risk.

As this trend expands, more employees will be asked to choose their investment options, usually from among several mutual funds. Most employees will make their choice with little investment advice other than a brochure, opting for the type of mutual fund with the best recent returns. This model will induce a lot of people to get into equity mutual funds during a bull market, only to switch back to guaranteed investments during the bear market that follows.

Many employees fail to understand the potential risks of the shift from defined benefit to defined contribution plan. If you are one of the many who have been forced into a defined contribution plan, take extra care in the investment of those funds. You would be smart to try to get some professional advice about your choices, since the psychological impact of watching a pension plan lose assets seems greater for most investors. My suggestion is to keep those assets in a low-risk fixed income type investment and concentrate on the stock market with other funds.

INSTITUTIONAL INVESTORS STRUGGLE TOO

I have discussed the balance problem only as it affects individual investors so far. You might think that professionals managing large pools of money for major corporations are too expert to need these balance rules. Nothing could be further from the truth. Pension plans, mutual funds, hedge funds, and others all struggle with this challenge of keeping their balance in all markets. The following fictional account of an institutional version of the balance problem is based on my real-life experience.

KEEPING YOUR BALANCE

The chairman of the meeting asked for quiet. Gradually the hum of conversation among the seven people in the room dwindled, and the guest speaker started his presentation.

"As portfolio manager of your pension plan I am here to review the past year's performance of your investment portfolio, answer your questions, and make recommendations for the next 12 months.

The total portfolio increased in value by 15%, with the equity portion up 25% and bonds up 5%. Your instructions to allocate 50% to stocks and 50% to bonds were followed, with only minor deviations during the year. The common stocks held by the portfolio matched the performance of the TSE 300 benchmark index, after deducting fees.

More details on the portfolio are in the handout. We are currently emphasizing common stocks in sectors such as technology, oil and gas, and metals and minerals."

The portfolio manager continued with the usual explanations of interest rate fluctuations, economic conditions, forecasts for the stock markets and bond markets, and then he asked for questions. His audience, the investment committee for a large pension plan, listened carefully.

One committee member spoke up.

"I have a question about asset allocation. When we met last year this committee discussed the wisdom of increasing exposure to the stock market from 50% to 60%. Several of us felt that, since the stock market provides higher returns over the long run, we should increase the equity exposure of this pension plan. After all, the pension plan has a long-term horizon since pension liabilities are spread out over many years. Some people were concerned about a decline in the stock market and the committee decided not to make a move. As I watched the market climb higher during this past year, I got more and more frustrated. I think we are making a mistake not to have more money in the stock market."

The other committee members shifted a little in their chairs. Last year, this questioner had argued forcibly for more stocks, bragging about his successes in the stock market with his personal portfolio. The other members were a little afraid of him, as he had clout with senior board members who make the appointments to the pension committee. Those who had argued last year against increasing the amount in stocks remained silent now, embarrassed by their excessive caution last year, grateful that no names had been mentioned.

The portfolio manager replied, "That's a very important question. It's really the responsibility of your committee to make a policy decision on asset mix. As portfolio managers we operate within your instructions and guidelines." He knew this was a hot potato and didn't want to get caught in any crossfire.

The questioner pressed; "But don't you agree that stocks should do better than bonds? Your own forecast indicates that you believe that to be true."

The portfolio manager started to perspire a little. "We certainly agree that the outlook for equities is more favourable than bonds, for the next year and over the long run. If you think as a committee that this pension plan can handle the additional risk involved in more stocks then it makes sense to have more stocks."

Other board members jumped in with varying degrees of agreement to the idea of getting more stocks. No members spoke up to object this time. They had learned their lesson. It was clear that the consensus was building to a decision to increase stock market exposure to at least 60% if not 70%.

As a result of this meeting, the committee decided to increase stock market exposure to 70%, buying more stocks and selling bonds for the pension plan.

Six months later a bear market started. After a few quarters of serious losses in the pension portfolio, new investment committee members were appointed, replacing those who had fallen out of favour with the executive committee. The new committee decided that a 30% exposure to equities was more appropriate for a conservative pension plan. This decision meant that common stocks were sold in large quantities with the proceeds placed in government bonds. A few months after these trades were completed the bear market ended and the next bull market quietly fell into place.

The long-term performance of this pension plan was seriously impaired by these "buy high, sell low" decisions made by sensible people with good intentions.

Statistics show that company pension plans drift toward common stocks with their asset allocation as the bull market progresses. Since companies are liable to meet pension needs of retired employees if there is any shortfall in the assets of a pension plan, these assets are still managed in a conservative, risk-adverse manner. The equity levels reached by these pension portfolios are normally limited at the direction of companies that are on the hook if markets turn down. Once the bull market is several years old the average institutional portfolio carries about 50% to 55% in equities. New developments in pension administration may mean that caution is replaced by more aggressive investing. An interesting illustration of this fact appeared in the January 1999 State of the Union address by the beleaguered President, Bill Clinton, when he suggested that the U.S. Social Security system invest in the stock market with a portion of its funds. While the suggestion met with some derision it could easily become public policy in a high-profile example of how greed grips people at all levels.

A TEST OF THE BALANCE METHOD

With the balance method the potential for buying high and selling low disappears. An illustration from the history of markets will help to show how powerful this method is. To determine if this balance method works, let us look at a very stressful period of stock market investing, 1925 to 1933.

The data for this example came from Ibbotson and Associates, a Chicago research firm. In this graph an earlier version of the S&P 500 index is used to represent common stocks. The proxy for bonds is also from Ibbotson, which publishes a long-term U.S. government bond index assuming

A balanced portfolio compared to 100% stocks and 100% bonds.

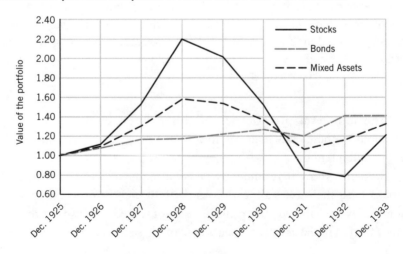

interest earned is reinvested. The third line follows the performance of a balanced portfolio with an asset mix of 40% stock and 60% bonds.

One striking fact from this graph shows up in the difference between the columns presenting 100% exposure to common stocks and the balanced portfolio with 40% exposure to stocks. Starting in 1925 at 1.00, the balanced portfolio never goes below 1.00. Its most severe one-year drop of 22% occurs from 1930 to 1931. The year prior, 1929 to 1930, the balanced portfolio declines by 11%. With this asset allocation, the Great Crash becomes a difficult but manageable two years that most investors could survive.

The 100% stock exposure portfolio plummets 24.9% one year and crashes the next year by 43.34%. Two years such as these would drive most if not all investors back to the safety of Treasury bills. Even a gain of more than 50% from 1932 to 1933 fails to bring the 100% stock portfolio back to a value equal to the balanced portfolio.

It appears clear that most investors with 100% exposure to common stocks would have given up on investing with two or three years of such devastating results. The more moderate volatility of the balanced portfolio gives a result that many investors could withstand.

This graph starts at 1925. Unfortunately, since most investors would have started investing later than 1925, only after several years of rising markets, they would have suffered more. If it is assumed that an investor started at the unlucky highest point on the index, December 1928, the balanced portfolio dropped by a maximum of 33% to the low point in December 1931. The 100% stock portfolio plunged a heart-stopping 61% over this same period. Some readers may be familiar with records that indicate the stock market was down 89% from the exact high to the exact low as measured by the Dow. The difference between this figure and the numbers from this chart is due to the use of the S&P 500, which is a broader index, and the choice of yearly observation points in December, rather than measuring from peak to trough.

The reality of a market decline of this magnitude is such that no technique would prevent most people from exiting the markets. The balanced approach still puts investors' portfolios lower in value four years after a peak. The fact that the decline pales in comparison beside the 100% stock portfolio may be of some comfort, but may not be enough to avoid a sell-out from fear. Still, these techniques give investors the chance to make it through even a 1929-type crash.

Mathematically astute observers will have noticed that while I said the balanced portfolio contained 40% exposure to equities, the actual level of equity participation varied as the fluctuations in the portfolio changed the balance. In fact, at one point in December 1928, the mixed asset portfolio metamorphosed to a 55% portfolio as stocks grew faster than bonds. This excess of stock market exposure over bonds continued the next year followed by three years of shrinkage, when stocks fell precipitously while bonds remained stable or grew. The bottom of stock market exposure in the balanced portfolio was reached in 1931 at 27% exposure to equities.

These fluctuations hurt the performance of the portfolio as the stock market participation reached a peak just before a huge decline and reached a bottom just before a violent rally. Could the portfolio have done better than this? Absolutely, with the help of the second part of the technique—re-balance.

IMPROVING PERFORMANCE WITH RE-BALANCE

Re-balancing means simply putting the portfolio back to the target asset allocation or equity exposure. Fluctuations in bond and stock markets often cause a discrepancy in the weighting of the portfolio. To correct these deviations from the target balance, assets must be shifted from stocks to bonds and vice-versa. Re-balancing can be monthly, quarterly, or annually. Studies show that the effect of re-balancing is very beneficial for lowering the volatility and risk of a portfolio.

In an article in the *Wall Street Journal*, published November 21, 1995, Jonathan Clements quotes extensively from a study done by T. Rowe Price Associates, a Baltimore mutual fund manager. An examination of a 25-year period from 1969 to 1995 showed that $10 000 invested in a 60% stock, 30% bond, and 10% Treasury bill portfolio grew to $145 000 re-balanced and $141 000 uncorrected. The uncorrected portfolio suffered greater losses during the 1973–1974 bear market, which caused the under-performance. The study concluded that re-balancing smoothed out the market swings and improved performance.

While the difference in the final amount of money was small, the re-balanced portfolio provided a much smoother ride. For example, in the 1987 crash, the uncorrected portfolio plunged 19.3%, while the re-balanced portfolio fell 15.7%

A Test of the Re-balancing Method

The re-balancing strategy works very well in normal markets with bull and bear phases. How did the re-balancing technique work in that king of all bears, 1929? We'll look at the same time frame as the previous graph to make our comparison.

A balanced portfolio (re-balanced vs. uncorrected) compared to 100% stocks and 100% bonds.

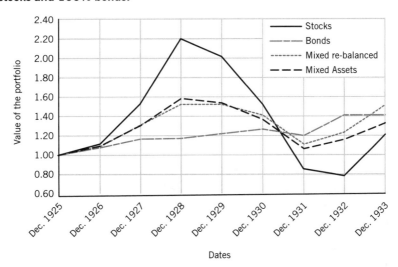

The re-balanced portfolio outperformed coming off the bear market bottom as investors forced themselves to add common stocks to their portfolio as the market declined. Re-balancing during the bottom year of 1932 when the uncorrected portfolio dropped to 33% equities meant adding substantial dollars into common stocks. This paid off handsomely as the re-balanced portfolio continued to outperform the 100% stock portfolio for 12 years after the bottom.

Obviously, 100% exposure to the stock market would be better than a balanced commitment, re-balanced or not. But for those who give up on their investment program during a bear market with an unsustainable 100% commitment to stocks, as most do, the balanced approach with re-balancing is infinitely superior.

So the tradeoff is clear. A portfolio with a balanced exposure, re-balanced periodically, gives you a good chance of surviving good and bad markets intact. You give up some of the upside of the stock market to improve your chances of surviving the bear market.

I continued this study to include the 1960s, 1970s, and 1980s and the results were the same. Re-balancing smoothed out the 1973–74 bear market especially. The 100% stock portfolio slid 14.66% and 26.47% in those two years back to back. The Dow Jones Industrial Average dropped more than 50% peak to trough. The re-balanced 40% portfolio declined 6.48% and 8.72% respectively, a very mild bear market experience.

Re-balancing works by forcing the investor to do the right thing at the right time, in spite of human emotions and temperament. By the bottom of a bear market, few investors consider adding to their stock market investments. The re-balancing investor does just that, without worrying about where the market is heading. As a bull market matures the investor following this program is trimming back on stocks, reinvesting profits from the stock market into bonds or Treasury bills. This money in bonds comes in handy for purchases of common stocks at inexpensive prices during a bear market.

You will recall chapter 1 when I described how the crowd pulls money out of the market as stock prices decline. This forces mutual fund managers to sell shares in excellent companies at fire-sale prices. As a re-balancing investor you would be buying just when the crowd is pushing the mutual funds to sell. Your source of funds would be the bond portion of your portfolio.

When to Re-balance

Re-balancing occurs usually once a year, unless there is a decline in the markets of more than 20% from peak to trough. In 1987 I asked my clients to sell some stocks in August and September as stock prices soared and bond prices plummeted. Interest rates on bonds reached 13% to 14% as the Federal Reserve tried to choke off the excessive speculation in the stock market. This affected bond prices negatively, which showed in portfolios as an imbalance in favour of stocks. I called my clients asking them to sell stocks and buy bonds. At that time I was looking more at the relative return on the stocks versus bonds as I was not fully committed to the balance and re-balance technique. When the market dropped 20% in one day in October I was caught up in the predictions of another 1929 scenario. A re-balancing move back into stocks after the October 1987 crash would have made all my clients and myself a lot of money. And with re-balancing it would have been done automatically.

Balancing and re-balancing guarantees that you do the right thing at the right time. You will buy low and sell high, without effort. You are not required to know anything about the future direction of the market or what stage exists in the market cycle. This mechanical approach takes all the guessing out of the market timing portion of the investment management equation. By removing the necessity to predict market cycles you can ignore the news about the economy, interest rates, and politics when thinking about how much to have invested in stocks. You need only look at your percentage.

While the technique is simple, it is not easy. Most investors would accuse their advisor of temporary insanity if he called to suggest an increase in equity exposure after a decline of 20% in the markets. All instincts call for the investor to run and hide from the pain of the market. With balance and re-balance doing the right thing when it feels all wrong is possible. Without balance and re-balance it seldom occurs, in my experience.

Re-balance your portfolio once a year and review your balance after a sharp rise or drop in the markets or after depositing additional funds.

Some investors imagine that the re-balance technique is a hidden strategy to increase brokerage commissions by justifying a lot of switching back and forth between bonds and stocks. This does not happen. Only extreme fluctuations in the market force a need for re-balance during the year. As a matter of practical experience I find that most investment portfolios need re-balancing just once a year. In addition to an annual review, the balance is reviewed every time a change is made in the portfolio, or after a sharp rise or drop in the markets. Investors depositing additional funds to their portfolios periodically readjust the balance by skewing the use of those funds toward the side of the portfolio that needs a boost. When a stock is sold in a rising market, some of the profits are directed toward bonds, re-balancing the portfolio.

The Psychological Benefits

Re-balancing helps investors in another way during difficult markets. Sailors have known for a long time that when the wind is blowing hard, keeping people busy works to maintain calm. The last thing a sailboat needs is a person in the grip of uncontrollable panic while a storm is raging. Experienced sailors have shared with me that they will give such a person a job, even a fabricated one, just to keep them busy. They might hold a line (known as a rope on shore) with instructions to pull whenever the boat rolls to port (left). Even though the line may not be attached to anything other than the rail of the boat, the calming effect on that person is substantial. A busy person on a sailboat does not have time to think too much about how bad things are and what might happen. Re-balancing acts the same way during a bear market, helping to avoid panic. Re-balancing also gives an investor the feeling of being in control, which is extremely important to most of us.

Balance and re-balance guarantees a buy low, sell high attitude to the stock market. You have the perfect tool to escape the trap of market timing.

With this information, you have enough knowledge to enjoy success in investing well beyond the average investor. By following these suggestions you put yourself ahead of more than 90% of investors.

You now have the tools to keep your independence from the mutual fund crowd, to maintain a balanced portfolio of bonds and stocks, to use your advantages as an individual investor and to choose a coach as your advisor. The last step to investing success is the selection of individual stocks and the maintenance of your portfolio.

Part 5

*Portfolio Management
for the Independent Investor*

Nine

Selling the Winners and Keeping the Losers

Investors, speculators, and stock market traders find that selecting individual companies, deciding when to keep them, and deciding when to sell them can be the biggest challenge of all. While this process can be difficult at times, stock market decisions do not need to be complicated. Most investors feel that the stock selection process is beyond their abilities and choose to give up their independence instead. As a result, managed product salespeople discover receptive investors at every turn. Investors turn themselves into consumers of investment products hoping to avoid the pain of stock market investing, usually after some bad experiences with individual stocks. These unfortunate mishaps result from the investor falling into one of the traps that spring themselves on investors. For these traps to be avoided you need to know where they are, in order to find a different path.

One of the most troublesome potential problems starts as soon as an investor is an owner of common stocks. He starts to review performance, of the total portfolio and of each stock separately. Some investors forget why they bought a stock almost immediately after buying it and start worrying. It seems they worry more about losing a profit than they fear experiencing a big loss.

This habit leads to a very serious error for many people. Human nature causes most investors to develop an uncontrollable urge to sell a stock that rises in price significantly or even a little. On the other hand, investors are reluctant to sell any stock at a loss, clinging to the notion that a loss is not permanent until a stock is sold.

This tendency is sometimes known as "small profits, big losses." Al Pearlstein, a stockbroker in Toronto, first brought this to my attention in 1979.

> ## THE SMALL PROFITS, BIG LOSSES TRAP
>
> **Investors tend to sell their promising stocks too early, taking a small profit and missing out on market gains. They also tend to keep poorly performing stocks too long, leading to big losses when they eventually sell.**

As an illustration, consider a garden. Flowers grow and flourish when watered and given some care. Unfortunately, weeds sprout aggressively right alongside. Weeds are obviously undesirable and get pulled out as soon as the gardener recognizes them. Culling the weeds ensures the success of the flowers and improves the health of the garden. The weeds, if left to spread, would eventually choke off the flowers.

A stock portfolio works in a similar manner. Some stocks emerge as winners, giving the investor capital gains on paper. Other stocks sag, causing a sinking feeling and declining value for the portfolio. The sensible thing to do is to pick the weeds, by culling the portfolio of the losers and help the flowers grow taller, by keeping the winners, perhaps buying more of the stronger companies if they still represent good value.

Human nature dictates the opposite. Most investors left to their own devices will sell the winners and keep the losers. A common phrase heard as an investor prepares to dump a good stock overboard is "you never go broke taking a profit." There are few attitudes among investors that cause more problems and poor performance.

In his 1930 book *The Art of Speculation*, republished by Wiley in 1997, Philip Carret put it as follows:

> A proverb every trader hears…You'll never get poor taking profits…As a matter of fact, the trader can insure his ultimate failure no more certainly than by taking profits.

THE DISPOSITION EFFECT

The tendency for investors to sell winners and hold on to losers has been labelled the disposition effect by researchers in the new field of behavioural economics. Terrance Odean of the University of California published a paper in July 1998 detailing the results of a study that examined the trading patterns within 10 000 investment accounts at a large discount brokerage house between 1987 and 1993. Odean showed that a definite pattern exists among investors to sell their winners quickly and hold their losers. He also showed that the winners that were sold went on to outperform the remaining stocks in the portfolio.

One explanation for this tendency is the importance that traders place on the initial purchase price as a reference point for decision-making. If someone paid $20 for a stock that rises to $30, there may be an unconscious feeling that the stock is headed back to $20, so the traders sells. On the other hand, if the same stock falls to $15 the trader holds because of the same belief, that the stock is headed back to $20. In other words, the investor believes that the correct or natural price for the stock is the price that investor initially paid.

Odean identified another factor influencing traders. Traders misapply the statistical concept of "regression to the mean," which suggests that high and low values in a series of numbers will eventually revert to the average or mean. While this regression tendency works with stock market sectors, individual stocks can and do break free of the constraints of average price levels. The value of good companies tends to increase over the years. The stock price of a good company is not constrained to move back toward some number or average.

Odean estimated the cost of following this flawed strategy as 4.4% per year, not counting the additional negative of capital gains taxes triggered by selling winners. No investor can afford to give up 4.4% per year in returns!

How to Get Poor Taking Profits

Let us examine the mechanics of the process. When buying a stock investors make a judgement that the chosen company will outperform the rest of the stocks available for purchase. If they thought otherwise they would buy another stock instead. Once that stock joins the portfolio the investor watches with interest. Will his expectations be proven right? Will the research that pointed to that company as exceptional turn out to be valid? If the price of the stock rises he is gratified. His confidence increases in his stock-picking ability. And he starts to worry about something happening to cause him to lose his profit.

If, on the other hand, the stock price sags the investor starts an argument with the stock market. Perhaps a mistake was made. Or, and this is a dangerous line of thought, the stock market is wrong and does not understand the company the way the investor does. Instead of closely examining the possibility that he made a mistake he commits himself to the stock and waits for the market to realize its error. This can be an expensive habit. An old saying from the days of the ticker tape says: Don't fight the tape!

A PORTFOLIO OF LOSERS

It is interesting to examine what happens to a portfolio when an investor consistently sells the winners and keeps the losers. A properly diversified stock portfolio holds 10 or more stocks. Let's assume about 1/5 of the stocks in a portfolio become huge winners and 1/5 become losers. The other 3/5 move along with the averages, rising and falling moderately with the market. The 1/5 of the stock portfolio that become huge winners represent about two stocks in this example. These two stocks provide a disproportionate percentage of the gains in any stock portfolio. Without some big gains a portfolio will lag behind the market, pulled down by the losers.

Investors need to have some big winners from time to time. In his book *One Up on Wall Street*, Peter Lynch talks about "fivebaggers" and "tenbaggers." A tenbagger is a stock that increases 10 times from the original purchase price. These gains are essential to cover the losses from the occasional mistakes that creep into the portfolio.

The mathematics of a portfolio illustrate how essential the winners are. Of the original ten stocks there are two stocks that have risen substantially after a certain time. If these are sold their replacements are likely to be winners or losers in about the same ratio. One stock carries the expectation statistically of being a big winner 20% of the time. So it would take five tries to get another big winner. Let's give our investor the benefit of the doubt and assume he gets one winner and one average. If he again sells the winner and keeps the other, there is a one in five chance of this stock being a winner. This time imagine that he gets a mediocre stock which he keeps.

The following table shows the portfolio after the investor sells his winners in two rounds of changes.

The Results of Selling the Winners

	Winners	Losers	Average
Original portfolio	2	2	6
After 1st Change	1	2	7
After 2nd Change	0	2	8

This table assumes that one of the two new stocks in the first round is a winner. The actual odds are that the new stocks will not contain a big winner. Obviously if the investor keeps selling off his winners and keeping his other stocks he will descend into mediocrity or worse. Many investors own portfolios that look horrible after a couple of years of "not going broke taking a profit."

Investors then call their advisor and berate him or her for being a poor stock picker. Often investors forget about the winners a few months after they are sold. By hanging on to the losing trades in the portfolio each look at the portfolio is a reminder of the mistakes that were made.

The tendency to want to unload a stock that is performing well betrays a lack of confidence in the stock market process. Investors are first surprised and then worried when a stock surges to new highs soon after purchase. Perhaps investors believe they do not deserve to make money in the market. They get a feeling that the gains are somehow illicit and want to pull them out before they are caught. By not being confident about their stock selection ability, investors feel that they need to get a profit before their luck runs out.

An investor that is forewarned about the tendency to sell the winners and keep the losers might think that it will be easy to avoid this trap. Unfortunately, this trap is so deeply embedded in human nature that constant vigilance by the investor and the broker is needed to catch it before it creeps in. Time and time again I have to force myself to consider selling a weak stock rather than a winner. It should be easier for me as I see the results on many portfolios every day. It never gets easy to do the right thing when it comes to selling stocks. In the next chapter I provide some sensible guidelines for knowing when to sell and when to hold on.

THE PSYCHOLOGY OF SELLING THE WINNERS AND KEEPING THE LOSERS

Why do investors turn on a stock that has performed for them? When the stock is purchased the investor expects an increase in price. The investor usually is impressed with some facet of the business of that company or perhaps is acting on a tip. The outlook for the company or the industry looks good, in the eyes of that investor.

Buyer's Remorse

Almost immediately after purchase the honeymoon period ends and the investor starts looking for flaws. All the positive attributes that led to the purchase in the first place seem less important, while any negative attributes grow larger. The stock buyer develops a version of buyer's remorse. He starts to wonder if another stock might have been a better investment. Something strange happens to the investor when that stock rises in price. The investor starts eyeing the stock with suspicion, wondering if a precipitous drop looms just around the corner. All of the positive expectations dissipate and a wariness develops. What if the stock drops and all the profits are lost? Fear grips the investor, especially if he did not participate much in the selection of the stock. The main attribute of the stock for the investor becomes the stock price. Focussing too much on stock prices leads to selling the winners and keeping the losers.

Small Profits and Big Losses

Adding to the pressure, the stockbroker calls and discusses the portfolio. It is only human for the investor and the broker both to enjoy discussing their successes. By paying attention to the stocks that rise in price the inevitable question emerges. Should the investor take a profit? From the stockbroker's point of view a trade in a stock that is up in price is much easier to generate. Stockbrokers who operate on a commission basis need some activity to get paid. If it is two or three times easier to convince a client to sell a winning stock than a losing stock one can expect the broker to take the easier path. A discussion about a winning stock turns into a decision to sell. The client and the broker pat each other on the back and "nail down that profit."

Brokers and investors find it more difficult to talk about a stock that is down. Even more intimidating for the broker is broaching the subject of the sale of a losing stock. Once that stock is sold a mistake is made permanent. The client and the broker both find it easier to say something like "just hold on and it will come back." This attitude results from thinking that the original choice was accurate but the stock market does not understand the stock yet. The wisdom of the broker and the investor is considered superior to the market, just a little ahead of the market. This type of flawed thinking costs money.

Ego

Ego is a big factor in this stock trading challenge. The human ego likes to recognize success and deny failure. Investors as a class of people may be more likely to have this tendency. Aggressive investors are more common than easygoing ones. Successful people have money to invest in the stock market, and when they invest they expect to be winners.

Admitting a mistake is difficult for most. Many stockbrokers are reluctant to admit a mistake in choosing a stock. Brokers often create unrealistic expectations about their stock-picking abilities in order to get new clients. While it is ridiculous to expect every stock to be a winner, it is not that unusual for an unwritten contract to develop between investor and broker. The contract says that the stock picks are all good, the market just gets it wrong sometimes.

The Myth of the Zero-Sum Game

A common misconception about the market among novice and experienced investors alike is the myth of the zero-sum game. A zero-sum game is a game that has one loser for every winner. If one person wins, another person must lose. The stock market is not a zero-sum game. In theory everyone who owns shares could be a winner over the long term. The stock market increases in size as the world economy grows. The size of the total pie is growing. When the occasional bear market comes along the market shrinks for a time, and then resumes growing. Even after a severe bear market when prices drop 50%, the market hits new highs one, two, or ten years later. After every bear market in the last 200 years the stock market eventually hit new highs. Investors fail to appreciate the significance of this fact.

The investor who feels a strong desire to pull profits out of a winning stock perhaps believes that the market is like a game of roulette. After a few wins the profits will be lost if all the money is left on the number. If the investor does not take some money off the table it will be given back to the house. This is true in Las Vegas but not on Wall Street or Bay Street. Unlike a roulette wheel, the market can provide winnings that grow over a long period of time. If a company is doing well the stock price will increase over time as that company grows.

The equally difficult time for investors comes when a stock price declines below the purchase price. This happens frequently, and is usually a temporary phenomenon. No investor picks stocks exactly at the low or sells exactly at the high.

Investors develop a certain stubbornness about a stock that declines. They start to fixate obsessively on their purchase price, thinking that they will sell when the stock returns to that price. Getting out "even" becomes very important psychologically. It is very important to realize that the market does not care what price you paid for a stock.

Not all Companies Recover

Not all companies with a declining stock price will recover. Some continue to slide into oblivion. Great care needs to be taken to avoid getting caught with a losing stock. More time should be spent on the losing stocks than the winners. The winners can be left to themselves unless they become so hot that they lose touch with reality. On the other hand, the losers can be very damaging for a portfolio as they may cause a complete loss of funds.

A decline in a stock price acts as a warning bell for successful investors. With such a position it is important to review the stock and the company. Has there been a change for the worse in the business of the company? Did something that was assumed to be true turn out to be false? You would do better to sell quickly while the loss is still small if there is a problem. If the company remains attractive for fundamental reasons it is advisable to hold the stock since stocks in out-of-favour sectors often decline just because they are not in fashion. Perhaps the purchase was made a little too early. The important thing is to ask the question: Is there a problem with this company?

Instead of "small profits, big losses" investors need to "let the profits run and cut the losses."

Limiting Your Chances

Some investors develop an investment practice that encourages them to sell their winners and keep their losers. The practice involves placing orders at a specific price when buying and selling stocks. These orders are known as limit orders. Limit orders are buy or sell orders entered at a specific price requiring that the broker execute the order only if the price target is met.

When buying a stock some investors try to buy at a price below the current market price by entering a limit order below the trading price. For example, when attempting to buy a stock trading between $32 and $33, an order is placed to buy at $30. The limit price means that the broker can only buy the stock if it becomes available at $30 or less.

When selling, these investors also insist on placing an order with a limit above the market price, so that when the price reached that level the broker would automatically sell the shares. If the same stock were trading at $45 to $46 a limit order might be placed at $50.

While on the surface it might look like a smart strategy, if perhaps a little greedy, this limit order practice risks triggering the limit order trap.

THE LIMIT ORDER TRAP

Using limit orders forces the broker to buy companies when their stock prices sink and sell those whose stock prices rise. Stocks that are at the beginning of a rise in price are never purchased, and good performers are jettisoned. Weaker companies get added every time using limit orders.

When using limit orders to buy a stock, stocks that weaken below the current market price are bought while those that strengthen in price never make it into the portfolio. This is a filter to keep out the stocks with good price action and select the stocks with poor price action.

The entering of limit orders below the market price to buy a good company's stock makes little sense. The investor's attitude is full of contradictions. She is saying that she likes the company, thinks the stock price will rise, but expects the stock price to do a dip first so it can be purchased before it makes its climb. This is asking for too much. If you identify a good company trading at a reasonable price, perhaps in an out-of-favour sector, then buy it. It might not stay low-priced for long.

When selling, the limit order filters out those stocks that keep rising in price, eliminating them from the portfolio as they reach the selling price limit. On the other hand the stocks with weak price action often never get sold as they fail to reach the price limit and then drift lower.

The limit order seller is asking for a convenient blip in the stock price to accommodate the higher-priced limit order to sell. If there is a good reason to sell the stock, it's better to get out as soon as the decision is made. Asking to get a higher price than the current market is just asking for trouble. Chances are that others have recognized the need to sell and will push the stock price lower.

HOW TO INVEST DANGEROUSLY

Hot Tips from Friends and Relatives

The experienced voice in *Reminiscences of a Stock Operator* by Edwin Lefevre (John Wiley & Sons Inc., 1994) extolled:

> I don't believe in tips. If I buy stocks on Smith's tip I must sell those same stocks on Smith's tip. I am depending on him. Suppose Smith is away on holiday when the selling time comes around? No, sir, nobody can make big money on what someone else tells him to do.

Many first-time investors call me with a specific stock in mind, usually a speculative one. Often these speculations are in a junior company on a junior exchange. In Canada the junior exchanges are Vancouver and

Alberta, as well as the unlisted market in Toronto. Junior companies are those with little or no business track record, a lack of revenues or earnings, few assets, and a tendency to rely on stock market issues to survive.

The speculative desire is triggered by a friend or relative who has "promoted" a stock to them. These would-be investors usually lack experience in the stock market. Few serious investors will push a junior stock onto another person, especially a relative. Experienced investors know that each investor must find a path that suits individual temperament and tastes. On the contrary, the hot tip usually comes from another person "playing" the market who is inexperienced himself. Perhaps he wants to appear wise about investing to his friend. A typical scenario goes as follows.

WHY WOULD YOU HEAR ABOUT A HOT TIP?

A person hears from someone who knows someone else who works for the company in question. The employee of the company, which is usually a junior company trading on a junior exchange, insists that the president of the company says that the stock will go to $2.00 by Christmas from its current price of 50 cents. On the strength of this whisper of a rumour the first-time investor wishes to take the plunge. The actual information offered about the company's business is minimal. The most frequently mentioned type of stock depends on the hot sector at the time. When gold shares were hot in 1996 the favourite hot tip was in mining. At other times the "flavour of the month" is biotechnology. Other "concept" stocks used for promotional purposes are computer technology, waste disposal, advanced materials, and Internet stocks.

What does that first-time speculator really know about the target company? Usually the person who gave the tip owns the stock as well. Why would they go to the trouble of pushing the stock unless they did? The employee of the company may own the stock and normally does, perhaps through stock options. The president of the company invariably owns lots of shares in the company, directly and through stock options. The president of the company would like to see the stock go higher. The only way the stock will go up is for an excess of buyers over sellers to appear on the stock market. By spreading the word the president tries to make this happen. By the way, promoters of both the innocent and the professional variety spread the word about a stock only after they accumulate their position, usually at lower prices.

Promoters

Professional promoters use more direct methods also. Stock promoters phone stockbrokers trying to gather support for pushing the stock higher. These promoters work out of their home with several phone lines and a script. When they get a stockbroker interested they offer a telephone meeting with the president. Often they get the broker involved by offering inducements in the form of stock at low prices.

The only useful information that can be known for sure is that someone, usually the president and other insiders, owns the stock and would like it to go higher. The reason they would like it to go higher is to make money. The only way they can make money is to sell the stock when it goes higher.

A significant hurdle to overcome for speculators buying on a tip is their lack of conviction. Knowing this, promoters often phone repeatedly with more positive news to pump up conviction because they do not want selling pressure on the stock just when they are getting ready to unload some of their own stock. If the stock keeps rising the speculator feels good and may even buy more stock. If the stock falls the speculator may want to get out but there is no informed way to make a decision. So hot tip traders usually just hold on, clinging to the last positive rumour they heard, until the stock slides to pennies after the insiders are out and the promotion ends. Seldom if ever does someone phone and tell them to get out.

Promotions on stocks happen more often during a hot market after the price of a stock moves up. The president and others purchase their shares during a quiet period in the market when the price is very low or prior to the stock going public on the stock market. The insiders sell the stock during the promotion phase when the share price is much higher. For the insiders the game is to buy low and sell higher. For the speculator the game becomes buy high, and hold until the promotion phase ends. Eventually the shares are sold much lower, for a tax loss. This sequence represents a buy high, sell low trap for the speculator.

THE HOT TIP TRAP

Unsuspecting investors are persuaded to purchase a stock whose price is rising solely due to the efforts of a rumour campaign. When the campaign reaches its peak the insiders sell their stock, the price falls, and the investor is left with a loss.

Once in a while a speculator hears about a stock before the promotional phase begins and the stock goes much higher. Or the stock movement may not be a promotion at all, but may turn out to be a real improvement in the value of the company. For this reason it is difficult for the stockbroker to say definitively that a tip is a bad deal. What if the stock goes much higher and the speculator misses out on a big profit? Most brokers go along with the tip, taking the path of least resistance. This agreement on the part of the broker is not an endorsement of the stock or the method. It is usually just a public relations attempt to avoid losing a client or potential client.

Some brokers get actively involved in the promotion, loading up their clients on a junior stock in the belief that things will work out. Occasionally brokers develop some real skill at playing this type of stock market game and make money for their clients and themselves. This is very rare.

Why do tips hold such an attraction for many people? The greed factor must be a part of the story. But there are many stocks available that could be bought to satisfy a "get rich quick" motive. One difference with a tip involves the comfort of the implicit support of other people. Some personalities need to know that a group is involved before they will invest. Most people love to be part of a group. The fact that others have selected the stock relieves the speculator of some of the responsibility for making a choice. If that friend who passed on the tip turns out to have made a mistake, the speculator can blame the friend for the mistake. He or she does not have to take responsibility for making a choice.

The best approach for the serious investor is to avoid hot tips entirely. For every tip that eventually makes money there are 30 or 40 that fizzle out, leaving the stock much lower or off the market altogether. With such terrible odds the best course is to rule out tips altogether as a method of stock selection.

DERIVATIVE TRADING AND OPTIONS

The practice of selling the winners and keeping the losers appears in disguise sometimes. Derivative trading is one example.

Derivatives occasionally attract a lot of attention in the markets, usually when a bear market hits as happened in the autumn of 1998. The U.S. market had declined about 20% as measured by the Dow, when a U.S.-based hedge fund named Long Term Capital got into trouble. A bailout was arranged by the major U.S. investment banking firms, with the help of the Federal Reserve. Many industry observers questioned the role of derivatives in the Long Term Capital problem, wondering if the use of derivatives could jeopardize the world monetary system. This concern has faded for the time being as the markets recovered.

The type of derivative most frequently encountered by individual investors is called an option.

Options are time-sensitive instruments that give an investor the right to buy or sell a stock at a set price for a specified period of time. The right to buy is referred to as a "call" option and the right to sell is called a "put" option. Options are also available on bonds, currencies, gold, futures contracts, and stock market indexes. Options expire after a short period of time, usually less than nine months. The longer the time to expiry the greater the cost of the option. This cost is called the "premium" and represents the extra cost of gambling with options compared to buying the stock itself.

Trading Options

Most investors fail when trying to trade options. The price paid to speed things up is very high as options carry an expensive premium. They are similar to lottery tickets. Most purchasers of lottery tickets lose all the cost of the ticket while a few win a lot of money.

The attraction for purchasers of options is the opportunity to put down a small amount of money for a potentially big payoff. The risk of options is due to the relatively short period of time in which the stock must make a big move in the right direction for the option player to win. The option buyer must be right twice—both in the direction of the change in price and the time period. The gamble seldom succeeds and the speculator loses the total cost of the options. As in Las Vegas, the casino always wins in the end.

Covered Call Writing

A different strategy with options appeals to investors with larger amounts of money. This strategy, known as covered call writing, involves buying a block of stock and then selling an option against it. This strategy pays off more consistently than purchasing options but there is a major flaw in covered call writing. I mention covered call writing specifically because sooner or later you may be offered the chance to do this if you invest in common stocks long enough.

The investor purchases the stock first. This could be in the form of a balanced, diversified 10-stock portfolio. Then call options are sold on those shares to a speculator who thinks that stock is about to go up quickly. A blue chip stock trading at $20 might carry options trading at $.50 that give the buyer the right to sell the stock at $22.50 for three months. The owner of the stock portfolio receives the 50 cents for offering this option on his stock. Most of the time the stock option never comes into play as the stock fails to rise above $22.50 and the option becomes worthless. The investor keeps the 50 cents and the speculator loses his bet. If this option selling is done four times in one year the operation yields $2.00, giving a 10% additional return on the stock. And the investor gets to keep the stock. Brokers who promote this type of trading suggest that the option seller is taking the side of the casino while the option buyer is the gambler.

You may notice that the option seller gets to keep the stock if it stays level in price or drops. Only if the stock rises quickly enough to reach the option price does the covered call seller lose the stock position. The main difficulty with this strategy is that it ensures a small profits, big losses philosophy. The portfolio retains the stocks that stagnate and loses the stocks that perform, guaranteeing a "sell the winners, keep the losers" strategy. In addition, if the stock drops in value sharply, the investor still owns the stock and carries all the risk. The income of 50 cents every three months is not enough to compensate for losing some of the big winners and being stuck with the losers. Devotees of the covered call writing strategy counter this argument by suggesting that investors buy back the good stocks that get away, but in practice this seldom happens.

Derivative trading appeals at first glance to many investors. As with covered call writing there is usually a hidden trap. The easy way to avoid trouble is to stay away from all derivative or exotic trading strategies. Let the professionals fill up their time with these complicated strategies. All you need is to own ten good quality companies.

MOMENTUM INVESTING

A popular fad for investing in the late 1990s is momentum investing. Momentum investing is based on the premise that a stock that is moving higher will continue to move higher. Computers and Internet-based day trading have encouraged more momentum traders, as a computer is a natural tool to track unusual activity in a particular stock or a sector or the market as a whole. Momentum investing is a trap for many speculators who wish to succeed in investing without using much patience or skill.

THE MOMENTUM INVESTING TRAP

Speculators buy stock based on the fact that it is trading actively and the price of the shares is going up. The underlying value of the company is not examined, and momentum traders must be very nimble to avoid losing money when the stock price corrects.

Many traders have been using a less sophisticated version of momentum investing for a long time. When stock traders say that a stock is acting well they mean that relative to the market the stock is holding up well. Perhaps the traders have noticed a tendency for the stock to trade up on most days. This is called momentum. The price of a stock is rising in a falling market, or rising more quickly in a rising market. Traders look for signs of positive momentum in a stock before they buy.

Price-momentum investing is popular partly because it uses computers. Professionals always try to find ways to use computers in investing and stock picking. Price-momentum is an ideal application, because it is easy for a computer to detect an increase in the volume of trading on a stock relative to a previous pattern of trading. An increase in trading might happen just before a company is acquired on a takeover. A stock attracts momentum buying when mutual fund managers start to buy a stock in large volume. The purchases of one mutual fund manager attract purchases by other managers (who are oriented to momentum investing) and it becomes a self-reinforcing spiral. Buying begets more buying and the price rises.

Recently I noticed an incident that brought to light some of the dangers day-traders experience who follow the momentum style. The following account, based on a real-life incident, uses fictional company names, and illustrates some of the pitfalls of momentum investing.

MOMENTUM INVESTING TAKEN TO THE EXTREME

A take-over bid at $50 per share was announced on a stock issued by SPI Corporation. Within seconds the stock symbol SPI started to respond, jumping from $27 to $35. As the symbol flashed across the screen more buyers were attracted to the stock, moving quickly for fear of missing out. I imagine that few of these buyers knew the type of business SPI Corporation handled, nor did they care. I had never heard of it myself.

A few minutes later the stock symbol showed an "h" beside it, indicating a halt, at the request of the either the company or the stock exchange. Curious, I selected the news report with my cursor.

The halt turned out to be at the request of the company, as they had no idea why their shares were surging higher. This company, called Safe Products International, happened to carry the stock symbol SPI but was not the corporation subject to a takeover at $50. As it was explained in a subsequent story, SPI Corporation had a symbol slightly different from its corporate name, along the lines of SPC. The momentum investors got caught assuming that the SPI symbol belonged to SPI Corporation.

This mistake cost many people a lot of money as the trades were unwound. This incident couldn't happen without the prevalence of traders that are looking just for volume and price action, and not checking the fundamentals.

In the days, years ago, when all trades went through stockbrokers this case of mistaken identity would not have happened. The broker would be responsible for checking for the correct symbol and if a mistake was made, the broker would pay, not the client. But things were much slower then.

I do not recommend the price-momentum method for individual investors. It requires a nimbleness in jumping in and out of stocks that is difficult even for pros. While momentum investing can be rewarding, there are too many full-time traders playing this game. The portfolio-oriented individual has no edge here and many disadvantages. Momentum investing also means leaving behind ideas of value and out-of-favour sectors. Usually momentum players are trading hot stocks in hot sectors, paying ever higher prices for stocks that are no longer in touch with fundamental values.

The momentum method is also described as the "bigger fool" theory of investing. The bigger fool theory says that while I may be a fool for paying such a high price for a stock there is an even bigger fool (I hope) who will pay an even higher price, allowing me to make a profit. This method can also be called buying high and selling higher. Often this turns into another buy high, sell low trap as investors fail to get out quickly enough, the bigger fool does not arrive and the momentum dies.

Knowing that investors are using price momentum, mutual funds with large positions to unload in a stock have been known to do a burst of buying in the stock, to attract momentum players to the stock. After attracting some buy orders from momentum players who took the bait, the fund slowly feeds in sell orders, trying not to disrupt the price momentum players so as to use them to sell out a large position.

Mutual funds did not invent this game. In *Reminiscences of a Stock Operator,* the author describes pool operations that were used to support stocks in the 1920s. These pools were organized groups who used their combined buying power to create a false picture of activity in a stock. This unusual trading would attract buyers and thus prepare the stock so that an insider could sell his position for a profit. There is little new in the stock market game, it seems.

Most mutual fund buyers are momentum investors since they rely on a history of rising prices in a fund to select their investments. The better the past rate of return in the fund, the more they like the fund. Of course, momentum players dislike a declining trend in a stock or a fund, which is why they exit from these investments after a downtrend is well established.

BORROWING MONEY TO INVEST

Many investors succumb to the temptation to speed up the process of using investments to get rich. A common way to accelerate the process involves investment loans from a bank or buying "on margin" from a brokerage firm. Brokerage firms lend up to 75% of the value of a purchase of shares to clients. The interest rate is usually 1.5% above the prime rate, or less on larger margin loans.

Margin loans allow the investor to leverage the stock market. In chapter 1 you saw how the leverage of investing with other people's money affected the Crash of 1929, wiping out most participants.

Borrowing money to invest would actually work if investors chose to borrow at the end of a bear market. Of course, they never do as their fear is too great. Without exception, margin accounts become popular toward the end of a long bull market. As investors and traders develop a confidence that the market is going higher they start to take larger and larger positions. When they run out of new capital to invest they look for ways to leverage the capital they do have. When the bull market peaks and starts to decline, margin accounts are common.

As the bear market takes hold brokerage firms demand more money from the margin account holders. They issue margin calls, asking that investors replenish the equity in their accounts. If the investor refuses to send in more money, which is usually the case, the brokerage firm sells out enough stock to meet the margin call.

This practice of buying stocks on margin just makes the buy high, sell low cycle more painful. Investors become speculators who buy more stock than they can afford at a high price and then make a forced sale later when the price is lower.

The sellout of a margin account occurs over a period of months. In the first phase the speculator believes that the market will come back, and sells the most conservative and boring stocks to meet the margin call, while keeping the more aggressive positions. Later, the speculator finds that some stocks cannot be sold easily and is forced to sell the blue chips to get enough money to meet a margin call. In the final stage of market meltdown the whole account is liquidated by the brokerage firm, sometimes with the speculator still owing money after all the stocks are sold.

DAY TRADING ON THE INTERNET

In a highly unusual move reported in the Wall Street Journal May 5, 1999, the chairman of the Securities and Exchange Commission in the United States, Arthur Levitt took exception to the online brokerage industry advertisements "focusing on the get-rich aspect of online investing." He thinks that these ads are doing "more harm than good for both Wall Street and the public."

In chastising these firms for creating "grandiose and unrealistic expectations" the SEC chairman is highlighting a phenomenon that is unique to the 1990s. Millions of traders are going online everyday, buying and selling stock without the benefit of investment advisors, trying to make a killing in the stock market. Employers are expressing concern about lost productivity at work as addicted traders hook up to the stock markets instead of performing their jobs.

This craze is just the present-day version of many different manias that have swept the stock market world from time to time over the last 100 years. The difference here, if there is any, comes from the dominance of the computer and the abundance of information available to the trader. The results will still depend on the quality of investments purchased and the ability of the individuals involved to keep their feet on the ground in times of turmoil.

In the 1920s an older version of this game prevailed. Trading operations, known as bucket shops, allowed individuals to bet on the short-term price movements of common stocks. Orders placed in a bucket shop paid off if the shares went up. If the price of the stock stayed the same or dropped the bucket shop kept all of the customer's money. Stories abounded of the rare individuals who made money trading this way, and mythical legends developed around a few names. One of these individuals was Jesse Livermore, the person behind the book *Reminiscences of a Stock Operator*, where he describes these trading operations.

My experience with day trading goes back to the late 1970s, before discount brokers appeared on the scene. At that time individuals who wished to try to make a killing trading the market came to stockbrokers and usually were assigned to the rookie in the office. As the rookie I picked up a few of these traders. Calling several times a day these traders watched the market for small price movements and tried to cash in. Invariably they all managed to lose their stake to the market after a period of time mostly because of their tendency to get caught in the "small profits, big losses" trap described above. As new brokers in the office we tried to keep these day traders alive as long as possible, not realizing that they would all disappear at the end of the bull market.

While not all online trading is day trading, the rapid growth in market share for brokerage firms such as Charles Schwab and E-Trade in the United States is undoubtedly linked to this attempt by individuals to trade their way to riches, especially through the exciting and dangerous Internet stock sector.

There is no evidence of any continuous success over a period of time through speculative trading on the stock market, online or bucket shop, or through regular brokerage channels. However, it is clear that during long and exciting bull markets excesses of this type always appear, with some initial success. After many speculators become enthralled with the adrenaline-pumping thrill of trading and even make a lot of money for a time, eventually the bull market fades and most, if not all of these traders give back all of their winnings to the markets. As both the QAIB and the Odean studies showed, excessive trading in the markets served to lower performance, by an amount that makes stock market investing less rewarding than the risk-free alternatives of government bonds and Treasury bills. The entertainment value of their "thrills and spills" in the trading world will be the only reward for these adventurous people.

An investor who wishes to remain independent of the crowd and exercise patience to make money in a steady and safe manner needs to resist the temptation of day trading in the markets at all times.

All of these trading traps leave the investor with grave difficulties that are entirely avoidable. Many of these traps involve an attempt to speed up the process of getting rich. Individuals lose their advantage over the pros as soon as they try to accelerate the process. If investors focus on the idea of owning 10 good companies and making changes when necessary to improve the portfolio, the stock market will make them rich, slowly. Time is on the side of the portfolio investor who has patience.

Ten

Using Professional Advice to Manage Your Portfolio

Most investors find it difficult to balance their need for help with investment decisions with a desire to maintain control and take responsibility for their decisions. Some people go to one extreme and decide to turn their money over entirely to others by purchasing a managed product. Others go to the other extreme and try to do it all themselves, spending countless hours in front of computer screens.

Few potential do-it-yourselfers have the time and expertise required to research all the different stocks and make selections without outside assistance. Other investors who put their faith in money managers eventually lose confidence in them, feeling a complete lack of involvement and control. In both cases the investor suffers from a lack of access to good information and advice that becomes critical at some stage in the market cycle.

The successful independent investor avoids both extremes. All the investor really needs is to find a way to build and manage a personal portfolio. This portfolio consists of ownership of 10 companies, hopefully purchased at reasonable prices, as well as some safe government bonds. Ongoing monitoring and decision-making is required to maintain and improve the quality of the portfolio. Most investors realize their need for help in the form of a coach and advisor as well as access to research on individual companies.

WHERE TO GET INFORMATION

The role of a coach looms larger when individual stock selections are made. A coach and an investor together find the companies that will provide a diversified portfolio that grows with the market. In order to provide a short list of options to their clients, most coaches need help themselves. Using additional outside help to provide research on dozens of companies that might fit in the portfolio does not frighten a confident coach, nor does having the client do research on their own.

Using the Internet

The arrival of the Internet improves your chances of success in investing. Access to information on the Web puts an individual investor at less of a disadvantage in the pursuit of quick and accurate information. As with most other revolutionary changes, the Web also has the potential to cause serious difficulties for some investors.

The best source of free reliable information comes from the financial reports filed at most companies' Web sites. Many companies of any size have their own Web site where they post their annual reports and quarterly financial reports as well as news releases. Since the directors and officers of publicly traded companies are legally liable for misinformation, these reports are usually reliable. Caution is still in order, however, as that infamous company, BRE-X, had one of the most impressive Web sites of its time.

I especially recommend reading a series of periodic company reports to see if management outlined and then followed through on their plans in a consistent manner. Investors need to avoid a company that frequently changes direction from quarter to quarter or fails to warn investors about negative developments.

Another source of information is research reports that can be purchased over the Internet. Investment analysts prepare these reports on individual companies. Since your coach can provide similar research reports for no additional charge, only "do-it-yourselfers" need to take this route.

Learning more about companies through the Internet and other sources will enhance your chances of success. Your involvement in the information-gathering process will demonstrate to your coach that you are committed to investing and knowledgeable about the process. You may find yourself bringing new information to your coach's attention, resulting in a stronger partnership and more confidence for you.

Research Analysts

Every brokerage firm employs analysts who research industries and companies to find attractive purchase candidates. These analysts also make "sell" recommendations on companies that should be avoided, in their opinion. In a well-run brokerage firm research analysts carry the responsibility of distinguishing the good from the bad. The research analysts specialize in a sector or subsector. As an expert in their sector they are expected to know that industry inside and out. Each major company in the industry must be familiar to them. In most cases, research analysts spend many years working in their chosen industry before entering the stock market business. Analysts hold extensive academic qualifications, including specific training in the industry they study as well as the Chartered Financial Analyst designation. Stock market analysts often carry a Masters of Business Administration and other graduate degrees.

Many analysts enjoy number-crunching activities more than passing time in small talk. Endless hours spent in the front of computer-generated spreadsheets are normal for these technical wizards. While a few analysts find it easy to sell their ideas to investors, most prefer to write reports instead of giving speeches. Some of the best analysts suffer from an inability to promote themselves. These analysts rely on the power of the written word to carry their message. Nevertheless, part of the analyst's job is to sell stock recommendations. They sell internally in the brokerage firm to stockbrokers and externally to institutional investors. Analysis without action does not bring in enough revenue to pay the bills.

The personality type of many professional money managers matches that of the analysts. Mutual fund managers hold similar academic qualifications and backgrounds. There is a two-way flow between analyst positions and money manager jobs. Many analysts move over to the "buy" side of the street to become portfolio managers. The term "buy side" refers to institutional clients such as mutual funds and pension plans that have money to buy stocks. The "sell side" is the brokerage community.

Since professional investors identify easily with research analysts and vice versa, research is used extensively by most professionals. In fact, institutional money managers' commissions pay for the research departments of most brokerage firms. Retail investor commissions would not justify the cost of a fully staffed research department. While commissions from professional investors pay for research, brokerage firms allow stockbrokers to disseminate the reports to individual investors also.

Any research report produced by an investment firm is available to all clients, retail and institutional. This research is valuable in making decisions about which stocks to buy. A successful independent investor makes use of the research available as one way of avoiding some of the stock trading traps discussed earlier. Unfortunately, only a small fraction of individual investors and brokers make use of the research available.

Understand What Makes the Analyst Tick

Research analysts have limitations. Analysts, in my experience, have a focus that is too specific to allow them to always see overall market trends. Industry-specific analysts spend most of their time looking at very fine distinctions between companies in an industry. Financial ratio analysis is the jumping-off point to differentiate between companies. Thorough analysts talk to competitors, suppliers, customers, and company executives to get a feeling for the present state of a company. Future trends for earnings are the main focus of analysis for these specialists.

Every analyst reaches a point in their career, often more than once, when all the companies in their assigned industry are doing poorly. Business is bad in the industry, and only some of the companies are making money. This is a very difficult time for the analyst, whose income depends on generating interest in the sector. At such times the industry is usually out-of-favour in the stock market also. Professional investors, with their short-term focus, give little notice to these cool sectors. As mentioned in chapter 4, analysts whose sectors go out-of-favour become discouraged, worrying about their jobs as those important institutional commissions slow to a trickle. The pros' negative feeling toward the sector sours the outlook of the analyst. Professional investors and research analysts maintain a close relationship that leads to a form of tunnel vision when a sector is either hot or cold. An analyst in a cool sector makes a poor judge of the timing to buy into that sector.

As contrarians, independent investors look for companies in sectors that are out-of-favour because of the value to be found there. An analyst who takes a negative approach to his sector when it is scorned by the pros might lead other investors to overlook a wonderful buying opportunity. A successful individual investor needs to ask the right question of the analyst to get a useful answer. The question for the research analyst is:

Which are the top three companies in your industry for a three-to-five year hold?

The wording of this question becomes important when you recall that professional investors (and therefore analysts) have a short time horizon. How often have you read in the newspaper that a certain analyst likes a stock fundamentally but would avoid it for the next six months? The time horizon of six months targets the pros, who need quick action to generate performance. Your concern needs to be longer term than that.

A competent analyst distinguishes between the best and the worst companies in the sector. In addition, some analysts are able to judge where the most attractive investments can be found within the best companies. The outstanding investments are the best companies at a stock market price that is reasonable. The analyst provides better information when asked to rank the companies in the industry against each other. Unfortunately not all brokerage firms use the same ranking system to report their research. Some brokerage firms allow the analysts to have mostly buy recommendations or mostly sell recommendations, depending on how the analyst feels about a particular sector. Because the analysts are so close to the professional investors the mood in the sector affects the analysts' recommendations. If the sector is hot, then all the research reports say buy. If the sector is cold, the few research reports that get written have a distinctly negative slant to them. Often it is difficult to find research of any kind on a cold sector as all the analysts had to find other work to survive. This situation is recognized as an opportunity by experienced investors.

Regardless of the degree that a sector is in-favour or out-of-favour, some companies in that sector are stronger than others. An independent investor looks to the research analyst primarily for distinctions between the stronger and weaker companies in that sector. Research analysts lose their usefulness when they are so enthusiastic about their sector that all their stocks rate a buy ranking. A buy recommendation can be misleading when most companies in the sector are buy rated. An overly enthusiastic analyst is a signal that an industry is hot. In such cases, the institutions are already heavily invested. The analyst's boosterism is often sympathetic to the large positions of his clients, the institutional investors. Individual investors who buy into sectors at this stage take a risk the professionals may start to exit the sector and stock prices will plummet. You already know who the analyst will call first when he decides the stocks in the sector need to be sold.

On the other hand, a sector may be cold due to a lack of interest from the pros. Research analysts become gun-shy after 10 or 20 rejections of their best ideas by the professional money managers. At times like this, their recommendations reflect a lack of confidence in the attractiveness of the sector. Only the best research analysts have the experience and self-confidence to overcome the negative pressure of money managers who are out of a sector.

Earlier you saw how attractive a sector can be that is cool and untouched by professional investors because of their short time horizon. This is exactly the situation where the independent investor gains the advantage over the pro. Coaches and investors both must take care not to get swayed by the collective malaise hanging over a sector that is not popular with the pros. This is the ideal opportunity for a value investor who has patience. With the magic of time, the sector eventually attracts new buying interest from astute investors, usually contrarian investors initially. When the sector starts to move up momentum investors and professional money managers pile in with buy orders, driving prices up rapidly. Independent investors want to be in the sector before this happens. Ideally, you want to buy in shortly before the heating-up process begins.

USE RESEARCH AND SECTORS AS A SCREEN

The simplest solutions work best, and the organization of the research department offers an attractive starting point to our stock selection challenge. In a typical research department, each analyst covers an industry sector or sub-sector. At the Toronto Stock Exchange there are 14 sectors. Most large firms employ 20 or more analysts. Some sectors are large enough to have sub-sectors and so may have more than one analyst. For example, industrial products is just one sector. Included in that sector are companies in the steel industry and the computer technology industry. These sub-sectors are very different from each other, requiring different analysts. In 1999 the high technology sector in some brokerage companies justified four analysts or more. Could this be a sign that a sector is overheated and the time to get out is near?

If each of the 20 analysts carry recommendations on an average of 15 stocks the universe of stocks with research available totals 300 stocks. This total coverage list includes the buys and the sells, as well as the holds. When I am building a portfolio I focus on the buy list. The number of buys varies between sectors and analysts. Most analysts recommend at least two or three of their 10 to 20 stocks as buys. Some recommend as many as half of their stocks as buys, which is less useful. The coach needs to talk to those analysts to find out which three stocks on the buy list are the best of the lot.

By asking the right questions of the analyst, the coach will discover two or three companies of interest in each analyst's domain. This process results in 40 to 60 good quality companies, representing more than 15 sectors and sub-sectors. With some further work the coach identifies five to seven sectors as cool or out-of-favour. Within these sectors, 15 to 20 top quality stocks will appear as the analysts' top picks. So far the investor has very little time invested in studying individual companies. But the coach and the investor have a list of 15 to 20 solid companies, diversified by industry and sector. Usually the independent investor asks the coach to do further study on these 20 companies and recommend a selection for the final decision. Some investors prefer to choose the stocks for the portfolio themselves. The final decision will be based on the relative value of the companies on the list and the need for proper diversification and balance.

WHEN A SECTOR OR A STOCK REPRESENTS GOOD VALUE

As an independent investor it is important to remember that you do not need perfection to succeed. If a sector and a stock is misjudged completely and you buy at the wrong time, you may have a long wait for a stock to perform. Unfortunately this happens. It is not the end of the world because the process described above still results in the ownership of 10 good-quality companies. The initial purchase price and timing become less and less significant as time goes on. As long as that company continues to be—or will become—a strong company, time is on the side of the investor. A mistake in the timing of a purchase is a minor irritant. Some purchase prices will turn out to be low and others high, viewed from six months or a year down the road. The important thing is the quality of the companies chosen for the portfolio.

Changing Perceptions of Value

Occasionally a bear market creates a climate for investment that produces very appealing bargains.

BUYING A VALUE INVESTMENT IN A BEAR MARKET

At the darkest time of the 1982 bear market my investment firm underwrote a new issue offering at $20 per share for Bell Canada, the largest telephone company in Canada.

The climate for investment offerings was difficult, to say the least. Treasury bills paid 18% while government bonds provided income of 14% to 15%. Investors were spooked by a stock market 30% to 40% lower than the year before, and a bond market where prices fell 20% in a few months.

I decided that this Bell Canada convertible preferred share offering was ideal for many of my clients. When our manager asked for "expressions of interest" I committed to 5000 shares. Since the offering price was $20 I was on the hook for $100 000 worth of stock. While the firm would not force me to keep the stock if I could not sell it, turning back stock was just not done.

The first few calls I made alerted me to my precarious situation. Investors were convinced that interest rates were going higher. They also believed that several oil and gas firms were on the brink of bankruptcy, along with the banks that financed them. One bank had failed around that time in the United States and, in Alberta, where the price of oil determined the fate of many businesspeople, the outlook was grim. Many local businesses were going under, including eventually two banks.

The features of the preferred share were compelling, I felt. The shares paid a dividend of $2.70, or 13.5%. Dividends generated a dividend tax credit, which meant individuals received approximately 30% more return after tax than they would with interest income. Thus the interest rate equivalent was over 17%. I thought this fact alone justified purchase of these shares.

Bell Canada was offering even more, however. In recognition of the difficult investment climate these shares included a conversion privilege. These shares could be converted, at the investor's option, into common shares of Bell Canada at any time for 10 years, on a share for share basis. So not only did they pay 17%, but they had unlimited potential for growth if the telephone company's share price rose. As a telephone company with a monopoly in Ontario and Quebec, the company represented the ultimate in safety as an investment. Even in a recession people kept their telephones, and the telephone charges were regulated by the government to ensure a profit for the phone companies.

While I was convinced of the merits of these shares, my clients felt a little differently. They were loath to leave a comfortable 15% return with government-guaranteed Treasury bills and bonds. The placing of those shares stretched my abilities to the limit. Some of the brokers in the office sympathized with my plight, while others quietly shook their heads at my foolhardiness. But, with persistence and a great deal of arm-twisting, I eventually found buyers for every share, earning some decent commissions during one of the slowest periods in a decade.

I will never forget how reluctant those investors were to take on such a high quality investment. If those investors had held their investment until today they would have earned 17% interest-equivalent income for ten years, and currently hold shares that are trading at over $60, (equal in value to $120 after a 2 for 1 split). In other words the shares still pay better than 17% interest equivalent income on the original investment amount, while the investment value has increased six times from $20 to $120.

Someone buying these shares today at a price more than six times more expensive and a yield of a mere 3.3% would not be getting anything like the bargain available back in 1982. And yet these shares sell infinitely more easily today than back in 1982. The explanation is simply that the investment climate is much more favourable toward equities than it was. The risk today is perceived as much lower than it was in 1982. This difference in the perception of risk changes from bull market to bear market. What was obviously a great value investment seemed too risky to most investors then. Now the same company is regarded as an excellent growth investment by some.

In a bull market finding value investments can be more difficult. But even in the most exciting times of major bull markets careful investors find good companies that are selling at bargain prices. One method involves looking for sectors ignored by other investors.

Identify an Out-of-Favour Sector

An accessible method to identify an out-of-favour sector is by reading a financial newspaper to track the return of each sector for the last twelve months. Usually there is a ranking of the sectors from best performing to worst performing. The TSE 300 itself will often be in the middle of the pack.

The statistical principle of "regression to the mean" mentioned above is important in this analysis. This tendency pulls the extreme occurrences back down (or up). This principle works well with stock market sectors. The only unknown is the time period. In practical terms, a sector with a heavy weighting (of more than 5%) in the TSE 300 that is underperforming or outperforming for more than one year usually reverses its position on the list in the subsequent year or two. An important group of stocks that makes up a large portion of the index will not deviate for very long from the average. A word of caution: While this expectation is realistic for a sector of the market, especially one that is weighted heavily, the principle of regression to the mean is not valid for an individual stock. Sometimes below-average stocks just keep getting worse.

When to Invest

A look at the five-year history of the market and its sectors reveals how these cycles occur. Each down cycle is followed by an up cycle for that sector. Exceptions are rare. On occasion the cycles take ten years instead of four to five. At other times the cycles last only a few months.

Investors experienced a particularly long cycle in Canadian economic history when inflation peaked in 1981, followed by at least 18 years of disinflation. This period was difficult for the resource sector stocks. Mining and forest product stocks demonstrated many minicycles during that period but the general trend was down. Portfolio diversification became very important for investors in these sectors. The downtrend in mining and forestry was countered by an uptrend in financial services and industrial products (especially the technology sub-sector).

In most instances a sector that has underperformed for two or three years will contain companies that can be purchased at very reasonable prices. These companies, sometimes called value investments, will give great rewards if the investor has patience. With luck sometimes a sector will turn around soon after purchases are made.

A company that is trading at a relatively low stock price may be a value investment regardless of the state of the sector. In some sectors there is limited cyclicality and few instances where value investments appear. For example, technology stocks run on their own energy, moving forward due to innovation and rapid change. Microsoft has never been described as a value investment since its inception on the market. Because it has always been expensive, few value-oriented investors had the courage to buy it, yet many investors are millionaires because of Microsoft. The challenge in finding a bargain in technology stocks is to pick an outstanding growth company like Microsoft or find one that is experiencing a temporary setback. The difficulty comes in determining when a setback is not life-threatening to a company. There is always a danger that a low stock price means trouble, but it is especially tricky with computer technology and biotechnology companies. Some investors avoid these stocks altogether because of this.

INVESTMENT STYLES

A plethora of books clogs the shelves of libraries and bookstores on the topic of stock market values and pricing. For those who are especially interested it can be fun to explore the various indicators. Book value, price-earnings ratios, trend lines, debt to equity ratios, and earnings momentum are just a few of the indicators.

When deciding which stocks to buy investors often follow a single style of investing, categorized by the types of companies that are purchased or by the techniques used to select companies. Among other techniques, there are three popular ones: value investing, growth investing, and cyclical investing. Investors will find that their personality is better suited to one type of investing, usually either growth or value investing.

Value Investing

Value investing means buying companies that are inexpensive compared to other stocks. This relatively inexpensive state is usually discovered by examining financial ratios that are well-known to value investors.

In the 1951 book, *Security Analysis,* by Ben Graham and David Dodd (McGraw Hill, 1951), considered the foundation of modern investment analysis, Ben Graham writes about value investing. His definition of investing "chiefly for profit" is:

> Purchase of representative common stocks when the market level is clearly low as judged by objective, long-term standards...(or) Purchase of individual issues with special growth possibilities, when these can be obtained at reasonable prices...(or) Purchase of well-secured privileged senior issues (or) Purchase of securities selling well below intrinsic value.

The author goes on to suggest that "speculation" is:

> Buying stock in new or virtually new ventures (or)...Trading in the market (or)...Purchase of growth stocks at generous prices.

Graham's early experience was obtained in the 1930s, 1940s, and 1950s when "values" in the stock market were extremely inexpensive. A value investor according to the method attributed to Graham would have found it very difficult to participate in bull markets of the 1980s and 1990s. Few worthwhile companies are cheap enough today to fit the strict value measure in the fourth criteria for investment, that the securities sell well below intrinsic value. While the Graham definition allows for the purchase of "issues with special growth possibilities...at reasonable prices" most observers feel that Graham would have found today's prices generally in the speculative category.

Notwithstanding the problem of reaching the standards of value espoused by Graham and others, there is merit in trying to find investments in common shares of companies that are relatively inexpensive. The advantage of using what is usually meant by the term "value investing" is that it keeps investors from buying expensive stocks. Only stocks that are very low-priced in relation to their assets are selected. Ben Graham wrote his book after the Great Depression had wreaked havoc with stock prices. He was reacting to the devastation in stock prices that followed a decline of 80% in the Dow from 1929–32. Due to unpopularity of the stock market for two decades after the low in 1932 it was possible to find many publicly traded companies that fit the stringent criteria for value that Ben Graham established.

Value Criteria for Investing in Stocks

Value investors try to buy stocks that meet one or more of several criteria that measure inexpensive stocks. These measures can be absolute or relative. Inexpensive can be compared in relation to the past or just against other stocks currently. Absolute definitions used by some are so rigid that in some markets no stocks can be bought.

For example, one well-known Graham measure is to buy a stock when you can buy it for less than its current assets, the "sub-current-asset" issues. It was possible to find common shares trading at these levels for most of the 1930s, 1940s, and the early 1950s. In the 1970s a few stocks met that test after the bear market of 1973–74. Very few stocks in the 1980s and 1990s would qualify. Following this criterion, devotees of strict value investing would have been out of the market from about 1983 onward, missing the move on the Dow from 1100 to 11 000 and higher. Professionals today who profess to follow strict value investing are probably exaggerating their adherence to the value techniques. Warren Buffet, the most famous disciple and student of Ben Graham, would admit that most of his investments would not be made today if value principles such as these were adhered to rigidly.

This is a danger in value investing based on absolute criteria. Strict adherence to value measures leaves the investor in a group of stocks that are often poor performers for long periods of time. In bull markets very cheap stocks get that way for a reason. It takes great skill to select those stocks that are very low-priced for reasons that are temporary. No one wants to buy a low-priced stock that is going to stay that way forever. Even more important is the fact that cheap stocks are often an indicator of serious trouble with a company, trouble that may result in bankruptcy. Only those individuals with lots of experience and skill are qualified to select stocks in this high-risk field of hidden land mines. If you use the screening method of asking the analysts for their three best companies first and then apply value principles to those companies you should avoid the possibility of buying a cheap stock at death's door.

Less rigid value measures are more helpful, ones that are more relative than absolute. Value measures can be used to identify individual companies that are trading at below average prices compared to their peer group of similar companies. Smart investors try to buy the less expensive stocks in an industry group.

Value measures can also be employed to identify sectors that are cheap relative to the market. A coach tries to find the less expensive groups using these indicators. Groups of stocks can get inexpensive as the market rotates from one sector to the next. An out-of-favour sector will contain some inexpensive stocks. One method of discovering out-of-favour sectors is to search for value-priced companies. When several turn up in one sector the odds are good that the sector is out-of-favour.

A Cheap Stock May Be in Trouble

A naive value investor might jump at a stock trading at depressed levels, thinking he has found a bargain. He might delude himself into thinking that no one else can see what a great company this is, selling for a price-earnings ratio well below other stocks. If he is foolish he might think he is so much smarter than other investors that they cannot see what he sees. Investors with this attitude usually lose a lot of money before they learn the required lessons.

A more beneficial attitude to take is to start to ask questions about the "bargain." What makes this stock so cheap, when it looks so attractive? What is it that others can see that I have missed? Why is the stock trading at such a low price? When a stock looks like an obvious bargain to me I need to understand what makes it unattractive to others.

As there are many professional investors in the market who spend all day scouring stocks for bargains, it is a good policy to assume that your obvious bargain stock has been examined and discarded by many professional investors. It would be foolish to ignore this fact and purchase the stock thinking you have discovered something no one else can see. The sensible thing to do is to question an apparent bargain first, eliminating the obvious and digging for deeper factors. A big ego combined with an inflated sense of skill in stock picking is an expensive attitude to take into the stock market. Your coach can quickly determine why a stock is cheap with one call to the research analyst covering that sector.

Before anyone gets too discouraged by the impossibility of the task of finding bargains in the market, I can reassure you that there are many opportunities at all times in the market, especially in companies and sectors ignored by the pros.

Growth Investing

Growth investing involves the purchase of companies that are growing either their earnings or their revenues faster than their industry or the economy. In order to do this, growth companies need to make acquisitions or take market share away from competitors. Microsoft is an example of a growth company that takes market share away from competitors and is involved in a growing industry—computer software. In fact, they took market share away so aggressively that there is a government inquiry into their business practices.

There have been many growth companies, such as McDonalds, in the fast food industry. An industry expansion allowed companies to grow quickly as more and more people ate meals in restaurants. This is true also in the computer industry, where the purchase of computers continues to increase every year and companies like Dell Computer thrive.

Institutional investors, especially mutual funds, spend a lot of time examining, buying, and selling the growth stocks. They spend a large amount of professional energy and time trying to find the best picks. It is a very competitive field for the individual investor. Jumping in and out of stocks as they move through the growth stages is difficult for the individual investor. Many growth companies eventually hit the wall and suffer a sudden setback, causing the stock market to re-evaluate their stock value.

For example, a former high-flying growth company in the waste disposal industry, Laidlaw Industries, peaked at $25 in 1989. Bought at the right time prior to this peak, Laidlaw made many people rich. In 1989 the management of the day made some mistakes and the share price plummeted, reaching as low as $7, and stayed down for several years. By 1999 the company was transformed into a transportation and ambulance service provider and traded at Can$10. Ten years was a long and difficult waiting period for the investor who sits. Mutual fund companies cannot afford to wait this long as their quarterly performance pressures are too great. So the professionals jump out of the stock at the first sign of trouble. I like growth stocks that have survived a setback such as this. The pros are usually out of the stock, the price is cheap and the management is either completely changed, as in the case of Laidlaw, or they have learned a valuable lesson about flying too high.

By definition growth stocks are successful companies that are doing better than the average company. They usually sell at a premium stock price. This premium stock price can rise as their success grows. Eventually the premium is removed by problems that develop, either in the company or the industry. The nimble investor can get in when the stock is rising and get out before problems develop. For most people this means buying an expensive stock and selling it when it is even more expensive. This is a tall order, especially when one is competing with most of the professionals. Any individual should ask themselves if they have the skill and time to compete with others in getting into and out of high flying growth stocks before attempting it.

I select growth stocks carefully for client portfolios. Only when a stock is in the early stage of the growth story do I feel confident enough to add it to the portfolio. Once the growth story becomes hot individual investors are advised to leave the growth stocks to the professionals who watch the stocks all day, every minute, and can jump out at the first sign of trouble.

Investing in Cyclical Companies

Cyclical companies make up a big component of the Canadian stock market and are less common in the United States. Cyclical companies are spread throughout many sectors, such as forest products, mines and minerals, oil and gas, and some industrial products like steels. All stocks are cyclical to a degree. The economic cycles make stocks rise and fall with some regularity, if not predictability. Some companies are more cyclical than others. Auto manufacturers have been very cyclical in the past. Telephone and cable stocks are less cyclical. Chemical companies are cyclical as plants are built in good times, leading to excess capacity and a glut of supply of the chemical product. Paper and forest products are the same. High prices for the commodity lead to large profits, which bring on more building of new plants and eventually a surplus of supply.

Oil and gas companies are cyclical but on a different time clock than the rest of the economy. Oil and gas companies are a much bigger factor in the Canadian market than in the United States. Manufacturing companies are more cyclical than others. In the case of Gillette, the demand for razor blades fluctuates less than the demand for cars and houses. Tobacco and liquor companies are not very cyclical as the demand for their products does not fluctuate much at all.

Some cyclicals can be bought when earnings are good and expected to get better. Cyclicals that lose money for a period of each cycle are better purchases when they are losing money. Buying cyclicals when earnings are peaking can be an expensive mistake. Price-earnings ratios are tricky to read when it comes to cyclical companies. As the earnings rise through an economic cycle the price-earnings ratio shrinks on most cyclical stocks. If a stock earns $1 per share and trades at $20, it has a P/E of 20. As the cycle progresses the earnings increase to $5 but the cycle is closer to ending. The price earnings ratio contracts to 5 times so the stock now is at $25. The novice investor who bought at $20 is surprised that the ratio has come down to 5 times. Experienced investors are aware that $5 per share earnings are not sustainable for much longer. An inexperienced investor or broker might try to put the initial price-earnings multiple of 20 on the $5 number and think the stock will go to $100. More likely the company will be losing money in the next cyclical downturn before it gets anywhere near $100. Some investment experts leave the cyclical companies alone because of the difficulty of timing the cycles.

TWO REASONS TO SELL A STOCK

Regardless of the method used to select companies for your portfolio there will come a time when some changes must be made if the portfolio is to continue to hold good companies that represent good value. Like the garden, the portfolio needs some weeding on occasion.

Many investors find the decision to sell a stock extremely difficult. Coaches too have problems in this area. There are several useful suggestions to help with this dilemma. According to Carret,

> ...there is no reason why the stockholder should terminate his commitment, [to a stock] unless strongly convinced that stock prices in general

have far outrun values. With this exception, the only logical reason that the speculative investor can have for selling a stock he holds is a change for the worse in the position of the stock.

While I take issue with Carret's hint about market timing when he says "prices in general have far outrun values," I agree that there are really only two good reasons to sell a stock. One occurs when that stock gets so expensive relative to other good companies that a substitution can be made for a less expensive investment in a company of equal or better quality. The other, which is the more important, is when a company gets into trouble.

When a Company Gets into Trouble

A sale of a common share needs to occur when the company gets into trouble of a serious nature. A company in serious trouble would no longer qualify as one of the top companies in the sector. As a warning of trouble, the research analyst usually drops a company to the hold category or the sell category, although not always.

The determination of when a company is in "serious" trouble poses a problem. Independent, contrarian investors look for some trouble either in the company or the sector when they buy stocks. It is the troubles that make a sector cool, and the difficulties create an environment where bargains can be found. So it is often the presence of trouble that attracts us to the stock in the first place.

Acceptable trouble that creates a buying opportunity must be capable of resolution by management or industry factors. Value investors exercise patience as long as a company is on the right track. Management must demonstrate that they are dealing with their problems, not denying their existence. When it becomes clear that management cannot or will not solve the problems, and the difficulties are longer term in nature the investor may decide to sell the stock.

At this point the wise investor does not hesitate. Investors who procrastinate on the sale of a stock because they are taking a loss are not being honest with themselves. Invariably if a company gets into trouble most investors who hold the stock have purchased it at higher prices.

The purchase price of the stock for any investor is not relevant to a decision to sell because of serious trouble in the business.

If the stock is headed down, it will go down regardless of the loss incurred by any single investor. An old saying is worth heeding—your first loss is your best loss. Loosely translated this means sell when the idea first strikes you. Most of the time companies that get into trouble experience greater difficulties as time goes by. Experience helps in developing the ability to discern a temporary setback from major trouble. When in doubt, if there is trouble, err on the side of selling.

Difficult judgement calls require the assistance of an experienced coach and competent research analysts. The intelligent investor discusses the problem openly with a coach, not laying blame on the coach for the mistake of buying the company. The focus needs to be on the decision to cull the stock from the portfolio or to keep it.

DECIDING TO SELL OR TO HOLD

I experienced a difficult decision to sell or hold a stock recently. Having purchased Rogers Communications after the stock price declined from $25 to $15 and the analyst added it to his buy list, I watched the price decline to $4.80 over a two year period. Although the share price declined, the fundamental story remained the same: Rogers was a cable company that owned shares in a nationwide cellular company and many other assets and had a lot of debt. The net asset value of the company when I purchased the stock was estimated at $25. After some time the estimated net asset value declined to about $15 but the analyst never took the stock off his buy list. My clients became very upset with the stock, not least because the newspapers kept printing stories of a negative nature about the company. Articles emphasized the debt of the company while repeatedly stating that Rogers was short of money to fund all requirements. I knew from the analyst that Rogers was investing heavily in both the cable and cellular operations, spending perhaps $800 million per year when available cash flow after debt service was $400 million. So Rogers looked a little desperate when they needed to raise money. Each time an article appeared clients called wondering if they should sell. I checked the analyst's comments and found the courage to recommend that the clients hold and add to their position. The analyst pointed out that the breakup value of the company was in the high teens even though the stock was trading down at $5.

In 1999 the stock broke through $30 per share, just fifteen months after bottoming at $4.80. Now the company has become associated with the Internet companies as U.S. telephone companies such as AT&T acquire cable firms to use as Internet and local telephone suppliers. None of the actual business activities of Rogers is new, just the perception. Was the company ever in serious trouble? I suppose if interest rates had soared to 10% a year this company would have been in trouble. I believe that the problems were more of investor understanding and perception.

Given the difficulty in distinguishing between real trouble and temporary setbacks, I composed the following list of signs of trouble in a company. This list is not exhaustive:

- Abrupt changes in senior managers
- Accounting practices being questioned
- Cancellations of financing arrangements
- Analysts complaining about lack of information
- Senior managers changing their story
- Two or more consecutive quarters of negative earnings surprises

A rule of thumb for deciding if a company is in serious trouble is to ask the question: Can the difficulties be fixed in one year or less? If the answer is no, then, in most cases, it would be better to sell. The goal here is to avoid getting caught with a company that gives us a catastrophic loss.

Difficult decisions like selling a company that may be in trouble require the help of a competent coach who is interested and experienced in common share selection and portfolio management.

When a Stock Gets Very Expensive

The second reason for selling a stock is less important than the first. As was pointed out in the discussion of the disposition effect, most investors need help in trying to hang on to stocks that go up, not encouragement to sell. With that qualification it can make sense to sell if the stock has become expensive relative to other good companies available in the stock market. You do not want to sell a good company just because it has done what you wanted—increase its stock market value. But, if you can replace a very expensive stock with an equally good company trading at a value price then you may improve the portfolio by making a change. Usually the best replacement is found in another sector since the sector of the stock to be sold probably contains mostly expensive stocks. The pros may be trading in a sector that has become very hot. The prudent investor looks for a cool sector where there are good values.

To sell a stock solely because of a profit is not smart investing. As discussed in the description of the trap known as "small profits, big losses," an increase in the stock price should not be taken as a trigger to sell, "to nail down that profit." The increased stock price is probably just telling you that you made a good decision to buy in the first place. To determine if you have a good company with an overpriced stock, you have to examine further the question of relative price for the stock. If you own a stock in an industry that has become the darling of the pro traders and speculators alike it makes sense to look at investments trading at more normal prices.

In any case, if you fail to act and the stock is held and the pros exit the sector causing the stock price to settle to a lower price, the harm done is much less than not selling a company that is in trouble. The stock of a good company can be held for years, as long as the company is one of the best two or three in the sector.

So the emphasis needs to be placed on the first reason for selling, not the second. If a company gets into serious trouble, sell without regard to the price or your ego or your purchase price. And if a stock becomes seriously overpriced, look for a replacement that is an equally good company at a reasonable price.

YOUR LIFE AS AN INVESTOR

Low Turnover in Your Portfolio

The frequency of trading in a portfolio determines the cost of managing that portfolio in the pay-as-you-go system. While your coach needs to get paid for helping with your portfolio, a good coach puts the need for portfolio management ahead of the need to earn commissions. Investors and coaches working together can find the balance. As a guideline only, trading costs for an actively managed, 10-stock portfolio vary between 1% and 2% a year. This cost level compares favourably with mutual funds at 2% and higher and discretionary portfolio management costing around 2.75% for average-sized accounts.

It costs approximately 1% a year to maintain a turnover of 20% of the stocks in a portfolio or 2% for 40% turnover. In a 10-stock portfolio turnover of 20% means changing two stocks per year. If the portfolio is 1/2 bonds and 1/2 stocks then the cost will be 0.5% to 1.0% per year for a 20% to 40% turnover if there are no bond trades. This is a very low-cost method of portfolio management. Most coach-style brokers will be happy to manage a portfolio on this basis if a client is reasonable about demands on the coach's time. For this low-turnover type of business the coach needs to have a fairly large clientele of portfolio investors who are following the same list of good quality companies.

Keep a Written Record

A client who has worked with me for more than 20 years gave me an idea about record keeping. Most investors keep track of the buying and selling costs of the stocks owned. This investor keeps a hand-written book with each purchase and sale recorded. He started a new page each time he bought a new stock. The stock that was sold remained in the book with a date and price for the sale.

To improve on his method I suggest you start a book that will become a permanent record of stock market activity. The ideal type of book is a three-ring binder with loose-leaf sheets. Each time a stock is initially purchased the date and price are recorded. In addition, a note is kept of *the reason for the purchase*. When the stock is sold, the date and price are recorded along with the reasoning behind the decision to sell. After a sale, the sheet is moved to the back of the binder.

The biggest benefit of this practice comes from avoiding making silly mistakes. The necessity of writing down reasons for a purchase makes it difficult to act on impulse or a tip. Can you imagine writing down, in a permanent record, "I bought the stock because Joe, my brother-in-law, the one I never liked that much, said it was going to double in the next two weeks"?

Initially the book will contain 10 sheets, each sheet representing one stock. As a trade is made and a position is liquidated, the sheet goes to the back of the binder and a new sheet is started for the new stock. By the time 20 years are past there might be 40 to 50 sheets or more. Often a stock that was purchased and sold once may be re-purchased, when the price becomes attractive again. Other stocks may be held for 20 years, if they continue to do well.

There is no need to write down the number of shares purchased and sold. That information is kept elsewhere along with the portfolio valuations and income tax records. The purpose of this book is solely to develop a feel for stock market investing. If the stock market portfolio is left to children or grandchildren the book represents a record of stocks held, bought, and sold. The book may be the start of a stock market investing tradition for the family.

Reading a book called *The Battle for Investment Survival*, (Simon and Schuster, 1965) written in 1935 by the famous and successful investor Gerald Loeb, I found the following advice: "Writing down your cogent reasons for making an investment—what you expect to make, what you expect to risk, the reasons why—should save you many a dollar. Years ago, in the early Twenties, I was initiated into writing down my reasons pro and con before making a purchase or a sale. This was suggested to me by an investor who had amassed many millions." This must be good advice when successful investors from the 1930s follow it.

Portfolio Investing Is Simpler Than Many Think

A small amount of money invested in the stock market for 30 or 40 years grows to huge amounts as you saw in chapter 2. Investors who live long enough to see the benefits of this growth for themselves are amazed. Multigenerational fortunes are based on this type of investing for long periods.

You too can achieve such results with much less difficulty than you probably realize. Allow me to summarize the suggestions:

- Hold 10 high quality blue chip stocks.
- Own a few government-guaranteed bonds.
- Keep a fixed percentage balance in stocks.
- Re-balance periodically or after a big market move.

- Avoid managed products.
- Use a coach and research analysts for advice.
- Stay in the stock market throughout the cycles.
- Avoid trying to beat professional investors at their game.
- Keep most of your winners and cull your losers.
- Maintain proper diversification in your portfolio.
- And—above all—keep it simple and have fun.

You now have all the information you need to be successful in the investment game. You know where the pitfalls lurk and how to avoid them. You understand that the investing process is just as important as the result. In investing, as in other aspects of life, getting there is more than half of the fun.

TAKE ACTION RIGHT NOW

What can you do right now to get started on the path to successful investing? Perhaps you have most of your investment dollars in mutual funds. It may not seem realistic to make a wholesale change to a more independent style of investing. However it is important to take some action to get started while you feel some motivation.

The first step is to approach an investment advisor who is experienced in the selection of individual stocks. Most investment firms will provide a name if none of your acquaintances know of someone. In the first meeting tell the advisor that you want a balanced portfolio of stocks and bonds, stating your preferred percentage balance.

The advisor needs to know that you want to invest in ten good companies, selected from a minimum of five stock market sectors. You may wish to indicate that you would like 12 to 15 choices so that you are involved in the final selection of these stocks. You would be wise to tell the advisor that you expect his research department to have recommended these stocks as well. Arrange a second meeting with the advisor to review his suggestions.

In the second meeting review the stocks your advisor selects to see if you can agree on ten. If you cannot find ten that you like ask for more suggestions. Any advisor interested in stock selection will provide additional selections without much prompting.

Once you agree on the selections for stocks and bonds instruct your advisor to proceed. You need to make sure that enough money is invested in this program that you will pay attention. Although you may wish to wait before withdrawing money from mutual funds to avoid the exit charges, you can recover these cost in two to three years through saving the annual management fee and the lower cost of independent investing in a portfolio of stocks and bonds. The important thing is to get started right away with individual stocks with at least part of your money. If your readily available money is limited you can meet your target balance by switching some of your mutual funds to bond funds, usually for no charge if you stay in the same fund group. You can withdraw as much money as possible from mutual funds or other sources and get started with individual stocks outside of your mutual fund holdings. Invest the stock market portion of your portfolio directly in individual stocks, keeping your balance overall between the two portfolios.

If you are just starting out on your investing career I suggest that you start with some direct ownership of individual stocks and bonds. This may mean waiting until you have saved sufficient funds to achieve adequate diversification, but a competent coach will help you get started on the right track. The important thing to remember is the sooner you start the sooner the learning experience begins.

One of the most important factors in your enjoyment of this new style of investment management is the relationship you develop with your advisor/coach. Is the advisor committed to managing individual portfolios? It is important to pick an advisor/coach who believes in this portfolio management style to give it a fair test. If you look you will find an advisor who is willing to take the extra time and trouble to work with you on the independent path of portfolio investing. For these advisors their love of the stock market and the investing process as well as their concern for doing the right thing for their clients outweighs the additional effort involved.

Glossary

Annual report A report issued by a publicly traded corporation that provides all the relevant financial data as well as a report from management. Annual reports are frequently available without charge on the Internet, and at some public and reference libraries.

Asset Allocation The practice of dividing financial assets among the classes of cash, fixed income (bonds), and common equity (stocks).

Balance and Re-balance See Policy Asset Allocation.

Bear Market A period in the stock market when the general price level of common shares is falling. Can be interrupted temporarily by a sharp upswing in prices, called a bear market rally. A bear market usually lasts from two months to three years in North America. The average decline in the price level is 30%.

Blue Chip Stock An imprecise term referring to the common shares of companies that are well established, pay dividends, and have a record of consistent earnings.

Board Lot A group of 100 shares, also called a round lot.

Bond A financial instrument issued by governments or corporations (sometimes called a debenture) that promises to pay a fixed rate of interest, usually twice a year, and repayment of principal at the maturity date.

Book Value The amount of net assets belonging to shareholders based on the balance sheet value for assets.

Breakup Value An estimated value for a company if all assets were sold or liquidated and all liabilities paid.

Bull Market A period in the stock market when the general price level of common shares is rising. Can be interrupted by a sharp downturn in prices, known as a correction. A bull market can last for many years, but eventually ends because of excessive speculation in stocks, a sharp rise in interest rates, or an economic recession or depression.

Buy Side The investment professionals who work as money managers, portfolio managers, investment counsellors, and mutual fund managers. They make decisions to place money in stocks and bonds.

Call Option The right to buy a common share at a specified price for a short period of time. A type of derivative.

Capitalization The number of shares issued and outstanding in a company multiplied by the price per share. Companies are loosely categorized as large-capitalization (>$10 billion), mid-capitalization (>$1 billion to $10 billion) and small-capitalization (<$1 billion) These categories are labelled large-cap, mid-cap, and small-cap, respectively.

Cash Flow A measure of the net income of a company plus any non cash deductions taken by the company. Deductions such as depreciation, amortization, and deferred taxes are added back to net income to determine cash flow. See also Price Cash-Flow Ratio.

Closed-End Fund A type of mutual fund that has a fixed number of shares and trades on the stock exchange. Also known as an investment trust or investment company. Closed end funds were very popular in the 1920s and known as investment trusts then. See also Mutual Fund

Common Stock The basic ownership unit of most companies traded on the stock exchange. Carries the right to vote and represents the value of a company. If a company is wound up and its assets are distributed to creditors and owners, owners of common shares rank last after all fixed obligations such as bank loans, debentures, and preferred shares. Common shares have the most potential for capital gain and loss of any type of investment.

Compound Annual Return The gain (loss) in the value of an investment including any interest or dividends as well as the value of the capital. In a multi-year period the return includes the reinvestment of interest, dividends, and capital gains. See also the Rule of 72.

Corporate Finance see Underwriting and New Issues.

Coverage List A list of companies followed by an analyst in the research department. Usually categorized by industry or sector.

Cyclical Stocks While all shares move in cycles with the economic ebbs and flows, cyclical companies are especially sensitive to business conditions. Examples are steel manufacturers, paper companies, mining companies, auto manufacturers, and house builders. Non-cyclical stocks are issued by companies that are relatively immune to cycles. Non-cyclical companies include food producers, utilities, liquor companies, and funeral service providers.

Defined Benefit Pension Plan A pension plan that guarantees a fixed income on retirement.

Defined Contribution Pension Plan A pension plan where the employer commits to a fixed contribution but the investment

returns determine the amount of retirement income. This plan shifts the investment risk to the employee and is becoming increasingly popular.

Derivative A contractual relationship between two (or more) parties where payment is based on an agreed-upon benchmark. The purpose is usually to shift the risk from one party to another for a period of time. An example is a call option.

Discretionary Portfolio Management An investment advisor has discretionary power over a client's portfolio when securities are selected by the advisor without approval by the client. Discretionary portfolio management is growing in popularity as an alternative to mutual funds. See also Investment Counsellor.

Diversification Spreading the investment risk by selecting more than one type or class of investment, or more than one security. This technique is especially useful for avoiding catastrophic risk or company-specific risk.

Dividend A payment, usually quarterly, of income from a corporation to shareholders, either preferred or common. Dividend income from common shares is low compared to growth in the share price of successful companies.

Dow Jones Industrial Average An index of 30 large companies trading on the New York Stock Exchange. Also known as the Dow Jones or the Dow.

Earnings per Share The net income of a company divided by the number of common shares outstanding. Used to compare to the price per share of a company. See Price-Earnings Ratio.

EBITDA Earnings before interest, taxes, depreciation, and amortization. Similar to cash flow, this measure allows analysts to compare companies and their earning power on a standardized basis that eliminates the effects of different amounts of debt or higher tax rates.

Equities Another term for common shares or common equities or common stocks.

Represents the equity ownership base in a company. Theoretically the term also includes preferred shares, but in practice equities refer to common shares.

Fundamental Analysis A method of assessing the value of a company by examining its assets and earning power. The financial condition of a company is examined based on its financial statements. The most difficult and important part of this type of analysis is a forecast of the future earnings and prospects for the company.

Future A type of derivative that represents a contract to buy or sell an instrument or asset at a specified price within a given time period. See also Options.

Growth Investing A style of stock selection that concentrates on companies that are growing faster than their industry or the economy. Analysis involves future earnings growth with less emphasis on current value.

Hedge Fund A type of investment fund that tries to minimize risk by taking long and short positions at the same time.

Hot Tip A recommendation to buy a common stock, usually of a speculative nature, based on rumour from an acquaintance or relative. The best hot tip: buy low, sell high!

Income The total amount of interest and dividend payments received from an investment or portfolio.

Initial Public Offering (IPO) A new issue of common shares in a company that has never been publicly traded. See also New Issue.

Investment Advisor One of many terms for people who make a living selling financial products or financial advice. Other terms are financial planner (who often specializes in mutual funds and insurance), investment executive, account executive, financial consultant, or registered representative. Investment advisors are usually paid by commissions or management fees. See also Stockbroker.

Investment Counsellor An investment professional or company that manages portfolios for individuals and pension plans on a discretionary basis. One of the fastest growing areas of the investment business as investors switch from mutual funds to investment counsellors. See Discretionary Portfolio Management.

Investment Dealer A company that provides the services of stock and bond trading, corporate finance, underwriting, research, and investment advice to institutions and individuals.

Investment Dealers' Association (IDA) A Canadian self-regulatory body for the investment industry, managed by investment dealers. It is responsible for the registration, licensing, and discipline of securities industry employees. Authority is delegated from provincial governments through their Securities Commissions.

Involuntary Market-Timing The tendency for investors to get drawn into the stock market when share prices are high and get pushed out of the market when prices are low. See also Market Timing.

Limit Order A type of order entered on the stock exchange that restricts the price for buying or selling a stock or option. A limit means sell or buy at no more than or no less than a set price, called the limit price.

Liquidity The ability to buy and sell a security with ease. Liquidity is especially important in the stock market as liquidity varies from company to company.

Managed Products Investments that are controlled by a professional money manager where an investor has no involvement in decisions. Mutual funds are the most popular type.

Management Expense Ratio (MER) An annual fee charged by mutual fund companies for managing the fund. The fees are used to pay the fund managers and their staff, trailer fees for the salespeople, and other expenses such as for advertising agencies, etc. Fees are taken from the fund before performance is calculated.

Margin The deposit required to secure a loan for the purposes of stock market investment.

Market Timing An attempt by some speculators to guess when to be in the stock market and when to avoid the stock market.

Maturity The date when a bond ceases to pay interest and is repaid by the borrower.

Mutual Fund An investment vehicle that manages money for a large group of people who have pooled their money together in a fund. The term "mutual fund" commonly refers to an open-end fund where investors can redeem their shares at net asset value at the end of each business day. See also Closed-End Fund.

Net Asset Value The value of a mutual fund share calculated at the end of each business day and paid to shareholders redeeming shares or charged to new shareholders buying shares. Also for a company the total assets of a company minus its liabilities.

New Issue An offering of shares or other securities by a company for the first time. May be in conjunction with a secondary offering of shares owned by a majority owner or large shareholder. See also Initial Public Offering.

Odd Lot A group of less than 100 shares. See also Board Lot.

Option A type of derivative that gives the holder the right to buy (call) or sell (put) a stock or bond at a specific price for a fixed period of time. Covered call writing involves selling call options on shares owned by the investor.

Par Value Bonds have a face value of $100, fixed at the date of issue. Bonds trade above or below par depending on the current level of interest rates.

Policy Asset Allocation Also called Balance and Re-balance, this technique allows the investor to set a fixed percentage of assets to be invested in the various asset classes, especially equities or common stocks. The investor resets the percentage mix back to the chosen level when required due to changing market conditions..

Portfolio A widely used term that refers to a collection of common stocks, bonds, Treasury bills, and preferred shares, or some combination, managed as a single unit. Portfolio management refers to the activity of selecting securities for a portfolio that will provide safety, income, and growth for an investor.

Position A holding of common shares of a company.

Preferred Shares A type of equity issued by corporations usually paying a fixed dividend and considered more secure than common shares.

Price Cash-Flow Ratio The price of a common share divided by one year's cash flow. Provides a better comparison than Price-Earnings Ratio when two companies have different levels of non-financial deductions such as deferred income taxes or depreciation and amortization. See also EBITDA.

Price-Earnings Ratio The price of a common share divided by the earnings per share for one year.

Prospect A sales term for a potential investor, in the view of an investment advisor or salesperson.

Prospectus A legal document prepared for an issue of securities, usually common shares. The prospectus contains all material information about a company for review by an investor. Great care is taken in the preparation of these documents to avoid legal liability for a misleading statement.

Rate of Return The amount of increase or decrease in value of an investment or portfolio including changes in the market value and interest and dividend payments.

Redemption To "redeem" or sell shares back at net asset value to the fund company.

Research Analyst Investment professionals who analyze companies and recommend that investors buy, sell, or hold shares in that company.

Risk A term that, when used by professionals, indicates volatility or degree of fluctuation in the value of a security. The more fluctuation or volatility the more risk. Catastrophic risk or company-specific risk refers to the possibility of total loss of capital in the case of bankruptcy or failure to repay a bond. Market risk refers to the fluctuations in the market.

Rule of 72 A quick and easy way to determine the time it takes for an investment to double. If an investment earns 12%, as an example, it will take 6 years to double. To calculate the number of years to double take the rate of return and divide that number into 72.

S&P 500 An index of 500 U.S. companies considered by investment professionals as more representative of the stock market than the Dow Jones Industrial Average.

Sector A categorization of companies listed on the stock exchange by industry or type of company. A sub-sector is a further division of companies according to their activity.

Sector Rotation A style of investment management used by professionals and individuals that takes advantage of the cyclical nature of different sectors of the stock market. Investors try to sell stocks in sectors that are overpriced and buy stocks in sectors that are underpriced. Frequently used in conjunction with value investing.

Sell Side Salespersons and analysts who work for stockbrokerage firms and investment dealers providing research and ideas to institutional investors. See also Buy Side.

Short Selling A fascinating and dangerous way to make money in a bear market when share prices are falling. Short sellers sell shares in companies that they don't own with the goal of repurchasing the shares later at a lower price. If a takeover on a company is announced short-sellers can be wiped out in minutes as they have no time to repurchase the shares.

Stockbroker A term for the individual who deals with individual investors, usually advising them on security selection and portfolio management. Commonly this service is provided on a non-discretionary basis and payment is by commission on each trade. See also Investment Advisor.

Strip Bonds and Coupons A bond that has its interest payments removed or "stripped" is a strip bond. The interest payments or coupons that are removed are called strip coupons. These instruments give one payment on maturity with no periodic payments. Strip bonds and coupons fluctuate more widely in price when interest rates change than regular bonds but provide comfort to the investor due to the certainty of principal on maturity.

Technical Analysis The study of price and volume movements in common stocks, stock markets and commodities with the goal of predicting future movements. By studying the psychological forces affecting traders, technicians can predict with some accuracy when a stock will have trouble moving higher or lower through a specific price. See also Fundamental Analysis.

Term to Maturity The period remaining until a bond comes due for repayment.

Total Return The total return on stocks or bonds is the sum of the capital gain or loss plus any dividends or interest payments. In the case of an index the total return index assumes that all dividends are reinvested into additional shares of the index.

Trailer Fee A portion of the management fee of a mutual fund paid to the salesperson who convinced the investor to purchase the mutual fund.

Treasury Bills (T-Bills) A promise to pay issued by the government. Both Canadian and the U.S. governments offer T-Bills. T-Bills are sold at a discount and issued for one year or less. Interest earned on T-Bills is usually lower than government bonds, which are longer term instruments. A good place to keep the safe (fixed income) portion of a portfolio in a period of rising interest rates. Although T-bills are issued in $1 000 000 units by the government, investment dealers offer T-bills in denominations of $5000 and up.

TSE 300 An index of the 300 largest companies on the Toronto Stock Exchange weighted by their market capitalization. A company's inclusion in this index does not guarantee safety or stability.

Underwriting The practice of raising money for companies issuing securities on the public markets. Investment dealers who act as underwriters are acting on behalf of the issuer in selling securities. See also New Issues.

Value Investing The practice of analyzing companies based on the assets and liabilities and earnings. Value investing as a style of security selection emphasizes the search for companies trading at bargain prices. Price-earnings, price/cash flow, and price/book value ratios are examined closely. See also Growth Investing.

Value of a Company Several different measures of value exist such as Market Value, Book Value, Net Asset Value and Breakup Value.

Volatility The amount of fluctuation in the value of a stock, bond or portfolio of bonds and stocks. See also Risk.

Weighting In a stock market index the degree of importance given to a company based on its market capitalization.

Yield to Maturity The estimated annual return from a bond, taking into account any premium or discount from par value, the interest payments, and the term remaining to maturity.

Index